AUSTRALIA THE BEAUTIFUL COOKBOOK

AUSTRALIA THE BEAUTIFUL COOKBOOK

BY JOY HAYES AND JULIE GORRICK

PHOTOGRAPHY BY COLIN BEARD, PHIL WYMANT, ANDREW ELTON

Publishing Director and Project Co-ordinator: Daniel O'Keefe

Published by:
Kevin Weldon and Associates Pty Ltd
43 Victoria Street, McMahons Point NSW 2060

Advertiser Magazines Pty Limited
100 Pacific Highway, North Sydney NSW 2060

Copyright Kevin Weldon and Associates Pty Ltd – Advertiser Magazines Pty Limited
Produced in Australia for the Publisher
Typeset in Australia by Walter Deblaere and Associates
Printed by Griffin Press Limited, Netley, South Australia

National Library of Australia Cataloguing-in-Publication Data
Australia the Beautiful, Cookbook
ISBN 0 949708 00 3.
1. Cookery
641.5

Designed by John Bull, Bull Graphics

A KEVIN WELDON PRODUCTION

CONTENTS

INTRODUCTION

There is no subject as universally popular as food and cookery. Other passionate interests may come and go, but the enjoyment of a good meal – or something as simple as a slice of crusty bread and butter – lives on.

Australia has always had much to offer on this irresistible subject. The early white settlers noted the variety and wholesomeness of aboriginal food, as simple as it was.

Animals and fish cooked in their skins over hot coals or in camp ovens stayed tender and juicy, the skin (discarded after cooking) keeping flavour and nutrients intact. Seeds and nuts were ground to make flour; beautiful clear honey was collected from wild bees; turtle eggs were made into a kind of firm omelette; wild vegetables, fruits and berries added interest to the diet.

By the 1830s, the settlers themselves had gone a long way towards reproducing what was needed for British culinary traditions. Familiar vegetables and fruits were now flourishing in the new land, even such delicacies as asparagus and strawberries along with the staples. Beef, pork and mutton had been introduced, and the delights of Australian fish and shellfish were acknowledged. Visitors to Australia were astonished at the abundant meals offered three times a day. Dinner could hardly be distinguished from luncheon, except that more puddings appeared at the evening meal!

With the gold rushes of the 1850s, ships began bringing adventurers from every part of Europe, America and the Orient, and international culinary influences began. The Australian passion for Chinese food can be traced back to the influx of Chinese prospectors in the 1850s and 1860s – cannily turning their skills to market gardening and restaurants, gold mines that couldn't run dry.

Today, with almost one in four Australians of non-British descent, we are more than ever eclectic in our approach to food. Our food industry has also grown into one of the most self-sufficient in the world, producing virtually everything needed for good cooking – including some of the world's best, best-value wines to wash it all down!

And there is an extraordinary resurgence of enthusiasm for cooking itself, a desire to chop and slice again, to make sauces from scratch, to experiment and innovate.

Economy is one motivation, because it's certainly cheaper to spend your time in the kitchen than spend money on pre-prepared and packaged foods. But there is also increasing emphasis on cooking as a relaxing, creative art as well as an essential skill.

Politicians and executives find relief from their problems when they concentrate on a recipe. Young people enjoy using ingenuity to produce interesting meals from wholesome, bargain-priced finds at the markets. The artistic can show off their skills in the presentation of a dish. There is satisfaction for everyone in the kitchen.

May this book add to your own satisfaction.

Julie Gorrick, Joy Hayes

THE MEAT HERITAGE

From the early colonial days, red meat has been an integral part of the Australian diet, eaten fresh where possible, or cured and stored. In the past, monotony was avoided to a certain extent by making use of every part of the animal. Recipes of the 1800's were more numerous than they are today for such portions as tripe, sweetbreads, ox cheek, heart, kidneys, brains, tongue and even cow's heel.

Towards the end of the 19th century, the average meat consumption in Australia was 270 lb (135 kg) a year per person, compared with 109 lb (55 kg) in Britain, and an average of only 60 lb (30 kg) for other European countries.

Not so long ago, a big piece of steak or a couple of juicy lamb chops were considered suitable for breakfast as well as dinner – and a slice of cold roast lamb or beef was the preferred filling in a lunchtime sandwich.

Today, the average Australian can't afford to be so lavish with grills and roasts, although they are still popular dishes. Good sense and economy, and the example of our European neighbours, have taught us how to get the most flavour and nourishment from the more modest cuts of meat, and to extend them with grains, pasta and vegetables.

These recipes give you a choice, ranging from splendid "big occasion" dishes to economical casseroles and clever minced-meat ideas which are still full of flavour and interest.

Captions to preceding 6 pages.

Page 14/15   Cattle mustering, Victorian Alps. (photography: Colin Beard)

Page 16/17   Lamb and beef still star on Australian tables, as they have since colonial times, served with a variety of fresh vegetables. (photography: Andrew Elton)

Page 18/19   Family home Hamilton, Western Victoria.

Facing Page: Tasmanian Pastures. (photography: Colin Beard)

Swaggie's soup
(photograph right)

We've called it Swaggie's Soup because it's a carefree kind of brew — you can really add any vegetables you have on hand, and it's ready in 20 minutes.

5 cups beef stock (made with cubes)

1 large onion, chopped

2 large carrots, chopped

1 medium turnip, chopped

4 sticks celery, chopped

(You may add also chopped potatoes, parsnips, leeks)

6 cloves

Salt and freshly ground pepper

¼ cup finely chopped parsley

Bring the stock to the boil and add all the ingredients except the parsley. Cover the pan and simmer for 20 minutes, or until vegetables are tender. Taste for seasoning and serve in heated bowls, sprinkled with parsley. Serves 4-6.

Brandied pepper steaks
(photograph left)

There are many versions of pepper steak — this one is easy, with a simple but delicious sauce of brandy and creamy pan juices.

4 thick slices of Scotch fillet, rump or boneless sirloin

2 tablespoons black peppercorns, coarsely crushed

Salt

90g (3oz) butter

2 tablespoons brandy

½ cup cream

Trim excess fat from steaks. Press peppercorns into both sides, and allow to stand at room temperature for 30 minutes.

Heat the butter in a large, heavy frying pan. Add steaks and cook over moderately high heat for 2 minutes each side, or until well browned. Season with salt.

Lower heat to moderate and cook for another 2 minutes each side, or until done to your liking.

Remove steaks to a heated platter. Add brandy and cream to juices in pan, stir until slightly thickened, and taste for seasoning. Spoon over steaks and serve at once. Serves 4.

Horseradish beef casserole with golden topping

Tender, beautifully flavoured beef is finished with an unusual carrot and swede topping.

1 kg (2 lb) gravy beef

Plain flour seasoned with salt and pepper

2 tablespoons oil

2 large onions, sliced

Salt and freshly ground pepper

½ teaspoon dried thyme

¾ cup tomato puree

¾ cup water

2 teaspoons prepared horseradish or horseradish relish

For swede-carrot puree:

750g (1½lb) swede turnips, chopped

4 large carrots, chopped

1 medium onion, finely chopped

Salt and freshly ground pepper

Good pinch nutmeg

3 teaspoons brown sugar

30g (1oz) butter or margarine

After trimming excess fat and any gristle from the meat, cut into 2.5cm (1in) squares and coat with seasoned flour. Heat the oil, add meat and quickly brown all over. Drain and put into a casserole dish.

Add onion slices to pan, cook until softened. Add salt, pepper, thyme, tomato puree and water and stir until boiling. Pour over meat, cover dish and cook in a moderately slow oven (170°C/325°F) for 2 hours, or until meat is tender. Stir in the horseradish, swirl the puree over top. Dot with small pieces of butter or margarine and return to a moderate oven for about 10 minutes until puree is piping hot. Serves 6.

Puree: Place vegetables in a saucepan with enough salted water to cover. Boil until tender, drain, and puree in a blender or push through a sieve. Beat in remaining ingredients.

Carpetbag steak

Early commercial travellers stuffed their treasured wares into voluminous bags called "carpetbags" . . . which eventually gave their name to a thick piece of steak stuffed with oysters.

For each person, allow a piece of rump steak cut at least 4 cm (1½ in) thick, and 4-6 oysters. You will also need salt and freshly ground black pepper, a little oil, and pats of butter for garnish.

Trim excess fat from steak, and snip remaining fat at intervals so steak will remain flat while grilling. Cut a pocket in each steak, stuff with oysters, and fasten opening with small skewers.

Season steak on both sides with freshly ground pepper, and allow to stand for 5 minutes.

Preheat grill to very hot, and brush grill bars and steak with oil. Grill at high heat until brown and crusty both sides, turning once. Then lower heat to moderate, or lower steaks away from heat if you have an adjustable grill.

Allow about 4 to 5 minutes each side for rare steak, 6 to 7 minutes for medium rare.

When steak is cooked, remove skewers and season each side lightly with salt. Serve with a generous pat of butter on top and add saute potatoes and a green vegetable or salad.

Steak and cheese

Something that's a little bit different — good with freshly cooked spaghetti.

1 kg (2 lb) round or topside steak, cut in thin slices

¼ cup plain flour

½ teaspoon salt

¼ teaspoon pepper

¼ teaspoon garlic or celery salt

90 g (3 oz) butter

1 large onion, finely chopped

1 cup beef stock

1 cup grated, mature cheddar cheese

2 tablespoons finely chopped parsley

Pound steak out until it is about 5 mm (¼ in) thick.

Combine flour, salt, pepper and garlic salt and rub well into steak on both sides. Allow to stand for 5 minutes, then cut into 8-10 serving pieces.

Heat butter in a large, heavy frying pan and brown steak on both sides over moderate heat. Sprinkle with chopped onion and add stock. Bring to the boil, cover the pan, and simmer for 1 hour or until steak is tender.

Sprinkle cheese and parsley over the top, cover again, and cook another minute or so to melt the cheese. Serves 6-8.

Sharp steak

Spicy, and very easy to prepare — a good dish for beginner cooks.

1 kg (2 lb) topside or round steak

1 large onion, finely chopped

Salt and freshly ground pepper

Dash cayenne pepper or chilli sauce

1 teaspoon mixed dried herbs

2 tablespoons tomato sauce

2 tablespoons brown sugar

1 tablespoon Worcestershire sauce

2 tablespoons vinegar

1 cup beef stock or water

Chopped capers or gherkins to garnish

Trim fat and gristle from steak and cut into bite-size cubes. Arrange in a shallow casserole and sprinkle with onion.

Mix remaining ingredients except capers together and spoon over the meat. Allow to marinate for several hours or overnight, turning meat now and again.

Cover dish tightly with a lid or aluminium foil, and place in a preheated moderate oven (180°C/350°F) for 1 hour, or until meat is tender. Taste for seasoning, and serve from the dish sprinkled with capers. Serves 6.

Photograph right

Mildura Beef Stew is flavoured with thyme, tomatoes and olives.

Pan-fried steak with peppercorn mustard sauce

4 thick slices Scotch fillet or fillet steak

Salt and freshly ground pepper

1 clove garlic, crushed

60 g (2 oz) butter

1 tablespoon olive oil

⅔ cup cream

1 tablespoon Dijon mustard

1 tablespoon drained green or pink peppercorns

Trim any fat from steaks, and season them with salt, pepper and crushed garlic, rubbing it in.

Heat butter and oil in a heavy frying pan, and saute steaks on both sides for 3 to 5 minutes, or until cooked to your liking.

Remove steaks to a heated platter. Add cream to pan, stirring to get up crusty bits from the bottom. Add mustard and peppercorns and continue stirring over low heat until sauce thickens a little. Taste for seasoning, spoon over steaks, and serve at once. Serves 4.

Mildura beef stew
(photograph page 25)

Australia produces its own excellent olives in the Mildura district of Victoria. In this recipe we've added black olives to a rich beef stew.

1 kg (2 lb) stewing beef

Plain flour seasoned with salt and pepper

125 g (4 oz) pickled pork

2 tablespoons oil

1 large carrot, sliced

12 small onions, peeled

2 cloves garlic, crushed

2 large tomatoes, peeled and chopped

About 2 cups beef stock

2 teaspoons sugar

1 teaspoon dried thyme

Salt and freshly ground pepper

1 cup stoned black olives

Remove any fat or gristle from beef, and cut meat into 5 cm (2 in) squares. Roll in seasoned flour and shake off excess. Cut the pickled pork into small cubes.

Heat the oil in a heavy saucepan or Dutch oven, and fry the pork until the fat starts to run. Add the meat, and toss over moderately high heat until brown. Add remaining ingredients except olives, using just enough stock to cover the beef and vegetables. Stir to get up the brown bits from the bottom, cover tightly, and simmer for 2 hours or until beef is tender. Add olives and cook for a further 20 minutes. Taste for seasoning, and serve piping hot with crusty bread. Serves 6.

Boiled beef with caper sauce

A piece of topside, fresh silverside or bolar blade is often roasted — but try it this way for a change, with a piquant creamy sauce.

2 kg (4 lb) beef in one piece

4 sprigs parsley

12 peppercorns

4 sprigs fresh thyme (or 1 teaspoon dried thyme leaves)

2 bay leaves

1 large carrot, chopped

1 large onion, chopped

2 teaspoons salt

For caper sauce:

60 g (2 oz) butter

2 tablespoons plain flour

2½ cups broth from meat

1 egg yolk beaten with ½ cup cream

1 tablespoon lemon juice

1½ tablespoons capers

Salt and freshly ground pepper

Place beef in a saucepan with remaining ingredients. Cover with cold water, bring to the boil, and skim any froth from the surface. Cover the pan and simmer for 3 hours, or until beef is very tender. Drain, reserving 2½ cups of broth for sauce. Cover beef and keep warm.

To make sauce, melt butter in a heavy saucepan and stir in flour over low heat. Remove from heat and gradually stir in warm broth. Return to the stove and stir until smooth and thickened. Stir a little hot sauce into the egg mixture, then stir this back into the pot. Add lemon juice, capers, and salt and pepper to taste. Heat through, but do not allow to boil.

Cut beef in thickish slices and arrange on a heated platter. Spoon some sauce over, and serve rest separately. Serves 8.

Beef olives
(photograph right)

These olives have an interesting stuffing of minced pork and mushrooms.

750 g (1½ lb) topside steak, thinly sliced

90 g (3 oz) minced pork or pork sausage mince

½ cup soft breadcrumbs

90 g (3 oz) mushrooms, finely chopped

2 tablespoons grated Parmesan cheese

2 tablespoons finely chopped parsley

1 teaspoon dried sage

Salt and freshly ground pepper

2 tablespoons oil

1 small carrot, chopped

1 medium onion, chopped

1½ cups beef stock

1 tablespoon tomato paste

2 teaspoons cornflour mixed to a smooth paste with a little water

Pound the steaks between two sheets of plastic film to flatten them, and cut into pieces about 12.5 × 7 cm (5 × 3 in). Mix together pork mince, breadcrumbs, mushrooms, cheese, parsley and sage and season to taste with salt and pepper. Spread stuffing over steaks, and roll up firmly, tucking in the ends.

Tie with white string, or sew up. Heat the oil in a large, heavy frying pan and brown the rolls on all sides. Sprinkle carrot and onion over and add stock mixed with tomato paste. Bring to the boil, then cover the pan and simmer for 45 minutes, or until meat is tender. Remove rolls from the pan and keep warm, and strain the gravy. Return gravy to the pan, bring to the boil, and stir a little hot liquid into the cornflour paste. Tip this back into the pan, stir until gravy is smooth and thickened, and taste for seasoning.

Meanwhile, remove string or thread from rolls and arrange on a heated platter. Spoon gravy over and serve at once with creamy mashed potatoes and a green vegetable. Serves 6.

Beef Olives may be served from the same pan used for cooking them. Sprinkle with a little extra chopped parsley for colour.

Beef Coolgardie

(photograph below)

Piquant raw minced beef served with garnishes makes a superb appetiser. Here's an unusual way of presenting it.

185 g (6 oz) rump or fillet steak
2 egg yolks
1 tablespoon Dijon mustard
1 tablespoon tomato sauce
1 tablespoon grated onion
1 clove garlic, crushed
Salt and freshly ground pepper
¼ cup finely chopped parsley
1 medium onion, sliced and separated into rings
Extra Dijon mustard
Slivered gherkins or dill pickles

Remove any fat and gristle from steak, and mince meat finely or chop very finely by hand. Combine with egg yolks, mustard, tomato sauce, onion, garlic, and salt and pepper to taste. Shape into two thick patties, and roll edges in chopped parsley. Arrange on a platter with onion rings, extra mustard, and gherkins or dill pickles, and serve with crusty bread. Serves 6-8 as an appetiser.

Beef ribs with onion gravy

Beef ribs make an economical and hearty meal for winter appetites. This gravy is especially nice, with sugar adding richness and flavour to the onions.

1.5 kg (3 lb) beef ribs
Plain flour
2 tablespoons oil
Salt and freshly ground pepper
1 medium onion, finely chopped
½ cup water or beef stock

Gravy:

2 medium onions, finely chopped
2 tablespoons sugar
1½ tablespoons plain flour
2 cups beef stock
1 tablespoon vinegar
Salt and freshly ground pepper

Trim as much fat as possible from ribs. Roll ribs in flour and shake off excess.

Heat the oil in a large frying pan and brown ribs over high heat on all sides. Season generously with salt and pepper and transfer to a shallow casserole dish. Sprinkle with onion, pour water over, and cover tightly with a lid or foil. Bake in a preheated moderate oven (180°C/350°F) for 2 hours, or until tender. Turn

several times during cooking, and add more water if needed to prevent sticking.

Gravy: Add onion to same pan used for browning beef, and stir to get up brown bits from the bottom. Cook over moderate heat until soft, sprinkle with sugar, and stir for a minute. Sprinkle with flour and stir in, then add beef stock and vinegar and stir until gravy is smooth and thickened. Taste for seasoning, adding salt and pepper if necessary.

To serve, arrange ribs on a heated platter. Spoon some of the gravy over, and serve the rest separately. Excellent with creamy mashed potatoes, dill pickles, and buttered cabbage or spinach. Serves 6.

Herbed rissoles

3 slices white bread, crusts removed
½ cup milk
30 g (1 oz) butter
1 medium onion, finely chopped
1 kg (2 lb) lean minced beef
½ cup finely chopped parsley
1 tablespoon each chopped fresh oregano and thyme, or 1 teaspoon each dried
2 eggs, beaten
2 teaspoons salt
¼ teaspoon pepper
2 tablespoons oil
For gravy:
1½ tablespoons plain flour
1½ cups beef stock

Crumble bread and soak in the milk for 5 minutes. Meanwhile, heat butter in a small frying pan and fry onion until soft and golden. Combine bread, onion, beef, herbs, eggs and salt and pepper in a large mixing bowl — easiest way is to use your hands.

Shape mixture into 12 rissoles about 7.5 cm (3 in) across.

Heat oil in a large frying pan, and add rissoles (you will probably need to cook them in two batches). Cook over moderate heat for 4-5 minutes each side, or until they are well browned and cooked through.

Keep rissoles hot on a serving plate while making gravy: Pour off all but 2 tablespoons of drippings from pan, and stir in flour over low heat. Gradually stir in stock, and keep stirring until gravy is smooth and thickened. Taste for seasoning, and spoon over rissoles or serve separately. Serves 6.

Devonport calf liver casserole

Calf liver is economical and delicious. Here's an interesting way to cook it, with the added touch of apples and cider.

500 g (1 lb) calf liver, thinly sliced
Plain flour seasoned with salt and pepper
4 rashers streaky bacon, rind removed
1 tablespoon oil
1 large onion, thinly sliced
1 large tart apple, peeled and chopped
2 teaspoons sugar
½ cup chicken stock
½ cup cider or apple juice
1 cup fresh breadcrumbs
A good knob of butter

Remove any membrane and tubes from liver and dust slices with seasoned flour. Chop the bacon into small squares and fry over moderate heat until the fat runs. Remove with a slotted spoon and set aside.

Increase the heat, and add the oil to the pan. Quickly fry the liver slices on both sides until golden brown. Arrange in a shallow casserole dish, and scatter bacon over the top.

Add onion and apple to the pan, and stir until they start to soften. Stir in sugar, stock and cider and taste for seasoning. Pour over the liver, sprinkle with crumbs, and dot with butter.

Cover with a lid or aluminium foil, and bake in a preheated moderately hot oven (190°C/375°F) for 45 minutes, or until liver is tender.

Remove lid or foil, and bake for a further 10 minutes to crisp the crumbs. Serve from the casserole. Serves 4.

Creamy veal and mushrooms

Quickly made and beautifully flavoured — a dinner party dish that's ready in 20 minutes.

1 kg (2 lb) veal steak
90 g (3 oz) butter
Salt and freshly ground pepper
2 cloves garlic, crushed
4 shallots, finely chopped
500 g (1 lb) button mushrooms
½ cup dry white wine
2 cups sour cream
2 tablespoons finely chopped parsley

Trim fat from veal and cut meat into strips about 7.5 cm (3 in) long and 1 cm (½ in) wide. Heat butter and toss veal strips over moderately high heat for 6 minutes, or until golden grown. Season generously with salt and pepper and remove with a slotted spoon. Add garlic, shallots and mushrooms to the pan, season, and saute for 5 minutes. Stir in wine, sour cream and parsley and heat, stirring.

Return veal to the pan and stir gently through the sauce to reheat. Taste for seasoning and spoon into a heated serving dish. Serve with buttered noodles and a green vegetable or salad. Serves 6.

Baked veal parcels

There's an especially delicious stuffing in these tender little parcels.

12 thin slices veal steak
Salt and freshly ground pepper
60 g (2 oz) butter
1 tablespoon olive oil
1 large onion, finely chopped
2½ cups fresh white breadcrumbs
½ cup grated Parmesan cheese
1 tablespoon chopped fresh marjoram, or 1 teaspoon dried
½ cup sultanas
½ cup chopped walnuts
1 cup tomato puree
1½ cups beef stock
2 teaspoons sugar

Beat steaks with a rolling pin until very thin, and season with salt and pepper.

Heat butter and oil, and fry onion until soft and golden. Mix in breadcrumbs, cheese, marjoram, sultanas and walnuts and season to taste.

Divide stuffing among steaks and roll them up firmly, tucking in the ends.

Arrange seam-side down, close together in a shallow casserole dish. Heat tomato puree with stock and sugar, pour over the veal, and cover tightly. Bake in a preheated moderate oven (180°C/350°F) for 45 minutes, or until veal is tender. Serve from the dish with buttered rice or noodles. Serves 6.

Tarragon veal fricassee

(photograph right)

Pale, creamy stews were very popular in our grandmothers' day. Chicken, lamb chops and veal were often "fricasseed" as a change from brown stews. Here's a streamlined version, using cream and sour cream to give richness and the necessary pale colour to the sauce.

750 g (1½ lb) stewing veal
Plain flour seasoned with salt and white pepper
60 g (2 oz) butter
1 large onion, finely chopped
1½ cups chicken stock
1 tablespoon chopped fresh tarragon, or 1 teaspoon dried
½ cup sour cream
½ cup cream
1 tablespoon lemon juice
Finely chopped parsley to garnish

Remove any fat and gristle from veal and cut the meat into bite-size cubes. Roll in seasoned flour and shake off excess.

Heat the butter in a heavy saucepan, and toss the pieces of veal until pale gold — don't let them brown. Add onion, stock and tarragon and bring to the boil. Lower heat, cover the pan, and simmer until veal is tender, about 40 minutes. Stir in sour cream, cream and lemon juice and bring to the simmer. Taste for seasoning, and sprinkle generously with chopped parsley to serve. Serves 4.

Note: If you like a thicker sauce, stir in a paste of 1 tablespoon cornflour mixed with a little water after adding the cream, and simmer, stirring, for 2 minutes.

Marmalade-glazed corned beef

Add interest to a faithful old friend with an easy, sweet-sour glaze.

2 kg (4 lb) corned silverside
1 cup marmalade (any kind)
1 tablespoon brown sugar
2 teaspoons dry mustard
2 tablespoons light soy sauce
2 tablespoons vinegar

Cook corned beef in gently simmering water for 3½ hours, or until tender.

Drain, and place in a shallow baking dish fat-side up.

Chop marmalade into fine pieces if it's the chunky kind, and combine with remaining ingredients. Spoon over beef. Place in a preheated moderate oven (180°C/350°F) for 30 minutes, basting once or twice with drippings that have collected in the dish.

Allow to stand for 20 minutes before carving. Serves 6-8.

Homestead beef and vegetable stew

750 g (1½ lb) lean stewing steak
Plain flour seasoned with salt and pepper
60 g (2 oz) butter
1 tablespoon oil
2 cloves garlic, crushed
4 medium onions, cut in quarters
8 small carrots
4 sticks celery, cut in finger lengths
1 large turnip, thickly sliced
1 bay leaf
2 teaspoons chopped fresh thyme or ½ teaspoon dried
3 cups beef stock or water
Salt and freshly ground pepper
4 small potatoes (optional)
Finely chopped parsley to garnish

Trim excess fat from steak, and cut meat into bite-size cubes. Toss in seasoned flour and shake off excess.

Heat butter and oil in a heavy saucepan or Dutch oven and brown meat on all sides. Remove with a slotted spoon. Add garlic and vegetables to pan, and toss for a few minutes. Return meat and add bay leaf, thyme and stock. Bring to the boil, taste for seasoning, and simmer covered for 2 hours, or until beef is tender. During last half hour, add potatoes if desired. Sprinkle stew generously with parsley to serve. Serves 4.

Hurry-up beef hash

Here's the simplest way we know to turn leftover roast meat (or even meat loaf or sausages) into a good, hot, main course.

60 g (2 oz) butter
1 large onion, finely chopped
2 cups chopped, cooked meat
2 large potatoes, boiled and chopped
Salt and freshly ground pepper
3 eggs, beaten with ½ cup milk

Heat butter and fry onion until golden. Place in a bowl and mix well with meat and potatoes, seasoning to taste. Spoon into a greased pie plate or casserole, and pour egg mixture over the top.

Bake in a preheated moderate oven, (180°C/350°F) for 20 minutes, or until egg is set and top of hash is golden. Serve with tomato sauce and a salad. Serves 4-6.

Squatters steak and mushrooms

You can cook this on top of the stove, or in a covered casserole in the oven.

1 kg (2 lb) lean stewing beef
Plain flour seasoned with salt and pepper
60 g (2 oz) butter
1 tablespoon oil
1 large onion, finely chopped
250 g (8 oz) mushrooms
2 tablespoons chopped parsley
1 teaspoon mixed dried herbs
3 cups beef stock or water
Salt and freshly ground pepper

Cut meat in 2.5 cm (1 in) cubes, after removing any fat or gristle. Roll in seasoned flour and shake off excess.

Heat butter and oil in a saucepan or flameproof casserole and fry onion until soft and golden. Add meat and stir over medium heat until meat is brown.

Wipe mushrooms with a damp cloth, and cut into slices if large. Add to pan with herbs and stock and bring to the boil, stirring. Taste for seasoning and cover tightly. Simmer on top of the stove, or place in a preheated moderate oven (180°C/350°F). Cook for 1½-2 hours, or until meat is very tender. Serve with boiled rice, noodles or mashed potatoes. Serves 6.

Tarragon veal fricassee is an old-time favourite using today's ingredients and interesting seasonings.

Meat loaf in an overcoat

Inside the loaf are tiny bits of cheese, outside has a creamy "overcoat" of parsley-flavoured potatoes.

750g (1½ lb) minced steak
¾ cup cornflake crumbs
¾ cup evaporated milk
1 egg, lightly beaten
1 teaspoon salt
1 teaspoon dry mustard
Good pinch pepper
½ teaspoon mixed herbs
1 small onion, grated
¾ cup diced, processed cheddar cheese
750g (1½ lb) old potatoes
15g (½ oz) butter or margarine
2 tablespoons chopped parsley
Salt
Good pinch cayenne pepper
Pinch nutmeg

Place meat and crumbs in a bowl with the evaporated milk, egg, salt, mustard, pepper, mixed herbs, grated onion and diced cheese. Mix until combined.

Pack into a lightly greased loaf tin, and bake in a moderate oven (180°C/350°F) for 1 hour. Meanwhile, boil potatoes until tender, drain thoroughly and mash well with the butter or margarine. (A little hot milk may be necessary to give a spreading consistency). Stir in the parsley, salt, pepper and nutmeg.

Remove loaf from oven, leave in tin 4 minutes, then pour off the fat and carefully turn loaf out on to an oven tray. Swirl the potatoes all over the loaf and return to a hot oven for 4-5 minutes to brown the potato coating. Serves 6.

Roast saddle of lamb with stuffed tomatoes
(photograph right)

A saddle, as you would imagine, is the back of the lamb, with the chops on either side still joined together. The average weight is about 3 kg (6 lb) so it's a lovely cut for a dinner party for 8.

1 saddle of lamb weighing about 3 kg (6 lb)
3 cloves garlic, cut into slivers
Salt and freshly ground pepper
1 cup beef stock
1 cup Madeira

For tomatoes:

8 medium tomatoes, peeled
Salt and freshly ground pepper
30g (1 oz) butter
1 medium onion, finely chopped
125g (4 oz) mushrooms, finely chopped
3 tablespoons finely chopped parsley

Cut tiny slits all over lamb, and insert slivers of garlic. Rub with salt and pepper. Place meat (back side upwards) on a greased rack in a greased baking dish, and bake in a preheated moderate oven (180°C/350°F) for 1½ hours. Pour off all fat that has accumulated in the dish, and place lamb directly in dish. Pour stock over and bake for a further 20 minutes, basting two or three times with the stock. Remove lamb to a heated platter and allow to rest for 15 minutes before carving. Skim as much fat as possible from the liquid in the baking dish. Strain into a small saucepan, and taste for seasoning. Add the Madeira. Reheat and serve as gravy with the lamb.

For tomatoes, cut a lid from each, scoop out flesh with a teaspoon and chop flesh roughly. Season tomato shells with salt and pepper. Heat butter and fry onion and mushrooms until onion is soft and liquid has evaporated. Add tomato and cook another minute. Stir in parsley and salt and pepper to taste and spoon into tomato shells.

Bake for 20 minutes with the lamb, and keep warm while lamb is resting. Serves 8.

Order a saddle of lamb from your butcher the day before for this spectacular party dish.

Orange-ginger lamb chops

Great for a barbecue!

8 thick lamb chump, shoulder or leg chops

½ cup oil

1 tablespoon grated lemon rind

Grated rind and juice of 1 large orange

1 cm (½ in) fresh ginger, finely chopped

3 tablespoons light soy sauce

3 tablespoons brown sugar

Salt and freshly ground pepper

Orange wedges to garnish

Trim excess fat from chops and arrange in one layer in a shallow dish. Combine remaining ingredients except orange wedges, seasoning to taste. Spoon over chops and marinate for several hours or overnight in the refrigerator, turning now and again.

Drain chops and grill for 5 to 8 minutes each side, depending on thickness. Baste with marinade every couple of minutes as they cook. Garnish with orange wedges to serves. Serves 4.

Leg of lamb with barbecue sauce

The leg is basted with a spicy sauce as it roasts. You can use the same sauce to baste a butterflied leg of lamb or chops cooked on an outdoor barbecue.

1 leg of lamb

For sauce:

1 cup chicken stock

1 fat clove garlic, crushed

1 large onion, grated

3 tablespoons olive oil

2 tablespoons mild chilli sauce

1 tablespoon vinegar

2 tablespoons brown sugar

1 teaspoon salt

½ teaspoon dried thyme

Place lamb on a greased rack set in a greased baking dish. Combine sauce ingredients in a saucepan and simmer for 5 minutes.

Roast the lamb in a preheated moderate oven (180°C/350°F) until done, allowing about 25 minutes for each 500 g (1 lb) and 25 minutes extra.

While lamb is cooking, baste frequently with sauce. If necessary, add a little water to the baking dish to prevent sauce scorching.

Transfer lamb to a platter and allow to rest for 20 minutes.

Skin any fat from juices in roasting pan, and taste for seasoning. If too thick, stir in a little water or chicken stock. Heat, and serve as gravy with the lamb. Serves 6-8.

Springtime lamb casserole

Everything about this casserole suggests spring — the tender lamb, the bouquet of vegetables, and the bright garnish of chives and parsley. Don't be put off by the long list of ingredients — it's not hard to prepare.

1.5 kg (3 lb) lamb chump or shoulder chops

2 tablespoons oil

30 g (1 oz) butter

1 large onion, finely chopped

2 tablespoons plain flour

2 cups chicken stock

2 large ripe tomatoes, peeled and chopped

¾ cup red wine

2 cloves garlic, crushed

1 bay leaf

2 teaspoons chopped fresh rosemary or ½ teaspoon dried

Salt and freshly ground pepper

Vegetables:

An extra 60 g (2 oz) butter

1 large turnip, peeled and diced

2 large carrots, thickly sliced

12 small onions

1 tablespoon sugar

8-10 small new potatoes

1 ½ cups shelled green peas

Chopped chives and parsley to garnish

Trim excess fat from chops. Heat oil and butter in a large frying pan and brown chops on both sides. (You will probably need to do this in batches.) Remove with a slotted spoon to a large casserole. Add onion to the pan, and cook until soft and golden. Sprinkle flour over and stir in, then add stock, tomatoes, wine, garlic and bay leaf. Bring to the boil, stirring, and add rosemary and salt and pepper to taste. Pour over lamb, cover, and bake in a preheated moderate oven (180°C/350°F) for 1 hour. Meanwhile, prepare vegetables.

Heat the extra 60 g of butter in a large saucepan, and toss turnips, carrots and onions for a minute or two until coated with butter. Sprinkle with sugar and toss until the sugar has melted. Put aside.

When lamb has cooked for 1 hour, add turnips, carrots and onions to casserole with potatoes. Cover and bake a further 20 minutes. Add peas and cook for 15 minutes or until the peas are cooked and other vegetables tender. Taste for seasoning, adding more salt and pepper if necessary. Serve from the casserole, sprinkled with finely chopped chives and parsley. Serves 6.

Fruity stuffed forequarter of lamb

125 g (4 oz) dried apricots, chopped

1 medium onion, finely chopped

30 g (1 oz) butter

¼ cup sultanas

1 cup soft breadcrumbs

3 tablespoons chopped walnuts

2 teaspoons grated lemon rind

Salt and freshly ground pepper

1 egg, lightly beaten

1 forequarter of lamb, boned

For gravy:

1 tablespoon plain flour

1 cup beef or vegetable stock

Salt and freshly ground pepper

Cover the apricots with boiling water, leave for 30 minutes, then drain. Fry the onion in the butter until softened, stir in the sultanas, apricots, crumbs, walnuts, lemon rind, salt and pepper. Add the egg and mix in.

Spread the stuffing over the meat, roll up, and tie in several places. Put into a greased baking dish and roast in a moderate oven (180°C/350°F) for 1¾-2 hours, or until lamb is tender. Put on a heated platter and leave in a warm place for about 15 minutes before carving. This sets the juices and makes the lamb easier to carve.

Meanwhile, make gravy: Pour fat from pan, leaving about 1 tablespoon. Stir in flour over medium heat until well blended, remove from heat and stir in stock. Return to heat and stir until thickened and smooth. Season with salt and pepper to taste and serve separately with lamb. Serves 6-8.

Rack of lamb Bendigo
(photograph below)

1 rack of lamb with 8 chops
1 teaspoon grated fresh ginger
1 clove garlic, crushed
2 tablespoons soy sauce
2 tablespoons dry sherry
1 tablespoon brown sugar
1 tablespoon honey
1 cup chicken stock

Place lamb in a baking dish, fat side up.

Combine remaining ingredients in small saucepan and bring to the simmer. Pour over lamb and bake in a preheated moderate oven (180°C/350°F) for 1 hour, or until lamb is nicely glazed and cooked through. Baste with pan juices while lamb is cooking and add extra stock to the pan if it seems to be drying out. Serves 4.

Crown roast of lamb

Your butcher will prepare a crown roast for you. It looks spectacular for a dinner party, but is easy to cook.

1 crown roast of lamb with 12-16 chops
1 teaspoon crushed black peppercorns
2 teaspoons salt
1 clove garlic, crushed
¼ cup oil

Combine peppercorns, salt, garlic and oil and allow to stand for 15 minutes. Brush roast inside and out with seasoned oil and place on a greased rack in a greased baking dish. Cover bone ends with foil to prevent charring. Roast in a preheated moderate oven (180°C/350°F) for 20 minutes for each 500 g (1 lb).

To serve, place crown on a heated platter. Remove foil and decorate bone ends with cutlet frills, button mushrooms or pitted olives. Fill centre of crown with buttered green peas, button mushrooms, tiny onions, pureed carrots etc. Cut in between the bones to serve, each diner receiving 2-3 cutlets. Serves 4-8.

Rack of Lamb Bendigo is basted with Chinese seasonings as it roasts for a deliciously different flavour. Serve with boiled rice and green peas or stir-fried young spinach

Tottie's lamb's fry and bacon

Soaking in milk has a magic effect on texture. Lamb's fry cooked this way is crispy outside and deliciously tender inside.

1 lamb's fry (young and pink)
Milk to cover
8 streaky bacon rashers, rind removed
About ¼ cup cornflour
1-2 tablespoons oil
Salt and freshly ground pepper
1 cup beef stock or water

Cut the lamb's fry in thin slices, removing any veins as you go. Place in a bowl, cover with milk, and refrigerate for several hours or overnight. Drain and pat dry. Cook the bacon rashers on both sides in a heavy frying pan until crisp. Remove and keep warm. Add oil to drippings in pan and heat.

Quickly dip the slices of lamb's fry in cornflour, shaking off excess. Add to the pan (do not crowd it) and cook over moderately high heat for two or three minutes each side, or until slices are crisp and brown outside. Season with salt and pepper and remove to a heated platter with the bacon.

Pour off excess fat from the pan, add stock, and bring to the boil, scraping to get up the brown crusty bits from the bottom. Simmer until gravy thickens, then strain over lamb's fry or strain into a gravy boat. Serve for breakfast with toast, or for lunch or dinner with vegetables. Serves 4-6.

Easy baked lamb shanks

When the Sunday lamb roast is being carved, lots of people ask for the delicious "knobbly bits" off the shank. Now everyone can enjoy the knobbly bits in a recipe that's almost ridiculously easy to make.

6 lamb shanks
1 packet dried onion soup mix

Cut 6 squares of aluminium foil big enough to wrap around the shanks.

Place a shank on each square of greased aluminium foil, and sprinkle with soup mix, rubbing it evenly over all sides.

Wrap tightly, and arrange in a greased baking dish.

Bake in a preheated moderate oven (180°C/350°F) for 1 hour, or until shanks are tender. Potatoes in their jackets can be baked at the same time.

Serve each diner his own packet, so he can enjoy the delicious aroma as he unwraps it for himself. Serves 6.

Sweet and spicy lamb breasts

Breast of lamb can be fatty and bland, but ask your butcher for meaty breasts, treat them this way, and you'll be delighted.

2 meaty breasts of lamb
1 medium lemon, thinly sliced
1 cup tomato puree
1 cup water or chicken stock
1 medium onion, grated
1 small can crushed pineapple
2 tablespoons light soy sauce
2 tablespoons brown sugar
1 tablespoon vinegar
1 teaspoon salt
Dash cayenne pepper or chilli sauce
Fresh pineapple slices to garnish (optional)

Remove as much fat as possible from outside of lamb, and cut lamb into serving size pieces.

Arrange in one layer in a baking dish, and top with slices of lemon. Bake in a preheated hot oven (200°C/400°F) for 30 minutes. Meanwhile, combine remaining ingredients in a saucepan and simmer for 5 minutes.

Pour off all fat that has accumulated in the baking dish. Reduce heat to moderate (180°C/350°F) and pour sauce over. Continue roasting uncovered for another 45 minutes, basting with sauce now and again. Serve piping hot, garnished with fresh pineapple if desired. Excellent with boiled rice. Serves 6-8.

Top hat lamb

Tender cubes of lamb are cooked with apple and onion and topped with a savoury scone crust.

500g (1 lb) boneless lamb from leg or shoulder
1 tablespoon plain flour seasoned with salt and pepper
2 large onions, thinly sliced
1 large tart apple, peeled and thinly sliced
2 teaspoons sugar
½ cup chicken stock
For scone crust:
1 cup self raising flour
¼ teaspoon salt
30g (1 oz) butter
1 tablespoon finely chopped parsley
1 teaspoon mixed dried herbs
½ cup milk

Remove fat from lamb, and cut meat into bite-size cubes. Toss in seasoned flour and shake off excess. Arrange lamb in a shallow 4-cup casserole dish, and top with onions and apple. Sprinkle sugar over, and add stock. Cover tightly and bake in a preheated moderate oven (180°C/350°F) for 1 hour, or until lamb is tender.

Increase oven temperature to very hot (220°C/440°F) and arrange rounds of scone dough over top. Continue cooking for 15 minutes, or until scones are cooked through and golden brown. Serves 4.

Scone crust: Sift flour and salt into a bowl. Cut butter into small pieces and rub through flour until mixture resembles breadcrumbs. Stir in parsley and herbs. Add milk and mix lightly with a fork to form a fairly soft dough. Pat mixture out on a lightly floured surface until it is about 2 cm (¾in) thick and cut into rounds or squares to arrange on top of casserole.

Hobart stuffed shoulder of lamb

An economical cut takes on special flavour with an apple-mint stuffing and minted gravy.

1 boned shoulder of lamb
30g (1 oz) butter
1 small onion, finely chopped
1 large cooking apple, peeled and grated
2 tablespoons finely chopped mint
½ teaspoon dried thyme
2 teaspoons grated lemon rind
2 teaspoons sugar
Salt and freshly ground pepper
1 egg, beaten
For gravy:
2 teaspoons plain flour
1 cup of stock made with lamb bone
1 tablespoon finely chopped mint

1 can peeled tomatoes

2 cloves garlic, crushed

1 teaspoon sugar

45 g (1½ oz) butter

¾ cup breadcrumbs

¼ cup finely chopped parsley

Place the beef in a bowl. Soak the bread in milk until soft, and add to beef with egg, onion, herbs and salt and pepper to taste. Combine lightly. Shape into two long rolls, and arrange in a greased baking dish, leaving a space in the middle.

Brush tops of meat with soy sauce and bake in a preheated moderate oven (180°C/350°F) for 20 minutes. Meanwhile, chop tomatoes finely and combine tomatoes and their juice with garlic, sugar, and salt and pepper to taste.

Fry the breadcrumbs in butter until golden, toss with parsley, and season with salt and pepper.

When meat has cooked for 20 minutes, spoon tomato mixture in the middle and sprinkle breadcrumbs on the top. Bake for a further 15 minutes, until loaves are cooked through and breadcrumbs crisp and golden. Serves 6.

Devilled kidneys

Good for breakfast with buttered toast, or for lunch or supper over boiled rice.

6 lamb kidneys

Plain flour seasoned with salt and pepper

60 g (2 oz) butter

1 small onion, finely chopped

2 teaspoons Worcestershire sauce

1 teaspoon dry mustard

Pinch cayenne pepper

2 tablespoons tomato sauce

1 cup water

Finely chopped parsley

Skin and core kidneys, and cut into thin slices. Dip slices in seasoned flour and shake off excess.

Heat butter in a heavy frying pan and fry onion until soft and golden. Add kidneys, and toss over moderately high heat until they have browned slightly.

Combine remaining ingredients except parsley, add to the pan, and stir until sauce boils and thickens. Taste for seasoning and serve at once, sprinkled with parsley. Serves 3-4.

Quick-Smart Loaf is ready in half the usual time!

Trim excess fat from lamb, heat the butter and fry onion until soft and golden. Mix with remaining ingredients, and spread over meaty side of lamb. Roll up, and sew or tie with string into a neat shape.

Place on a greased rack in a baking dish, and bake in a preheated moderate oven (180°C/350°F) until done, allowing about 25-30 minutes for each 500 g (1 lb) of meat.

Allow lamb to rest for 20 minutes before removing string and carving.

To make gravy, pour off all but 1 tablespoon of drippings in baking dish. Stir in flour over low heat, then gradually stir in stock and continue stirring until gravy is smooth and thickened. Add mint, and taste for seasoning. Serves 4-6.

Honied leg of lamb

The glaze of honey mixed with lemon juice and marjoram adds a delicious touch to the traditional Australian roast.

1 leg of lamb weighing about 2 kg (4 lb)

Salt and freshly ground pepper

2 tablespoons honey

1 tablespoon lemon juice

1 tablespoon chopped fresh marjoram or 2 teaspoons dried

Sprinkle lamb with salt and pepper, rubbing it well in. Put on a rack in a baking dish (add a little fat to dish if there is not much fat on the leg) and roast in a moderately slow oven (170°C/325°F) for 1¾ hours, or until tender. Baste with pan juices now and again.

About 20 minutes before cooking time is finished, mix together honey, lemon juice and marjoram, brush some over lamb. Continue basting with rest of honey mixture until lamb is cooked. Serves 6.

Quick-smart meat loaf

(photograph above)

Twin loaves bake quickly, and there's a savoury tomato mixture in the middle, so no sauce is needed.

750 g (1½ lb) minced beef

2 slices white bread, crust removed

¼ cup milk

1 egg

1 small onion, grated

1 teaspoon mixed dried herbs

Salt and freshly ground pepper

1 tablespoon soy sauce

Veal hotpot with cheese dumplings

Economical stewing veal is the basis of a nourishing all-in-one meal.

750 g (1½ lb) stewing veal

Plain flour seasoned with salt and pepper

3 tablespoons oil

2 cups tomato juice

2 teaspoons sugar

2 cups beef stock

Salt and freshly ground pepper

3 medium potatoes, peeled and cut into quarters

4 sticks celery, chopped

4 medium carrots, cut into quarters

Dumplings:

1 cup self raising flour

Pinch of salt and pepper

2 tablespoons grated tasty cheese

30 g (1 oz) butter

1 egg

½ cup milk

Remove fat from veal and cut meat into bite-size cubes. Heat oil in a heavy saucepan, and brown veal on all sides. Add tomato juice, sugar, stock, and salt and pepper to taste. Bring to the boil, then cover the pan and simmer for 1 hour. Add potatoes, celery and carrots, cover, and cook another 30 minutes or until vegetables are almost tender.

Meanwhile, mix dumplings (see below). Drop by tablespoons into hot, bubbling stew, cover tightly, and steam for 15 minutes without lifting the lid. Serves 6.

Dumplings: Sift flour, salt and pepper into a bowl. Rub in butter with the fingertips, then stir in the cheese. Beat egg with milk and stir in to form a soft dough.

Baked hamburgers

Here's an easy, foolproof way to cook hamburgers — bake them in the oven. A good idea if you're cooking a cake or pudding at the same time.

500 g (1 lb) finely minced steak

1 small onion, grated

1 tablespoon prepared horseradish

½ teaspoon dry mustard

2 tablespoons tomato sauce

1 teaspoon salt

Dash pepper

Combine all ingredients lightly but thoroughly. Shape into 4 or 6 hamburgers and arrange in a greased, shallow baking dish. Bake in a preheated moderate oven (180°C/350°F) for 35-40 minutes, turning once. Serve on a toasted bun with lettuce and pickles, or as a main course with chips and a salad. Serves 4-6.

Spicy meatballs

(photograph below)

The meatballs are browned first, then simmered in sauce, so they absorb the spicy flavouring.

For meatballs:

500 g (1 lb) minced beef

½ cup soft breadcrumbs

2 tablespoons finely chopped parsley

1 egg

1 small onion, grated

2 teaspoons grated lemon rind

Salt and freshly ground pepper

2 tablespoons oil

For sauce:

1 medium onion, finely chopped

½ teaspoon curry powder

1 teaspoon cinnamon

1 teaspoon ground cumin

1 teaspoon ground coriander

2 cups beef stock

¼ cup coarsely chopped raisins

Salt to taste

A little sugar (optional)

Mix together all ingredients for meatballs except oil. Heat the oil in a heavy frying pan and brown the meatballs over moderate heat. Remove from the pan and set aside while you make the sauce.

Add the onion to the same pan (you may need a little extra oil) and stir until starting to soften. Add curry powder, cinnamon, cumin and coriander, and stir for one minute. Add stock, raisins, and salt to taste and bring to the boil.

Return meatballs to the pan, cover, and simmer for 30 minutes.

Taste sauce and adjust seasoning, adding a little sugar if desired. Serve meatballs and sauce in a heated dish, with boiled rice, chutney and sliced cucumbers. Serves 4.

Braised knuckle of veal

An economical meat cut is meltingly tender and flavoursome cooked this way.

| 1.5 kg (3 lb) veal knuckle, sawed into pieces about 5 cm (2 in) long |
| Plain flour seasoned with salt and pepper |
| 90 g (3 oz) butter |
| 1 fat clove garlic, crushed |
| 1 large carrot, finely chopped |
| 2 teaspoons grated lemon rind |
| ¼ cup finely chopped parsley |
| About 2 cups beef stock |
| Garnish: 3 tablespoons finely chopped parsley mixed with 1 finely chopped clove of garlic and 1 teaspoon grated lemon rind. |

Roll slices of veal in seasoned flour and shake off excess. Heat the butter in a heavy saucepan and brown the slices on both sides. (You will probably need to do this in batches).

Return all pieces of veal to the saucepan and add remaining ingredients. Use enough stock to come half-way up the knuckles.

Bring to the boil, scraping to get up the brown bits from the bottom. Cover tightly and simmer for 1 hour, or until veal is tender but not falling from the bone.

Turn pieces over once during cooking, so pieces on top are immersed in liquid at the bottom.

When veal is cooked, remove lid and cook a further 5 minutes or so to reduce liquid to gravy consistency. Taste for seasoning, arrange on a heated platter, and sprinkle with garnish. Nice with boiled rice or boiled potatoes. Serves 6.

Irish stew

Only three main ingredients in this well-loved stew — but the flavour is rich and satisfying.

| 1 kg (2 lb) best-end lamb neck chops |
| 1 kg (2 lb) old potatoes |
| 500 g (1 lb) onions, peeled and sliced |
| Salt and freshly ground pepper |
| About 2 cups chicken stock, made with cubes |
| Finely chopped parsley to garnish |

Trim excess fat from chops. Cut ¾ of potatoes in thick slices and remainder in thin slices. Arrange the thin slices on the bottom of a deep saucepan. Arrange chops, remaining potatoes and onions in layers on top, seasoning each layer generously with salt and pepper. Finish with a layer of potatoes.

Add stock to come to the top of the potatoes, bring to the boil, then cover and simmer for 1½ hours, or until chops are very tender. Sprinkle with parsley to serve. Serves 4-6.

Note: The thin potatoes on the bottom thicken the gravy. The chicken stock is not strictly traditional but adds to the good flavour.

Beaudesert lamb and pumpkin cakes

Queensland is rightly famous for its beautiful pumpkins. Here's another way of using leftover mashed pumpkin, apart from those well-known scones.

| 2 cups cooked, finely chopped lamb |
| 1 tablespoon finely chopped gherkin |
| 1 medium onion, grated |
| 2 cups cold, mashed pumpkin |
| Salt and freshly ground pepper |
| 2 eggs, beaten |
| Fine, dry breadcrumbs |
| Oil for frying |

Combine lamb, gherkin, onion, pumpkin and salt and pepper to taste. Mix in half the beaten egg. Shape into 8 round patties, and dip in remaining egg and then breadcrumbs. Allow patties to set for 30 minutes or so in the refrigerator.

Heat enough oil in a heavy frying pan to give a depth of about 5 mm (¼ in). Add patties, and fry over moderate heat for 3-4 minutes each side, or until brown and crisp and heated through. Serve with tomato sauce or chutney and a salad. Serves 4.

Pan-fried liver in creamy sauce

For tenderness, liver should be cooked quickly, or long and slowly. Here's a quick approach, using lamb or calf liver. If you're a working cook, keep it in mind for a dinner party — it's ready in minutes.

| 750 g (1½ lb) lamb or calf liver |
| Plain flour seasoned with salt, pepper and paprika |
| 90 g (3 oz) butter |
| 2 cloves garlic, crushed |
| ¼ cup dry white wine |
| ¼ cup cream |
| 2 tablespoons finely chopped chives or parsley to garnish |

Remove any membrane and tubes from liver. Cut into thin slices, and then into finger-length strips. Toss in seasoned flour, and leave for 10 minutes to dry.

Heat butter in a large frying pan, add garlic, and fry until garlic starts to soften. Add liver and toss over high heat until brown on all sides.

Reduce heat and add white wine to pan, stirring to get up the crusty bits from the bottom. Stir in cream and heat through (do not boil). Taste for seasoning, and add more salt and pepper if necessary. Sprinkle with chopped chives to serve. Delicious with buttered noodles. Serves 6-8.

Hamburgers Diane

Here's all the flavour of the classic dish at a budget price!

| 1 kg (2 lb) best quality minced steak |
| 1 teaspoon seasoned salt |
| ½ teaspoon seasoned pepper |
| 2 tablespoons oil |
| 60 g (2 oz) butter |
| 2 cloves garlic, crushed |
| 2 tablespoons lemon juice |
| 1 tablespoon Worcestershire sauce |
| ¼ cup finely chopped parsley |

Lightly mix together minced steak, salt and pepper, gently shape into six hamburgers. Heat the oil, add hamburgers and cook over medium heat for 3-5 minutes on each side, or until done to your liking.

Remove to a heated platter and keep warm. Pour oil from pan, add the butter and garlic, heat until butter has melted. Add lemon juice, sauce and parsley and stir over low heat until well blended. Spoon over hamburgers and serve at once with creamy mashed potatoes and a green salad. Serves 6.

Note: If you have no seasoned salt and pepper, use ordinary salt and pepper and add 1 tablespoon grated onion and 1 teaspoon grated lemon rind to the hamburger mixture.

Australian meat pies

When people think of Australian meat pie they think of individual pies — a good square meal in themselves, and capable of being eaten in the hand.
Everyone has a favourite filling. Some like a plain mince, others steak and kidney or steak and vegetable. We like this filling, well flavoured with kidney and seasonings.

For filling
(make first and allow to cool)

2 tablespoons oil
1 medium onion, finely chopped
750 g (1½ lb) lean minced steak
2 lamb kidneys
1½ cups beef stock
Pinch freshly grated nutmeg
1 tablespoon Worcestershire sauce
1 teaspoon mixed dried herbs
Salt and freshly ground pepper
1½ tablespoons plain flour mixed to a paste with water

For pastry:

2 cups plain flour
1 cup self raising flour
¾ teaspoon salt
185 g (6 oz) butter or firm margarine
Squeeze lemon juice
About ½ cup iced water
Milk to glaze

Filling: Heat the oil in a large, heavy saucepan and fry the onion over moderate heat until starting to soften. Add mince, and stir until brown and crumbly. Stir in remaining ingredients except flour, seasoning well with salt and pepper. Bring to the boil, then cover and simmer for 1 hour. Stir a little hot liquid into the flour paste, then stir this back into the saucepan. Continue stirring until mixture thickens. Taste for seasoning and allow to cool.

Pastry: Sift flour and salt into a bowl. Cut butter into small pieces and rub through flour until mixture resembles breadcrumbs. Add lemon juice and ½ cup of water and mix to a dough with a fork. If too dry, add a little extra water. Knead the dough lightly, then wrap in plastic film and chill for 30 minutes before rolling out.

To make pies: Divide dough into thirds and grease 6 individual oval pie tins. Roll two thirds of the pastry out to line the tins. Roll the remainder out to cut into lids for the top. Divide meat mixture among lined tins, and moisten edges of pastry with water. Press lids into place and make a slit in top for steam to escape. Brush with milk, and bake in a preheated hot oven (200°C/400°F) for 30 minutes, or until pastry is crisp and golden. Makes 6 hearty pies.

Note: For a shortcut, you can use prepared sheets of puff or short pastry, or packaged pastry mix.

Colonial goose

Missing their traditional Christmas goose, early settlers stuffed a boned leg of mutton with seasoning — and so, Colonial goose!

1 leg of lamb about 2.5 kg (5 lb)
90 g (3 oz) butter
1 medium onion, finely chopped
2 lamb kidneys
2 cups fresh, white breadcrumbs
2 teaspoons chopped fresh rosemary (or ½ teaspoon dried)
2 teaspoons chopped fresh sage (or ½ teaspoon dried)
2 tablespoons chopped parsley
Salt and freshly ground pepper

For gravy:

1½ tablespoons plain flour
1½ cups stock made with lamb bone

Ask the butcher to bone the lamb for you and save the bone. Heat the butter and fry onion until soft and golden. Skin and core the kidneys and cut into small dice. Add to the pan and stir until lightly browned. Remove from heat and add breadcrumbs, herbs and salt and pepper to taste. Allow to cool a little, then stuff lamb and tie into a neat shape with string. Season with salt and pepper, arrange on a greased rack in a baking dish, and place in a preheated moderate oven (180°C/350°F).

Roast uncovered for about 2½ hours for well done lamb, basting now and then with juices that collect in the pan. Allow to rest for 20 minutes before removing string and carving.

Meanwhile, make gravy: Pour off all but 2 tablespoons of drippings in pan, and stir in flour over low heat. When well blended, gradually stir in stock and continue stirring until gravy is smooth and thickened. Taste for seasoning and strain into a gravy boat. Serves 6.

Note: Potatoes, pumpkin, onions etc, can be cooked in the baking dish with the lamb. If necessary, add a little oil or butter to the dish, and turn vegetables to brown evenly. Allow about 45 minutes for medium-size potatoes.

Shearer's casserole
(photograph right)

750 g (1½ lb) lamb's fry
Plain flour
2 tablespoons dripping or butter
1 medium onion, chopped
2 cloves garlic, chopped
1 teaspoon sugar
3 large ripe tomatoes, coarsely chopped
1 cup each tomato juice and water
Salt and freshly ground pepper
1 teaspoon sugar
¼ cup finely chopped parsley
4 rashers streaky bacon, grilled

Trim membrane and tubes from fry, cut into 2.5 cm (1 in.) cubes and toss in flour.

Heat the dripping in a large saucepan, and brown the liver on all sides. Add garlic, tomato juice, water, salt, pepper and sugar. Bring to the boil, then cover the pan and simmer for 1 hour, or until liver is tender. Add tomatoes to pot and simmer for another 5 minutes. Taste for seasoning. Spoon into a heated serving dish and garnish with parsley and grilled bacon. Serves 6.

Melbourne mixed grill

Remember when a mixed grill was the highlight of many restaurant menus? There's still nothing to beat it for lavish looks and downright good eating.

4 lamb loin chops
4 sausages
4 lamb kidneys
4 thick slices fillet or Scotch fillet steak, or 4 small pieces rump
8 large mushrooms
2 large firm tomatoes
Melted butter
Salt and freshly ground pepper
Chopped parsley and pats of butter to garnish

Trim excess fat from chops and steak. Parboil sausages for 2 minutes and drain. Skin kidneys, cut in half and remove cores. Wipe mushrooms with a damp cloth and trim stalks. Cut tomatoes in half crosswise. Season mushrooms and tomatoes with salt and pepper, and drizzle with melted butter.

Preheat grill and brush bars with oil. Arrange chops, sausages, steak and tomatoes on grill bars and grill until meats are brown and crisp on top. Turn meats, and then add the kidneys and mushrooms.

Turn kidneys after a minute or two, and keep a watchful eye on the other ingredients. Steak mustn't overcook. Season steak, chops and kidneys with salt and pepper, and arrange with other ingredients on a heated serving platter or individual plates. Top steak and chops with pats of butter, and sprinkle with a little parsley. Serve at once with chips or mashed potatoes and a green vegetable or salad. Serves 4.

Crumbed cutlets

There's not a person who doesn't seem to love them. Even the most sophisticated eater succumbs to juicy lamb in a crisp crumb coating.

8 lamb cutlets
Plain flour seasoned with salt and pepper
1 egg, beaten with 1 tablespoon water
Fine, dry breadcrumbs to coat
30g (1oz) butter
2 tablespoons oil
To garnish:
4 firm tomatoes
A little butter
Salt and freshly ground pepper
4 bacon rashers
1 tablespoon chopped mint (optional)

Trim excess fat and gristle from cutlets. Dip in seasoned flour, shaking off excess, then in egg and breadcrumbs. Chill for 30 minutes to firm crumbs.

Heat the butter and oil in a large, heavy frying pan and fry cutlets over moderate heat until crisp and golden each side and cooked through. (Don't have heat too high, or crumbs will scorch before meat is cooked).

While cutlets are cooking, cut tomatoes in half, season with salt and pepper, and top with a knob of butter. Place under a preheated hot grill.

Cut each bacon rasher in half, roll each half up, and secure with a toothpick. Grill bacon with tomatoes, turning to cook evenly.

To serve, arrange cutlets on a heated platter and garnish with tomato halves and bacon rolls. Sprinkle tomatoes with chopped mint if desired. Serves 4.

Note: Creamy mashed potatoes and green peas are the traditional and perfect vegetables with crumbled cutlets.

LIFE IN THE TROPICS

Did you know that 40 per cent of Australia is in the tropics? Over 50 per cent of Queensland, 40 per cent of Western Australia, and 80 per cent of the Northern Territory is above the tropic of Capricorn. This means that much of the remaining 60 per cent of the country enjoys sub-tropical conditions. Even in "temperate" cities such as Sydney, it is quite common to see palm trees, bananas, avocados and pawpaws growing in gardens and back-yards.

Whether your view of the tropics is romantic, visual or culinary, Australia has it, from rain forests, coral sands, exotic birds and fish, sugar plantations, sheltering palms and blue lagoons, to superb tropical fruits and technicolour sunsets. And of course, to give the final touch of magic to our tropical coastline there is the Great Barrier Reef – the world's finest coral reef, sheltering a necklace of beautiful islands.

When the weather is tropical, we like to eat tropical-style. Frosty drinks, cool salads, cold soups and desserts, luscious fruits, superb seafood – they're part of our way of life whether we live in Cairns or Canberra, Darwin or Devonport.

This chapter is devoted to cool, beautiful food to enjoy all year round.

Captions to preceding 6 pages.

Page 42/43   Sugar canefields near Cairns, Queensland. (photography: Colin Beard)

Page 44/45   All Australians can enjoy the lush fruits and cool, enticing dishes of the tropics. Note: The dish holding nuts is a traditional Aboriginal coolamon, made by the Pitjantjatjara. The cloth is a new development in an Aboriginal art, using age-old designs with a batik technique. (photography: Phil Wymant)

Page 46/47   Old homestead, Mossman, north of Cairns, Queensland. This home was built in 1883. (photography: Colin Beard)

Facing Page: Port Douglas, Queensland. (photography: Colin Beard)

Caviar – salmon pate

*How to make a small amount
of luxury ingredients go a long way!*

| 60g (2 oz) red caviar or lump fish roe |
| 60g (2 oz) smoked salmon, chopped |
| 125g (4oz) cream cheese at room temperature |
| 60g (2 oz) butter, softened |
| 1 tablespoon finely chopped onion |
| 2 tablespoons cream |
| 2 tablespoons lemon juice |
| 1 teaspoon Worcestershire sauce |
| Salt and freshly ground pepper |
| Dash cayenne pepper |

Place all ingredients in a blender or food processor fitted with the steel blade, and process until smooth. Taste for seasoning, spoon into a pretty pot, and chill for an hour or more. Serve with sliced French bread or crackers. Serves 8 as an appetiser.

Luau fish appetiser

*In many parts of the tropics,
raw fish is "cooked" in lime juice.*

| 500g (1 lb) firm white fish fillets |
| Juice of 2 large limes or 1 large lemon |
| 3 tablespoons dry white wine |
| 1 medium onion, grated |
| 1 clove garlic, chopped |
| ¼ cup mayonnaise |
| 2 teaspoons prepared horseradish |
| 1 tablespoon chopped fresh dill, or 1 teaspoon dried |
| 2 teaspoons sugar |
| 1 teaspoon celery seed |
| Salt and freshly ground pepper |
| Lettuce leaves, lime wedges and watercress to serve |

Remove skin and bones from fish and chop flesh very finely in a blender or food processor fitted with the steel blade (or chop by hand). Combine with remaining ingredients, cover, and chill for several hours or overnight. Taste for seasoning, and serve in lettuce leaves, garnished with lime wedges and watercress. Serves 6 as an appetiser.

*Island Salads! Sunshine Salad with cucumber
and banana, Harlequin tomatoes and
melon and prawn salad.*

Yoghurt and spinach iced soup

Deliciously light, cool and refreshing.

| 2 cups chicken stock |
| 1 large onion, finely chopped |
| 6 tender spinach leaves, stalks removed |
| 1½ cups plain yoghurt |
| 1 tablespoon finely chopped mint |
| Salt and freshly ground pepper |
| Grated lemon rind to garnish |

Bring chicken stock to the boil, add onion and spinach. Cover the pan, and simmer until vegetables are soft, about 5 minutes. Whirl until smooth in a blender or food processor fitted with the steel blade. Cover and chill.

At serving time, stir in the yoghurt and mint and season to taste with salt and pepper. Spoon into bowls and sprinkle each bowl with a little grated lemon rind. Serves 4.

Chilled avocado soup

| 2 large ripe avocados |
| A little lemon juice |
| 2 cups chilled chicken stock |
| 2 cups milk |
| 1 cup cream |
| Salt and freshly ground white pepper |
| 2 shallots, finely sliced |

Peel avocados, remove stones and chop the flesh into dice. Reserve about ½ cup of diced avocado to garnish the soup.

Sprinkle with lemon juice, and chill until ready to serve.

Place remaining avocado in a bowl with stock, milk, cream and salt and pepper to taste. Puree in batches in a blender and chill, covered.

At serving time, taste soup for seasoning and ladle into chilled bowls. Top each serving with small pieces of avocado and finely sliced shallots. Serves 6.

Chilled carrot-orange soup

*An unusual soup with a subtle,
spicy-sweet taste.*

| 6 medium carrots, chopped |
| 3 cups chicken stock |
| 1½ teaspoons ground cumin |
| 1 teaspoon ground cardamom |
| 2 teaspoons sugar |
| 2 tablespoons grated orange rind |
| 1 cup orange juice |
| 1 cup pouring cream |
| Salt and freshly ground white pepper |
| Thin orange slices to garnish |

Place carrots in a saucepan with all ingredients except orange juice, cream and salt and pepper. Bring to the boil, then simmer covered for 45 minutes, or until carrots are very soft.

Whirl in batches in a blender then stir in orange juice and cream. Cover and chill for several hours.

When ready to serve, taste for seasoning and add salt and pepper and perhaps a little extra sugar. Soup must be well-flavoured. Float a slice of orange on top of each bowl. Serves 6-8.

Avocado-anchovy dip

It's an unusual but delicious combination!

| 2 medium-size, ripe avocados |
| 1 cup sour cream |
| 2 teaspoons grated onion |
| 2 teaspoons lemon juice |
| 6 flat anchovy fillets, finely chopped |
| 2 teaspoons Worcestershire sauce |
| Salt and freshly ground pepper |
| A few drops of green colouring (optional) |

Peel and pit avocados, and mash the flesh. Blend in sour cream, onion, lemon juice, anchovies, sauce and salt and pepper to taste. Place a piece of plastic film directly on the surface of the dip, and chill until serving time.

If desired, add a drop or two of green food colouring just before serving. Serve in a bowl surrounded by corn chips, celery sticks, whole radishes, sliced French bread etc, for dipping. Enough for 8-10 as an appetiser.

Pineapple boats

Here's an exciting way to treat sweet Queensland pineapple — no-one will guess what makes the flavour so intriguing!

| 1 large pineapple |
| 4 cups iced water |
| 2 teaspoons salt |

Cut pineapple in half lengthwise, through the green top to the bottom.

Cut out the centre cores, then carefully cut around the flesh and remove it in two whole pieces. Cut these pieces into bite-size chunks (not too small) and chill in a covered container. Reserve the pineapple shells.

Above 20 minutes before serving, place pineapple in a mixture of iced water and salt. When ready to serve, drain pineapple and replace in shells. Serve with toothpicks for spearing. Serves 4-6 as an appetiser, or first course.

Seafood Pacific is a superb combination of fish, mussels and prawns in a creamy sauce flavoured with wine and brandy.

Salad dressings

Salads are part of the sunny Australian way of life, and we have a choice of many dressings to complement them. The first one given here is a special favourite — and thought to be an Australian culinary invention.

Condensed milk dressing:

| ½ teaspoon dry mustard |
| ½ teaspoon salt |
| 2 tablespoons condensed milk |
| 2 tablespoons vinegar |
| A little fresh milk |

Mix together mustard, salt and condensed milk. Beat in the vinegar, than add milk little by little to give the consistency you prefer. Taste for seasoning and store in a screwtop jar in the refrigerator. Serves 2-3.

Honey lemon dressing

So easy, and delicious. Try it tossed with grated carrots and raisins, or apple wedges, walnuts and sliced celery.

| ½ cup clear honey |
| ½ cup lemon juice |
| ¼ cup medium sherry |
| 2 tablespoons toasted sesame seeds |
| ¼ teaspoon salt |

Place all ingredients in a screwtop jar and shake until blended. Chill until serving time, then shake again before using. Makes about 1½ cups.

Pink lagoon dressing

If you like a touch of the exotic, here's a dressing for you — clear, pink and sweet. Toss through crisp salad greens, or spoon over a fruit salad.

| ⅓ cup sugar |
| 1 tablespoon paprika |
| 1 teaspoon dry mustard |
| 2 teaspoons tomato paste |
| ½ teaspoon salt |
| ½ cup white vinegar |
| 1⅓ cups oil |
| 1 tablespoon celery seeds |

Place all ingredients except oil and celery seeds in a saucepan. Bring to the boil stirring, then simmer for 2 minutes. Allow to cool. Gradually beat in oil, adding very slowly and beating constantly. Stir in celery seeds.

Chill dressing before serving. Makes about 2 cups.

Boiled salad dressing

A traditional dressing for shredded lettuce and cabbage, and very good with potato salad.

| 1 egg |
| 1 teaspoon dry mustard |
| ½ teaspoon salt |
| 1 tablespoon sugar |
| ¼ cup milk |
| 2 tablespoons white vinegar |
| 15 g (½ oz) butter |

Beat egg with mustard, salt and sugar. Mix in the milk, then the vinegar. Melt butter in a small saucepan over low heat, add egg mixture and stir until dressing coats the back of the spoon. Cool, then store in a covered jar in the refrigerator. Serves 4-6.

Note: You might like to add finely chopped shallots, capers or parsley to the dressing, or a pinch of dried herbs.

Blender lime mayonnaise

A quickly-made mayonnaise with refreshing flavour. If you can't find fresh limes, use lemon juice.

| 2 egg yolks, at room temperature |
| ½ teaspoon salt |
| ½ teaspoon dry mustard |
| Pinch cayenne pepper |
| 3 tablespoons fresh lime juice |

About 1½ cups oil (a mixture of olive oil and sunflower is good)

Put egg yolks, salt, mustard, cayenne, lime juice and ¼ cup of oil in the blender. Cover and blend at low speed. Remove cover and with the motor running, add a steady stream of oil from a jug. Blend just until very thick and smooth — don't use all the oil unless it's necessary. Cover and store in the refrigerator. Makes about 2 cups of mayonnaise.

Fluffy mayonnaise

A lovely dressing for coleslaw, sliced fresh fruits, and cold fish dishes.

| 1 cup mayonnaise (home-made or bought) |
| ½ cup cream, whipped with 2 teapoons sugar |
| 1 tablespoon lemon juice |
| 2 teaspoons grated lemon rind |

Gently fold all ingredients together, and chill. Makes about 2 cups.

Jellied beetroot salad

| 3 cups finely chopped beetroot (preferably home cooked) |
| ½ cup finely chopped celery |
| 1 small onion, finely chopped |
| 1 tablespoon gelatine |
| ½ cup wine vinegar |
| 1 tablespoon sugar |
| 1¼ cups hot apple or pineapple juice |
| Salt and freshly ground pepper |

Mix beetroot, celery and onion together. Soften gelatine in vinegar, then stir into hot apple juice with sugar. Season to taste with salt and pepper.

Leave in a cool place until beginning to thicken, then combine with beetroot mixture. Spoon into a wetted mould and chill until set. Excellent with cold roast pork, pickled pork and corned beef. Serves 6-8.

Celery-cucumber salad

This crunchy, creamy salad goes beautifully with any cold meats.

| 4 sticks tender celery |
| 1 large cucumber |
| 1 tablespoon Dijon mustard |
| 2 teaspoons lemon juice |
| ¾ cup cream |
| Salt and freshly ground white pepper |
| Dash cayenne pepper |
| 1 teaspoon dill seeds |

Cut celery into 1 cm (½") slices. Peel cucumber, halve lengthwise, scoop out seeds with a spoon and cut flesh into slices. Blend mustard and lemon juice in a small bowl and slowly stir in cream. Season with salt, pepper and cayenne and stir in dill seeds. Spoon over vegetables, toss lightly, and chill until serving time. Serves 4.

Daydream salad

Fish, potatoes and apples are the main ingredients in this deliciously different main-course salad.

| 750 g (1½ lb) firm white fish fillets |
| 3 large potatoes, boiled and peeled |
| 2 sticks celery, finely chopped |
| 2 crisp apples, peeled and cut into dice |
| 1 tablespoon lemon juice |
| 1 cup mayonnaise |
| 1 tablespoon sugar |
| 2 teaspoons prepared horseradish |
| 4 shallots, finely chopped |
| 2 tablespoons finely chopped parsley |
| Salt and freshly ground pepper |
| Extra chopped shallots to garnish |

Poach fish fillets in lightly salted water until white and opaque — about 6 minutes. Drain, remove skin and bones, and separate into large flakes.

Place in a bowl with potatoes cut into bite-size cubes. Toss with celery, apples and lemon juice.

In another bowl, combine mayonnaise, sugar, horseradish, shallots, parsley, and salt and pepper to taste. Add to fish mixture, toss to combine, and chill until serving time. Serve sprinkled with chopped shallots. Serves 6.

Salad superb
(photograph right)

When you want to impress a luncheon guest, serve this sumptuous salad. It's expensive — but worth it!

| ½ ripe avocado, peeled and cut into wedges |
| Squeeze of lemon juice |
| 1 cos lettuce, or ½ firm head of lettuce |
| 4 cooked asparagus spears, cut into short lengths |
| ½ chicken breast, cooked and cut into chunks |
| 125 g (4 oz) cooked prawns, peeled |
| Salt and freshly ground white pepper |
| ¼ cup mayonnaise |
| 2 tablespoons sour cream |
| 60 g (2 oz) sliced smoked salmon |
| 60 g (2 oz) black caviar or lumpfish roe |
| Celery leaves to garnish |

Squeeze a little lemon juice over the avocado. Make a bed of lettuce leaves on a serving plate, and arrange avocado, asparagus, chicken and prawns over it. Season with salt and pepper. Arrange salmon slices overlapping on top, forming a cup shape, and spoon caviar into the middle.

Combine mayonnaise and sour cream. Spoon some over the salad, and serve remainder separately. Garnish salad with celery leaves. Serves 2.

Crab sunshine salad

Whether you use Queensland mud crabs or sand crabs, or Sydney's blue swimmers, you will do justice to the delicate flavour of crab with this golden salad.

1 large lettuce
500 g (1 lb) cooked crab meat
1 large pawpaw or rockmelon
4 hard-boiled eggs, peeled
2 tablespoons snipped chives, or finely chopped shallots (including green tops)

For dressing:

½ cup mayonnaise
¼ cup French dressing
2 teaspoons finely chopped gherkin
1 tablespoon tomato sauce
Salt, freshly ground pepper and sugar to taste

Wash and dry the lettuce leaves and shred finely. Make mounds of lettuce on 4 plates, and pile crab meat in the centre.

Peel and seed the pawpaw or rockmelon, cut into thin crescents, and arrange around the crab.

Separate the whites from the yolks of the eggs. Push the yolks through a sieve, and sprinkle over crab. Chop the whites finely and sprinkle around the lettuce. Scatter snipped chives over all, and serve with dressing. Serves 4.

Dressing: Combine all ingredients, seasoning to suit your own taste with salt, pepper and sugar.

Salad bouquets

(photograph above)

A trio of salads that look as pretty as flowers, and are especially easy to prepare.

For Rice Platter: Make a bed of lettuce leaves. Toss together 3 cups cooked rice

(1 cup raw), 1 cup drained, whole kernel corn, and ½ cup French dressing. Pile on top of lettuce and garnish with tomato wedges, cucumber slices, and strips of red pepper. Serves 4.

For Celery and Olive Salad: Slice ½ bunch of tender celery, and combine with ½ cup of mayonnaise, a squeeze of lemon juice, 2 teaspoons sugar and ½ cup cream. Spoon into a serving dish and garnish with wedges of ripe pineapple and black olives. Serves 4.

For Tomato-Onion Salad: Cut 4 medium-size, firm tomatoes into slices. Arrange on a pretty serving plate and drizzle with French dressing. Thinly slice a large onion (the purple Spanish type if available), separate into rings, and scatter over the top. Serves 4.

Surfside salad

250g (8 oz) cooked ham, cut into cubes
2 sticks celery, sliced
1 small pineapple, peeled and diced
2 tablespoons mayonnaise
½ teaspoon curry powder
1 tablespoon pineapple juice
Celery sticks and grapes to garnish

Combine ham, celery and pineapple. Mix mayonnaise, curry powder and pineapple juice together and pour over ham mixture. Toss gently. Garnish with celery sticks and small bunches of seedless grapes. Serves 4.

Confetti salad

90g (3 oz) butter
1 medium onion, finely chopped
5 cups boiled rice
2 chicken stock cubes, crumbled
2 tablespoons tomato sauce
1 red or green pepper, cut into strips
2 sticks celery, sliced
250g (8 oz) ham, cut into cubes
250g (8 oz) peeled prawns
Mayonnaise to serve (optional)

Melt butter in a frying pan and fry onion until soft and golden. Add rice, chicken cubes and tomato sauce to pan and stir thoroughly over medium heat for 2-3 minutes. Add pepper, celery, ham and prawns to rice and allow to cool. Serve mayonnaise separately if desired. Serves 6.

Island salads

(photograph page 51)

A trio of easily prepared salads for sunny days.

Melon and prawn salad

1 small rockmelon, halved and seeded
¼ small watermelon, seeded
2 grapefruit, peeled and separated into segments
2 kiwi fruit, peeled and sliced
1 can mandarin segments, drained
250g (8 oz) peeled, cooked prawns
Lettuce leaves
¾ cup salad dressing, home-made or bought
Lemon wedges to garnish

Scoop rockmelon and watermelon into balls with a melon baller, or cut into cubes. Combine with remaining fruits and prawns, cover and chill.

At serving time, spoon into a bowl lined with lettuce leaves and top with salad dressing. Garnish the salad with lemon wedges. Serves 4-6.

Sunshine salad

(photograph page 51)

1 small lettuce, washed and dried
1 small cucumber, thinly sliced
1 can mandarin segments, drained
1 small onion, thinly sliced
1 banana, thinly sliced
2 teaspoons lemon juice
½ cup French dressing

Tear lettuce into pieces and place in a bowl with cucumber, mandarins and onions. Sprinkle banana slices with lemon juice and add to bowl. Chill until serving time, then toss with the French dressing. Serves 4.

Harlequin tomatoes

(photograph page 51)

4 medium-size, ripe tomatoes
Salt and freshly ground pepper
1 cup boiled long grain rice
¼ cup cooked green peas
¼ cup drained, whole kernel corn

1 medium-size red or green pepper, finely chopped
½ cup French dressing
¼ teaspoon dried oregano
Lettuce leaves to serve

Cut a slice from the top of each tomato and scoop out the seeds and some of the flesh. Season inside with salt and pepper. Chop the flesh and mix with remaining ingredients. Fill tomato shells with the mixture and arrange on lettuce leaves. Chill until serving time. Serves 4.

Stuffed nutty mushrooms

The delicate flavour of raw mushrooms is complemented by a creamy, blue cheese filling.

24 small mushrooms
Salt and lemon juice
¼ cup sour cream
60g (2 oz) blue cheese, crumbled
½ teaspoon mild curry powder
Dash cayenne pepper
2 shallots, finely chopped
½ cup chopped pecans
Watercress sprigs to garnish

Drop mushrooms into cold water with a dash of salt and lemon juice added. Leave for a minute, then drain, pull out stems, and dry mushrooms on paper towels.

Thoroughly combine remaining ingredients, except watercress, and stuff mushroom caps. Cover with plastic film and chill. At serving time, garnish each mushroom with a little sprig of watercress. Serves 12 as an appetiser.

Kingaroy creamed onions

An ambrosial vegetable dish that pays tribute to the Queensland peanut. It's rich, so serve with a plain roast or grill.

| 500 g (1 lb) small onions |
| ½ cup cooking liquid from onions |
| 1 cup thickened cream |
| Salt, pepper and freshly grated nutmeg |
| 30 g (1 oz) butter, melted |
| ¼ cup fine breadcrumbs |
| ¾ cup finely chopped peanuts |

Boil the onions in lightly salted water until just tender. Drain, and reserve half a cup of cooking liquid.

Place onions in one layer in a shallow casserole dish. Combine cooking liquid with cream, and season with salt, pepper, and a dash of nutmeg. (Go lightly on the salt if you are using salted peanuts).

Mix together melted butter, crumbs and peanuts and scatter over the top. Bake in a preheated hot oven (200°C/400°F) for 10 minutes, or until cream is bubbly and topping golden brown. Serves 4.

Salad Bedarra

(photograph above)

| 1 small lettuce |
| 2 medium carrots, cut into sticks |
| 8 slices rare roast beef |
| 1 cucumber cut into sticks |
| 2 medium tomatoes, sliced |
| 2 teaspoons chopped parsley |
| ½ honey dew melon, cut into crescents or wedges |
| 1 bunch radishes |

For dressing:

| ⅓ cup natural yoghurt |
| ⅓ cup sour cream |
| 1 teaspoon Worcestershire sauce |
| 4 tablespoons grated Parmesan cheese |

Shred lettuce and arrange on a platter with carrot sticks on top. Arrange beef slices and cucumber sticks on the sides of the platter. Add tomato slices and sprinkle with parsley, then add honey dew and radishes. Prepare the dressing by mixing all ingredients together thoroughly, and serve separately or spoon over the salad. Serves 4.

Herbed beef salad

Leftover roast beef makes a very special salad.

| 6-8 slices rare roast beef, cut into matchstick (julienne) strips (There should be about 2 cups) |
| 2 medium onions, thinly sliced |
| ¼ cup white wine vinegar |
| ½ cup olive oil |
| 2 tablespoons drained capers |
| 2 tablespoons chopped parsley |
| 4 shallots, finely chopped |
| 2 teaspoons chopped fresh marjoram, or ½ teaspoon dried |
| 2 teaspoons chopped fresh tarragon or ½ teaspoon dried |
| ½ teaspoon dry mustard Salt and freshly ground pepper |
| Lettuce leaves to serve |

Place beef in a bowl and add onion slices separated into rings. Toss with remaining ingredients, cover, and stand at room temperature for 2-3 hours, stirring occasionally. Serve in a bowl lined with lettuce leaves. Serves 4.

Avocado, fruit and cheese platter

Refreshing, colourful and substantial enough for a main course.

| 1 lettuce, washed and dried |
| 2 medium-size ripe avocados |
| 1 small watermelon or honeydew melon |
| 3 bananas, peeled and sliced |
| 2 tablespoons lemon juice |
| 1 small pineapple, peeled and diced |
| 125 g (4 oz) cheddar cheese, cut into cubes |
| 1 punnet strawberries, hulled |
| Pink lagoon dressing (see recipe in this chapter) |

Make a bed of lettuce leaves on a large platter. Peel avocados, cut in half lengthwise and remove pits. Slice flesh into crescents and arrange in centre of platter. Surround with cubes of melon.

Toss bananas in lemon juice and arrange on lettuce leaves with pineapple and cheese. Scatter strawberries over. Cover with plastic film and chill for 30 minutes or so. Just before serving, spoon dressing over. Serves 6.

Coconut prawns with pineapple sauce

500 g (1 lb) medium-size prawns

Plain flour seasoned with salt and pepper

1 egg, beaten with 2 tablespoons water

¾ cup fine dry breadcrumbs

½ cup desiccated coconut

Oil for frying

For sauce:

¾ cup pineapple juice

¼ cup white vinegar

1 tablespoon light soy sauce

1½ tablespoons sugar

½ cup finely chopped fresh or canned pineapple

1 tablespoon cornflour mixed to a paste with a little water

Peel and de-vein prawns, but leave tails on. Make a slit along the underside of each prawn, then flatten out a little into a butterfly shape.

Dip prawns into flour, then in egg mixture, then in coconut mixed with breadcrumbs. Chill for 30 minutes to firm the breadcrumbs.

Heat enough oil in a large frying pan to give a depth of 5 cm (2 in). Fry prawns a few at a time until golden, about 3 minutes. (Remove each batch with a slotted spoon, drain on paper towels, then keep warm in a very slow oven). Serve with pineapple sauce, and boiled rice if desired. Serves 4 as an appetiser.

Sauce: Combine juice, vinegar, soy sauce, sugar and pineapple in a saucepan and bring to the boil. Pour a little hot liquid into cornflour mixture, stir to combine, then stir this back into the saucepan. Continue stirring until sauce is smooth and thickened, and taste for seasoning before serving with prawns.

The Reef fish stew

If you can get them, use 4 or 5 kinds of Barrier Reef fish in this easily-made, delectable stew. Or use whatever firm, white-fleshed fish you can find at your fish market.

90 g (3 oz) butter)

1 large onion, finely chopped

2 cloves garlic, crushed

250 g (8 oz) mushrooms, sliced

Salt and freshly ground pepper

1.5 kg (3 lb) assorted fish, cut into 5 cm (2 in) slices

1 bay leaf

2 sprigs thyme

4 sprigs parsley

1 cup fresh breadcrumbs

1 bottle dry white wine

2 tablespoons brandy

3 tablespoons finely chopped parsley

Heat the butter in a deep, heavy saucepan and fry onion, garlic and mushrooms for 3-4 minutes, or until they soften. Season with salt and pepper. Add half the fish slices, season them, and top with the bay leaf, thyme and parsley tied together. Sprinkle the breadcrumbs over, add remaining fish, and season. Pour in the wine, and bring to the boil.

Heat the brandy, pour into the saucepan and ignite it. Cover the pan and simmer fish for 10-15 minutes, or until white and opaque. Remove fish with a slotted spoon to a heated platter. Take the bundle of herbs from the broth.

Taste the broth for seasoning, stir in the parsley, then spoon over the fish. Serve with crusty bread. Serves 4-5.

Surfer's buttery scallops

Quick cooking keeps scallops tender and juicy. This dish is literally tossed together in minutes. If you have a chafing dish, you might like to cook it at the table.

500 g (1 lb) scallops

½ teaspoon salt

½ teaspoon medium curry powder

1 small onion, grated

1 clove garlic, crushed

90 g (3 oz) butter

2 tablespoons fresh lime or lemon juice

2 tablespoons finely chopped parsley

Lime or lemon wedges to garnish

Pat scallops dry with paper towels. Combine salt, curry powder, onion and garlic, sprinkle over scallops, and toss lightly. Cover and allow to stand for 15 minutes. Heat butter in a heavy frying pan, add scallops, and toss over moderately high heat for 3 minutes, or until scallops are just tender.

Sprinkle lemon juice and parsley over and stir gently to combine. Serve at once, garnished with lime or lemon wedges. Good with boiled, buttered rice. Serves 4.

Fish and lobster salad

If expense is no problem, you could use all lobster in this delectable salad.

| 1 cooked lobster weighing about 500g (1lb) |
| 500g (1lb) firm white fish fillets, steamed and cooled |
| 3 hard-boiled eggs, coarsely chopped |
| 2 gherkins, finely chopped |
| 1 tablespoon drained capers |
| 1 medium onion, thinly sliced |
| 1½ tablespoons white vinegar |
| 1 teaspoon Dijon mustard |
| Salt and freshly ground pepper |
| 4 tablespoons olive oil |
| Lettuce leaves |
| Paprika |
| Watercress or parsley sprigs to garnish |

Remove lobster meat from shell and cut into bite-size cubes. Crack claws and reserve. Remove any skin and bones from fish and cut into bite-size pieces.

Gently toss lobster and fish with eggs, gherkins, capers, onion slices, vinegar, mustard and salt and pepper to taste. Cover and chill for an hour or more.

Just before serving, pour oil over, toss again, and taste for seasoning. Spoon on to a bed of lettuce leaves, sprinkle with paprika and garnish with lobster claws and watercress. Serves 6.

Gold coast barramundi

Simply pan-fried or grilled, barramundi can hardly be bettered, but you might like to add herbs and a dash of brandy for a dinner party.

| 4 large barramundi fillets |
| Plain flour seasoned with salt and freshly ground pepper |
| 90g (3oz) butter |
| 1 teaspoon fennel seeds |
| 1 teaspoon dried thyme |
| 2 tablespoons finely chopped parsley |
| ¼ cup brandy |
| an extra 30g (1oz) butter, cut into pieces |

Dry fillets with paper towels, coat with seasoned flour and shake off excess. Heat butter in a large frying pan and cook fillets for 3 minutes each side, or until golden brown and cooked through.

Remove to a heated platter and sprinkle with fennel seeds, thyme and chopped parsley.

Pour brandy into the pan and stir to scrape up the brown bits from the bottom. Whisk in the butter, bring to the boil, and spoon over the fish. Serve at once. Serves 4.

Seafood Pacific

(photograph page 52)

| 8 fillets firm white fish |
| ¾ cup dry white wine |
| ½ cup water |
| Few sprigs parsley and thyme |
| Salt and freshly ground pepper |
| 45g (1½oz) butter |
| 2 tablespoons plain flour |
| ½ cup fish stock |
| 1 can seafood bisque or cream of oyster soup |
| 2 tablespoons cream |
| 1 tablespoon brandy |
| 12-15 steamed mussels, or 1 jar mussels, drained |
| 250g (8oz) peeled prawns |

Remove any skin and bone from fillets and cut into serving pieces. Bring wine and water to the simmer, add fish, salt and pepper and herbs, and poach fish gently for 5 minutes, or until flesh is white and opaque. Drain fish and keep warm on a serving plate. Reserve ½ cup of fish stock. Melt butter in a heavy saucepan, stir in flour over low heat and cook for 1 minute. Stir in warm stock, then undiluted soup, cream and brandy. Add mussels and prawns and heat through. Taste for seasoning and pour sauce over fish. Serves 4-6.

Hot crab puffs

If you're lucky enough to catch your own crabs, you may be looking for new ways to serve them. Here's a splendid hot idea for a first course or luncheon dish.

| 500g (lb) cooked crab meat |
| 4 rashers streaky bacon, rind removed |
| Salt and freshly ground pepper |
| 4 shallots, finely chopped |
| ½ cup sour cream |
| 1 teaspoon dry mustard |
| 1 teaspoon mild chilli sauce |
| 1 egg, beaten |

Place crab meat in a bowl. Grill bacon until crisp, cut into small pieces, and add to bowl with salt and pepper to taste and shallots. Toss to combine, then divide among 4 individual buttered ramekins.

Combine remaining ingredients and spoon over crab. Place in a preheated hot oven (200°C/400°F) for 15 minutes, or until crab is heated through and topping puffy and golden. Serves 4.

Honey chicken with tropical dip

A tropical climate just naturally encourages outdoor cookery. Here's a sensational recipe for your next barbecue.

| 6 half-breasts of chicken |
| ½ cup liquid honey |
| ¼ cup lime or lemon juice |
| ¼ cup oil |
| 1 clove garlic, crushed |
| Salt and freshly ground pepper |
| **For tropical dip:** |
| 1 large ripe avocado, peeled and chopped |
| 2 teaspoons lime or lemon juice |
| 1 tablespoon honey |
| ¼ cup cream |
| ¼ cup pineapple juice |
| ½ teaspoon mild curry powder |
| Salt and freshly ground pepper |

Place breasts in a shallow dish. Combine honey, lime juice, oil, garlic and salt and pepper to taste and spoon over chicken. Cover and marinate for an hour, turning now and again.

Remove chicken from marinade and place in a greased, hinged griller. Grill over coals until brown on both sides and cooked through, brushing often with honey mixture. Serve with Tropical dip, a crisp salad and buttered rolls. Serves 6.

Tropical dip: Mash avocado well and combine with remaining ingredients, seasoning to taste with salt and pepper. Cover and chill until serving time.

Heavenly rockmelon

For a special occasion, serve scoops of sherbet in melon halves.

2 cups water
1 cup sugar
2 teaspoons gelatine
2 extra tablespoons water
Grated rind and juice of 1 large lemon
2 tablespoons sweet sherry
4 small rockmelon
2 egg whites
Mint leaves to decorate

Bring water and sugar to the boil, then simmer uncovered for 4 minutes. Soften gelatine in the 2 tablespoons of water, and dissolve in the hot syrup. Cool a little, and stir in lemon rind and juice and sherry.

Peel and seed one rockmelon, chop the flesh, and force through a sieve or puree in a blender. (There should be 1 cup of puree). Mix well with cool syrup, pour into ice-cube trays and freeze until mushy. Turn into a chilled bowl, add unbeaten egg whites, and beat until light and increased in volume. Return to tray and freeze until firm.

Halve remaining rockmelons, scoop out seeds, and fill melons with sherbet. Decorate with mint leaves. Serves 6.

Note: You might also like to sprinkle a little green Creme-de-Menthe liqueur over the sherbet.

Buderim ginger ham

The beautiful ginger from Buderim goes all over Australia in many forms. In this recipe, preserved ginger adds flavour to baked ham steaks.

4 ham steaks
4 pineapple slices, fresh or canned
30 g (1 oz) butter, melted
1 tablespoon brown sugar
1 tablespoon finely chopped preserved ginger
1 teaspoon grated lemon rind
1 cup pineapple juice

Arrange ham steaks side by side in a shallow casserole dish. Put a slice of pineapple on top of each. Mix together remaining ingredients and spoon over ham and pineapple.

Bake in a preheated hot oven, (200°C/ 400°F) for 10 minutes, or until ham is heated through and glazed. (Baste with liquid in dish several times during this period). Serve from the dish with boiled new potatoes and green peas, or a salad. Serves 4.

Frozen pawpaw delight

A fragrant, delicious iced dessert that almost makes itself.

1 medium-size ripe pawpaw
½ cup sugar
2 tablespoons lemon juice
Pulp 1 large passionfruit
1 cup cream

Peel and seed pawpaw and cut flesh into chunks. Puree in a blender or food processor fitted with the steel blade, or push through a sieve. There should be about 1½ cups of puree.

Mix with sugar, lemon juice, passionfruit and cream and spoon into an ice cube tray. Freeze at coldest setting until firm, stirring mixture now and again.

When firm, turn temperature to normal and allow to ripen for several hours before serving. Serves 4-6.

Frosty bananas

Bananas take on an entirely new taste when you freeze them, and serve with cinnamon and cream.

4 ripe bananas
1½ tablespoons sugar
2 teaspoons cinnamon
1 cup thickened cream
Grated chocolate to decorate

Peel bananas and wrap each one tightly in plastic film. Place in freezer and freeze until solid, about 4 hours or overnight.

When ready to serve, place bananas on a chopping board and cut into thin slices with a heavy knife.

Arrange in shallow dishes and sprinkle with sugar and cinnamon mixed together. Pour cream over so each slice is lightly coated. Sprinkle with grated chocolate and serve at once. Serves 4.

Little rum and raisin tarts

Absolutely delicious for afternoon tea,
or as a dessert.

For pastry:
90g (3oz) butter
¼ cup sugar
1 egg yolk, beaten
1½ cups plain flour, sifted

For filling:
250g (8oz) Ricotta cheese
2 tablespoons dark rum
1 tablespoon cream
1 tablespoon icing sugar
½ cup chopped raisins
Whipped cream to decorate

Cream butter and sugar until fluffy, then gradually add egg yolk. Stir in 1 cup of flour with a wooden spoon, then mix in remaining flour by hand. Shape into a ball, wrap in plastic film and chill for 30 minutes.

Place pastry between two sheets of lightly floured plastic film or greaseproof paper and roll out thinly. Using a floured cutter, or the rim of a glass, cut into circles to fit greased patty tins about 7.5cm (3in) in diameter. Prick all over with a fork and bake in a preheated moderate oven (180°C/350°F) for 10-12 minutes, or until lightly browned and crisp.

Remove from oven, allow to cool for a minute or two in the tins, then gently remove to a wire rack to finish cooling. When ready to serve, add a generous spoonful of filling and top with whipped cream. Makes about 18 tarts.

For filling: Beat cheese until creamy, then beat in rum, cream and sugar. Fold in raisins and chill until ready to fill tarts.

Quick rum sauce

The romance of the tropics lies in the
word "rum". Thanks to Queensland,
we can enjoy the home-grown
product in many ways, such as this
wonderful sauce for steamed
puddings, stewed fruit or custards.

½ cup vanilla custard
(home-made or bought)
¼ cup dark rum
½ cup cream, whipped

Mix custard and rum together, then fold in the whipped cream. Serves 4.

Cherry cream freeze

Here's a rich, delicious dessert
with only three ingredients.

2 cups sour cream
1 cup cherry jam
2 tablespoons cherry brandy

Stir ingredients together, spoon into an ice-cube tray and freeze for 30 minutes only (mixture should not be frozen hard). Serve in pretty glass bowls, each with a macaroon or sweet wafer. Serves 6.

Icecream meringue cups

Crisp pastry shells made with
ground almonds are the delectable
containers for icecream and
almond-topped meringue.

1 cup ground almonds
1½ cups plain flour
¼ cup castor sugar
150g (5oz) butter, cut in small pieces
1 egg yolk, lightly beaten

For filling and topping:
10 scoops very firm vanilla icecream
3 egg whites
⅓ cup castor sugar
2 tablespoons toasted slivered almonds

Combine almonds, flour and sugar. Add butter and rub in with fingertips. Stir in egg yolk and mix to a firm paste. (This can all be done in a food processor). Wrap in plastic film and chill for 30 minutes. Divide paste into 10 pieces. Using floured thumbs, press paste against sides and base of 10 large patty tins. Bake in a preheated hot oven (200°C/400°F) for 10 minutes or until golden. Allow to cool in tins.

Preheat oven to very hot (250°C/500°F). Beat egg whites until peaks form, then beat in sugar a little at a time to form a stiff, glossy meringue. Place a scoop of icecream in each almond cup, then cover completely with meringue, making sure it touches edges of pastry all round. Sprinkle with almonds.

Bake in a very hot oven for 2-3 minutes, or until meringue is lightly tinted. Serves 10.

Meringue cups are perfect for a special
dinner party.

Avocado icecream
(photograph left)

Delicately flavoured, prettily coloured, and so easy to make!

1 small carton (½ litre) vanilla icecream

2 medium, ripe avocados

2 tablespoons honey

2 tablespoons lemon juice

Chopped avocados to decorate (optional)

Allow the icecream to soften at room temperature. Peel and pit the avocados and mash the flesh with honey and lemon juice. Combine quickly but thoroughly with icecream, then return to freezer until firm, about 1 hour.

Serve in scoops or squares, and if desired decorate with avocado. Serves 6.

Coconut icecream
(photograph below)

1¼ cups desiccated coconut

3 egg yolks

3 tablespoons castor sugar

¾ cup cream

2 tablespoons chocolate cream liqueur

Toast coconut in a dry frying pan over medium heat, stirring constantly, until light brown. Combine egg yolks and sugar; beat until fluffy. Whip cream until stiff. Combine egg mixture with cream, liqueur and nearly all the coconut. Mix thoroughly, then pour into a cake tin or mould and freeze 4-5 hours. To unmould icecream, dip mould in hot water briefly and invert on to a serving dish. Allow icecream to soften for ½ an hour before serving, then sprinkle with remaining toasted coconut. Serves 6-8.

Jade fruits with rum icecream

(photograph above)

2 crisp eating apples
2 tablespoons lemon juice
4 ripe kiwi fruit
2 tablespoons sugar
1 small carton (½ litre) vanilla icecream
2 tablespoons light rum

Peel apples, cut into matchstick-size strips (julienne) and sprinkle with lemon juice. Peel and slice kiwi fruit, combine with apples and sprinkle with sugar. Chill until serving time.

Meanwhile, place icecream in a bowl, allow to soften slightly at room temperature, and quickly stir rum through. Freeze until firm.

Serve fruit in pretty bowls, topped with scoops or squares of icecream. Serves 4.

Golden glory icecream sauce

1 tablespoon cornflour
¾ cup orange juice
1 tablespoon lime or lemon juice
½ cup sugar
Pinch salt
1 tablespoon grated orange rind
Pulp of 3 large passionfruit
3 cups diced pawpaw

To serve:

Vanilla icecream and desiccated coconut

Blend cornflour in a small saucepan with ¼ cup of the orange juice. Add remaining orange juice, lime juice, sugar, salt and orange rind. Stir over medium heat until mixture boils and is clear and thick.

Remove from heat and stir in passionfruit pulp and pawpaw. Cool, then chill for an hour or more before serving.

Serve over icecream, and sprinkle each serving with coconut. Serves 6-8.

Lemon passionfruit flummery

This delicate, beautifully flavoured dessert is suitable for any occasion, from family meals to a formal dinner party.

6 eggs, separated
¾ cup castor sugar
2 medium lemons
2 large passionfruit
1 tablespoon gelatine
¼ cup white wine
1 cup cream, whipped

Beat the egg yolks with the sugar until thick and lemon-coloured. Grate the rind from the lemons and squeeze the juice. Stir the rind into the egg yolk mixture. Heat the juice to simmering point.

Soften the gelatine in the white wine then dissolve it in the heated lemon juice. Add the passionfruit pulp.

Stir this spoonful by spoonful into the egg yolks, then stir in the whipped cream.

Lastly, beat the egg whites until they hold stiff peaks and fold through. Spoon into a pretty glass bowl and chill until set. Serves 6-8.

Frozen Grand Marnier mousse

2 egg whites
Pinch salt
6 tablespoons castor sugar
1 cup cream
¼ cup Grand Marnier liqueur
1 tablespoon grated orange rind
1 punnet strawberries

For sauce:
1 punnet strawberries
2 tablespoons Grand Marnier

Beat egg whites with salt until they form soft peaks. Gradually beat in three tablespoons of the sugar. Using same beater, whip cream until stiff with remaining sugar. Fold Grand Marnier and orange rind into cream, then combine gently with egg whites. Spoon into 6-8 individual mousse pots or small moulds, and freeze until firm, about 4 hours. To serve, unmould on to dessert plates and spoon sauce over. Serves 6-8.

Sauce: Hull berries, wash lightly, and puree in a blender or push through a sieve. Stir in Grand Marnier.

Mango whip

This is a cross between a milk shake and dessert, to serve anytime you feel like something rich, cool and sweet.

1 cup milk
2 cups ripe, diced mango
2 tablespoons honey
2 drops almond essence
2 cups vanilla or strawberry icecream

Place milk, mango, honey and essence in a blender and whirl until smooth. Add icecream and whirl again. Serve at once, with a straw and a spoon. Serves 4-6.

Lime cream tarts

Try to get fresh limes for this luscious tart — they're appearing in more and more fruit shops throughout the country.

For crumb crust:
185 g (6 oz) plain sweet biscuits
90 g (3 oz) butter
1 teaspoon cinnamon

For filling:
4 eggs, separated
¾ cup castor sugar
3 teaspoons gelatine
⅓ cup lime juice
2 teaspoons grated lime rind
½ cup cream, softly whipped
Extra whipped cream to decorate

Crush biscuits into fine crumbs, combine well with melted butter and cinnamon, and press evenly over the base and sides of a 23 cm (9 in) pie-plate. Refrigerate for 30 minutes or until firm.

Beat egg yolks with ¼ cup of the sugar until thick and lemon-coloured. Soften gelatine in lime juice, then place over hot water and stir until dissolved. Allow to cool a little and stir into egg yolk mixture with lime rind. Place over simmering water and stir until custard coats the back of the spoon, about 5 minutes. Remove from heat, and cool until beginning to thicken.

Beat egg whites with remaining ½ cup of sugar until soft peaks form and fold into custard with the whipped cream. Spoon into cold crust, chill until set, and decorate with extra whipped cream. Serves 6.

Rum cream

A luscious party dessert!
1 tablespoon gelatine
⅓ cup dark rum
2 eggs, separated
½ cup sugar
Pinch salt
1 cup milk
½ teaspoon vanilla
½ teaspoon freshly grated nutmeg
½ cup cream, whipped
Extra whipped cream and toasted slivered almonds to decorate

Soften gelatine in rum. Beat egg yolks in a basin, then place basin over simmering water (water shouldn't touch the bottom). Add sugar and salt and beat well, then beat in milk. Continue beating until mixture thickens to a creamy consistency.

Remove from heat and stir in vanilla, nutmeg and gelatine-rum mixture. Cool, then chill until beginning to set around the edges, about 20 minutes.

Beat egg whites until they hold stiff peaks and fold in. Fold in the whipped cream. Turn mixture into a mould rinsed in cold water, and chill until firm. Unmould on to a serving plate, and decorate with whipped cream and toasted almonds. Serves 4-6.

Plantation iced tea

Australia now enjoys the pleasure of iced tea, served in long glasses with ice cubes. Here's a special Queensland version.

4 cups freshly made, double-strength tea
⅓ cup sugar
4 cups mint leaves, tightly packed
4 tablespoons lemon juice
4 cups unsweetened, chilled pineapple juice
6 spears fresh pineapple
6 sprigs mint

Combine hot tea, sugar and mint leaves. Stir well, cover, and allow to cool.

Strain into a large jug and add lemon and pineapple juice.

Pour over ice cubes in 6 tall glasses, and decorate each glass with a pineapple spear and a sprig of mint. Serves 8.

Light 'n easy drinks
(photograph right)

Six refreshingly different drinks made with healthy ingredients — perfect pick-me-ups for humid days.

Bloody Jane

There's no alcohol in this version of a Bloody Mary.

2 large ripe tomatoes, peeled and chopped
¾ cup tomato juice
2 tablespoons lemon juice
2 teaspoons sugar
Salt and freshly ground pepper
1 teaspoon Worcestershire sauce
Dash cayenne pepper
Celery sticks to serve

Place all ingredients except celery in a blender, and whirl until combined. Taste for seasoning and serve with a celery stick stirrer. Serves 2-3.

Golden fizz

1 medium carrot, chopped
1 large sweet apple, peeled and chopped
½ cup orange juice

Place all in a blender and whirl until combined. Serves 2-3.

Avocado smoothie

1 large, ripe avocado, peeled and chopped
½ small cucumber, peeled and chopped
2 tablespoons lemon juice
⅓ cup plain yoghurt
Salt and freshly ground pepper

Combine all ingredients in a blender, and whirl until combined. Serves 2-3.

Strawberry sundae drink

1 punnet strawberries, hulled
½ cup strawberry or vanilla icecream
2 cups milk

Place all in a blender and whirl until combined. Serves 4.

Orange flip

1 orange, peeled and chopped
1 egg
1 cup plain yoghurt
Dash sugar

Place all in a blender and whirl until combined. Serves 2-3.

Grapefruit mint cooler

1 grapefruit, peeled and chopped
½ cup milk
½ cup vanilla icecream
6-8 mint leaves

Place all in a blender and whirl until smooth. Serves 2.

These light 'n easy drinks are fun to make and serve: From the back, they are Bloody Jane, Golden Fizz, Strawberry Sundae, Avocado Smoothie, Grapefruit Mint Cooler and Orange Flip.

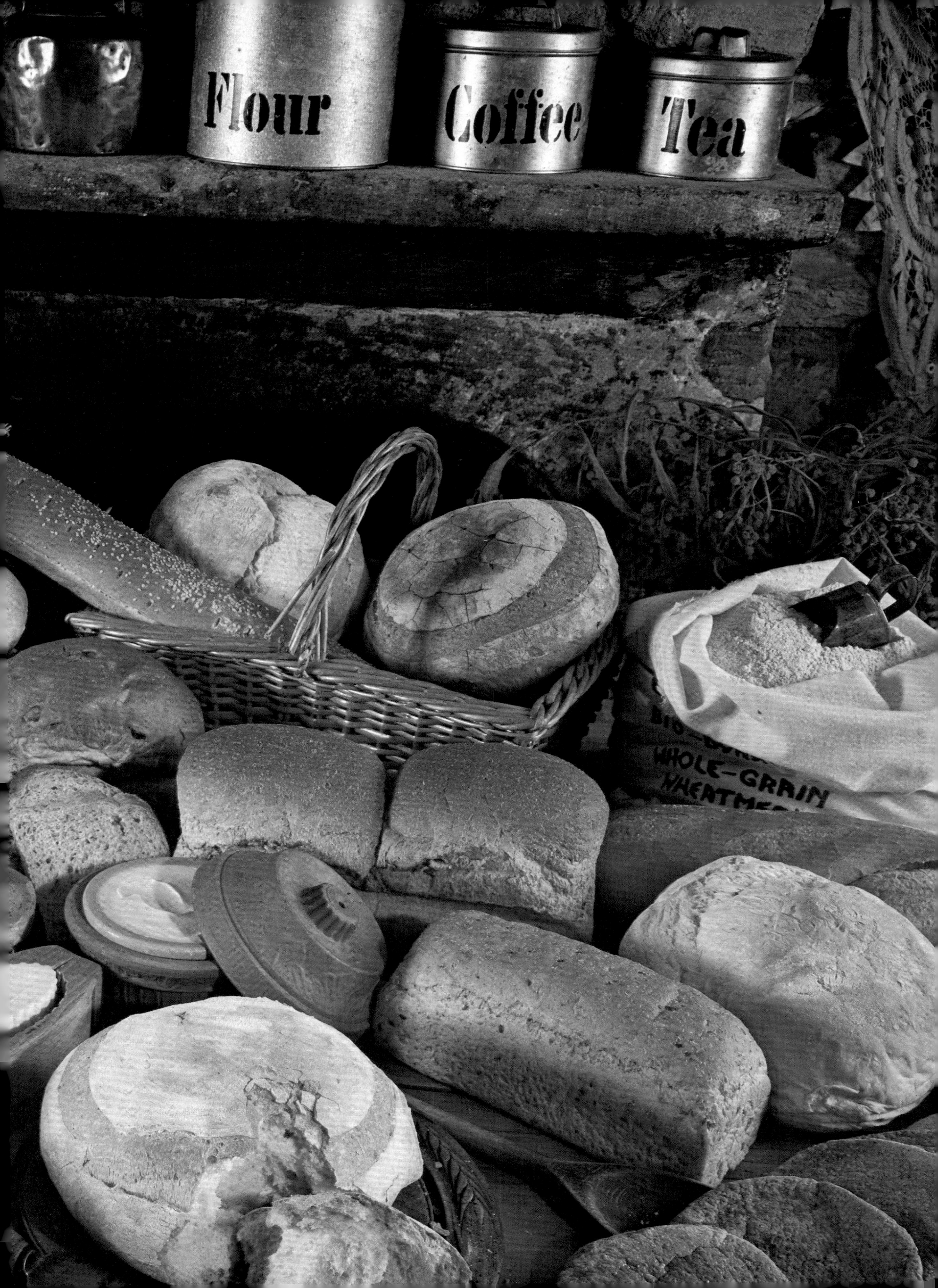
Flour
Coffee
Tea
WHOLE-GRAIN

THE VITAL GRAINS

One of the joys of childhood was Vienna bread still warm from the local bakery, delivered to the front door. The combination of soft bread, crisp crust and cold butter was irresistible at breakfast time.

Once again good bread is coming into its own – not only for the pleasure of eating it, but for its importance in the daily diet.

Dieticians say that it is healthy to eat more carbohydrates, and fewer foods high in fat, sugar and salt. Bread and cereal grains also supply fibre essential to good health and are an economical source of protein.

In Australia today we have a wonderful range of breads to choose from: rye bread, wholemeal bread, mixed grain bread, kibble bread, soya bread, rice bread, unleavened flat bread, milk bread, high fibre bread, fruit bread, black bread, bread rolls and muffins – the list seems endless.

We are also being educated more and more in the art of making our own breads, and finding it fun, as well as learning about the use of grains in good cookery.

Middle Eastern dishes made with barley and cracked wheat, brown and white rice dishes, home-made meusli and soups are only a few of the more popular foods among those of us who are interested in nutritious, creative cookery. Polenta (made from cornmeal) and semolina (from wheat) are the basis of interesting main courses and accompaniments. Oatmeal is delicious not only in porridge, but in wholesome lunch-box biscuits and slices.

In the selection of recipes which follow, for good nutrition and variety and at prices which won't dent the budget – we recommend the vital grains!

Captions to preceding 6 pages.

Page 70/71   Wheat fields with homestead, Victoria. (photography: Colin Beard)

Page 72/73   At the left of the picture, taking pride of place among breads made with Australia's vital grains, is damper — our traditional bush bread. (photography: Andrew Elton)

Page 74/75   Small homestead, southern New South Wales. (photography: Colin Beard)

Facing Page: Miss Maud's restaurant, Perth, Western Australia. (photography: Colin Beard)

Hot fruit and wheatgerm

A marvellous breakfast for cold weather — and made in a minute.

3 tablespoons wheatgerm

Dash salt

1 sliced banana or chopped apple

1 tablespoon sultanas

2 teaspoons honey

1 cup very hot milk

Put wheatgerm in a bowl with salt, banana, sultanas and honey. Pour hot milk over, and stir. Chopped nuts or chopped dried fruit may also be added. Serves 1.

Oatmeal porridge

We like the taste of bran and sultanas, in good old-fashioned porridge.

¾ cup oatmeal

2 tablespoons unprocessed bran

1½ cups water

1 tablespoon sultanas

¼ teaspoon salt

2 tablespoons honey

Place all ingredients in a saucepan and blend together. Bring to the boil slowly, then simmer for 5-10 minutes, stirring. Serve hot, with a little extra honey if desired, and milk or cream. Serves 4.

Fruit muesli

Some historians believe that muesli is almost as old as man himself — that our caveman ancestors lived mostly on a mixture of crushed grains, raw fruits and nuts. The combinations are almost limitless, so experiment with your own.

½ cup chopped dried apricots

½ cup sultanas

1 cup quick-cooking rolled oats

¼ cup wheatgerm

¼ cup bran, processed or unprocessed

¼ cup chopped walnuts, hazelnuts or almonds

¼ cup cracked wheat (burghul) or millet

2 tablespoons raw sugar

Mix all together and store in an airtight container. To serve, top with grated fresh apple or other fruits, and add milk, cream, buttermilk or yoghurt. Makes 8-10 servings.

Vegetable wheat soup
(photograph left)

Whole grains of wheat add pleasant texture to this simple country-style soup. You can buy whole wheat at health food stores.

5 cups beef stock

1 medium can tomatoes, with their juice

2 cloves garlic, crushed

½ cup wheat, soaked overnight in water

2 teaspoons sugar

Salt and freshly ground pepper

1 medium can butter beans or canellini beans, drained and rinsed

½ small white cabbage, shredded

2 teaspoons chopped fresh thyme or ½ teaspoon dried

30g (1oz) butter

Bring stock to the boil and add chopped tomatoes with their juice, garlic, drained wheat, sugar, and salt and pepper to taste. Cover and simmer until wheat is tender, about 1 hour. Add drained beans, cabbage and thyme and simmer another 10 minutes until cabbage is cooked. Taste for seasoning, stir in the butter, and serve in deep bowls with plenty of wholegrain bread. Serves 4-6.

Savoury burghul

Burghul (cracked wheat) can be used in the same way as rice to make savoury side dishes to go with meat and poultry.

90g (3oz) butter
2 tablespoons oil
1 clove garlic, crushed
1 large onion, finely chopped
2 cups burghul
3 cups hot beef stock
Salt and freshly ground pepper

For garnish:

2 tablespoons pine nuts or slivered almonds and ½ cup sultanas fried in a little butter

Heat the butter and oil in a large, deep saucepan and fry the garlic and onion until soft and golden, about 5 minutes. Add the burghul, and stir over low heat for 5 minutes. Add the hot stock and bring to the boil. Cover the pan and simmer gently until the stock has been absorbed and wheat is tender, about 10 minutes. Season with salt and pepper to taste and spoon into a heated serving bowl. If you wish, garnish with fried nuts and sultanas. Serves 6-8.

Beggar's pork

A sage-flavoured stuffing is traditional with roast pork, and apple sauce is the traditional accompaniment. Here, we've used the same flavours with marrow to make a budget-priced main course.

1 marrow about 1 kg (2 lb)
90g (3oz) butter
1 large onion, finely chopped
1 large tart apple, peeled and grated
2 teaspoons chopped fresh sage, or ½ teaspoon dried
½ cup chopped raisins
½ cup apple juice
1 cup cracked wheat (burghul)
2 teaspoons sugar
Salt and freshly ground pepper
1 egg, beaten
A little melted butter
Apple sauce to serve

Cut the marrow in half lengthwise and scoop out some of the flesh, leaving a shell about 2.5 cm (1 in) thick. Discard the seeds, and chop the flesh finely.

Heat the butter in a large frying pan, and cook the onion until soft, about 4 minutes. Add chopped marrow, apple, sage, raisins and apple juice. Bring to the boil, then simmer until marrow is soft. Stir in the cracked wheat and season with sugar, salt and pepper. Remove from heat, cool a little, stir in the egg.

Season the inside of the marrow halves with salt and pepper and spoon in the stuffing. Drizzle a little melted butter over the top, and place in a baking dish. Add about 5 cm (2 in) of water to the dish, and cover top of marrow with aluminium foil. Bake in a preheated moderate oven (180°C/350°F) for 45 minutes, or until marrow is tender. Remove foil for last 15 minutes to brown top. Serve marrow cut in thick slices, with apple sauce. Potatoes baked in their jackets at the same time would be perfect accompaniments. Serves 6.

Riverina rice crepes
(photograph right)

Delicious for breakfast with bacon, and honey or maple syrup. For dessert, top with strawberry jam and whipped cream.

1 cup plain flour
½ teaspoon salt
2 teaspoons baking powder
2 cups milk
3 eggs, beaten
2 cups cooked, short grain rice
A little oil for cooking

Sift flour, salt and baking powder into a bowl and make a well in the centre. Pour one cup of the milk into the centre, and gradually incorporate the flour, using a wooden spoon. Add the rest of the milk and the beaten eggs and mix to a smooth batter. Stir in the rice and allow to stand for 20 minutes.

Grease a crepe pan or small frying pan with oil, and heat. Using about 1½ tablespoons of batter for each crepe, cook one side until golden underneath and bubbly on top, then turn and cook the other side. Keep cooked crepes warm in a folded tea towel while frying remainder. Serves 4-6.

Corn pancakes with sour cream dip

(photograph below)

1 cup self raising flour, sifted
Salt and freshly ground pepper
1 egg, beaten with 1 cup of milk
1 cup cream-style sweet corn
Oil for cooking

For dip:

1 cup sour cream
1 tablespoon lemon juice
1 tablespoon finely chopped chives or shallots
Salt and white pepper

Place flour in a bowl and season with salt and pepper. Pour egg mixture over the top, and fold through (do not overmix). Stir in corn.

Heat enough oil to give just a thin film on the base of a large frying pan. Drop mixture by spoonfulls into pan, and cook over moderate heat until browned underneath and bubbly on top. Turn and cook other side. As each batch is cooked, place on a wire cake rack covered with a tea towel, and cover with another tea towel to keep warm. Add a little extra oil to the pan for each batch. Serve pancakes with a bowl of sour cream dip for spreading. Makes about 30 small pancakes.

Dip: Combine all ingredients, seasoning to taste with salt and pepper.

Burghul and honeydew salad

We are used to the lovely Middle Eastern salad called Tabbouleh, made with cracked wheat. Here's an Australian version with melon and pineapple.

1 cup burghul (from your health food shop)
2 cups diced honeydew melon or rockmelon
1 cup diced fresh pineapple
4 shallots, finely chopped
½ cup finely chopped parsley
½ cup finely chopped mint

For dressing:

1 tablespoon lemon juice
¼ cup pineapple or orange juice
1 teaspoon Dijon mustard
2 tablespoons honey, at room temperature
3 tablespoons walnut, apricot or olive oil
Salt and freshly ground pepper
Toasted sesame seeds to garnish (optional)

Soak burghul in plenty of cold water for 30 minutes. Drain well in a sieve and squeeze out as much moisture as possible. Spread out on a tea towel and allow to dry off for 20 minutes or so.

Place in a bowl with all other salad ingredients and toss together. Combine dressing ingredients by shaking together in a screwtop jar. Pour over salad and toss. Taste for seasoning. Spoon into a pretty bowl, and sprinkle with toasted sesame seeds if desired. Serves 6 as a first course, or as a salad with cold meats.

Lamb and vegetable couscous

Moroccan food is wonderful. In Casablanca, we learned to prepare it from a French diplomat's Berber cook, and couscous was one of the highlights. Failing a couscous steamer, and the wide range of spices used in Morocco, we have evolved this simplified recipe. It's still deliciously exotic, and you can't go wrong with the instant couscous (prepared semolina) now available from gourmet sections in department stores and health food shops.

750 g (1½ lb) boneless lamb shoulder
¼ cup oil
3 teaspoons ground cumin
2 teaspoons turmeric
½ teaspoon ground ginger
¼ teaspoon chilli powder
½ teaspoon crushed caraway seeds
1 teaspoon salt
2 large onions, cut into quarters
8 baby carrots
2 cups pumpkin, cut into chunks
2 large tomatoes, peeled and chopped
5 cups beef stock
4 sticks celery, chopped
6 small zucchini, cut into chunks
¼ cup chopped fresh coriander
1 can chick peas, drained and rinsed in cold water
1 cup sultanas
1 pkt. instant couscous, prepared according to packet directions

Remove excess fat from lamb and cut into 2.5 cm (1 in) cubes. Heat the oil in a large heavy saucepan and brown the lamb on all sides. Sprinkle lamb with spices and salt, and stir to coat evenly. Add onions, carrots, pumpkin, tomatoes and stock to the pan. Bring to the boil, and simmer covered for 1 hour, or until lamb is tender. Add remaining ingredients except couscous and simmer for another 10 minutes. Taste for seasoning — broth must be highly flavoured.

Arrange prepared couscous in the centre of a large platter, mounding it up to a conical shape in the middle.

Strain the meat and vegetables and pour 1 cup of the broth over the couscous. Arrange meat and vegetables around couscous, and serve remaining broth separately, as a sauce. Serves 6.

Pork 'n beans with corn
(photograph page 86)

A soup-stew that's hearty enough for a main course — and with corn for extra colour and nutrition. (When fresh corn is out of season, use frozen cobs or drained, canned corn).

2 tablespoons oil
750 g (1½ lb) lean pork, cut into cubes
2 medium onions, sliced
2 cloves garlic, crushed
1 teaspoon caraway seeds
1 tablespoon chopped fresh oregano, or 1 teaspoon dried
8 cups beef stock
Salt and freshly ground pepper
1 medium can kidney beans, chick peas or other dried beans, drained and rinsed
2 large carrots, sliced
3 ears corn, cut in thick slices
Lemon wedges and natural yoghurt to serve

Heat the oil in a large, deep saucepan and fry the pork over moderate heat until well browned. Add onions and garlic and cook until onion softens. Add caraway seeds, oregano, stock and salt and pepper to taste. Bring to the boil, then cover the pan and cook until pork is tender, about 1 hour. (This can all be done the night before, and the dish refrigerated until the next day).

Add drained beans, carrots and corn to the pot, and simmer until vegetables are tender, about 15 minutes. Taste for seasoning and serve in deep bowls, with crusty bread. Provide bowls of yoghurt to stir into the soup, and lemon wedges for added zest. Serves 8.

Note: If you don't like the flavour of caraway seeds, leave them out — but they do go well with pork.

Fantasia

This dish can be anything you want it to be — breakfast, lunch, dessert, snack, or campfire survival food.

3 cups milk or water

1 cup coarse cracked wheat (from the health food shop)

1½ cups chopped dried apricots

½ cup sultanas

½ cup chopped walnuts

Bring the milk or water to the boil, and add wheat a little at a time, so liquid doesn't stop boiling. Lower heat and stir in remaining ingredients, except sultanas and walnuts. Simmer covered until wheat is tender, about 20 minutes. Spoon into a bowl and sprinkle with sultanas and walnuts. Eat plain, with cream or milk, or with stewed or fresh fruit. Serves 4.

Barbecued sweet corn

(photograph below)

There are two basic approaches to roasting whole ears of corn. We give them both.

Corn in the husk: Make sure the corn is young and tender. (The time-honoured test is to pierce a kernel with your fingernail — if milk spurts out, the corn is young. If the fingernail test strikes you and the fruit shop proprietor as unhygienic, at least peel down the husk far enough to see that the kernels are smooth, small, plump and pale yellow — and not dried out.)

To prepare, gently pull down the husks without removing them, and peel away as much silk as possible. Smooth the husks back into shape, and tie into place at the pointed end with a strip of husk (use one of the outer ones). Soak the ears for ½ an hour in water, so they won't char too quickly, and drain. Arrange in a hinged, double-sized griller for easy turning, and grill directly on hot coals, or a little above them. Turn several times during cooking and allow about 10 minutes altogether. Allow to cool a little, then untie them, pull away the husks, and season corn generously with salt and pepper and melted butter.

Husked corn: Remove husks and silk from ears of corn and roll ears in melted butter. Arrange in a double-sided griller, and cook about 5 cm (2 in) above glowing coals for 3-4 minutes each side. (If some of the kernels blacken a little, don't worry — the black ones seem extra sweet and delicious). Season with salt and pepper and extra melted butter when cooked.

Note: Corn should be eaten in the hands so don't forget to provide plenty of paper napkins. Some kitchen shops sell special corn holders, but corn lovers don't think they're really necessary.

Photograph left. Pork 'n' beans with corn makes a satisfying meal in itself.

Rice and vegetable bake

(photograph right)

Brown rice is nutritious and has a pleasantly nutty texture and flavour. Combined with vegetables, milk and cheese, it makes a meal in itself.

3 cups cooked brown rice (1 cup raw)
4 sticks celery, sliced
2 medium parsnips, thinly sliced
1 small leek or onion, sliced
60 g (2 oz) butter
250 g (8 oz) mushrooms, sliced
3 tablespoons plain flour
¾ cup milk
¾ cup liquid from cooking vegetables
Salt and freshly grated pepper
1 cup grated tasty cheese

Spread rice in a greased casserole dish. Cook celery, parsnips and leek in salted water to cover until just tender, about 5 minutes. Drain, reserving ¾ cup of liquid. Arrange vegetables over rice. Heat butter in a saucepan and toss mushrooms until beginning to soften. Lower heat, stir in flour, and cook for 1 minute. Combine vegetable water and milk and stir in. Continue stirring until mixture is smooth and thickened, then season with salt and pepper to taste.

Spoon sauce over vegetables, and sprinkle with cheese. Bake in a preheated hot oven (200°C/400°F) for 15 minutes, or until heated through and cheese is melted. Serve with a green salad. Serves 4.

Creamy noodle squares

Grains are represented by pasta, as well as bread. This makes a delicious lunch, with salad, or you can serve it with grills or roast meats.

500 g (1 lb) egg noodles
1 cup creamed cottage cheese
90 g (3 oz) cream cheese
¾ cup sour cream
2 eggs, beaten
4 shallots, finely chopped
1 tablespoon lemon juice
Salt and freshly ground pepper
½ cup freshly grated Parmesan cheese
A knob of butter

Cook noodles until tender, according to packet directions. Drain well. Meanwhile, mix together cottage cheese, cream cheese and sour cream. Beat in eggs, shallots, lemon juice, and salt and pepper to taste. Combine with noodles. Spoon into a buttered casserole dish, sprinkle Parmesan cheese over the top and top with small pieces of butter. Bake in a preheated moderate oven (180°C/350°F) until brown on top, and firm. Cut into squares to serve. Serves 4-6.

Chelsea buns

(photograph page 72)

These light, fruity buns are a quickly made version, without yeast.

3½ cups self raising flour
1 teaspoon mixed spice
Dash salt
90 g (3 oz) butter cut in small pieces
1 cup warm milk
2 eggs, beaten
For filling:
90 g (3 oz) butter, softened
½ cup brown sugar
1½ cups mixed dried fruit
1½ teaspoons cinnamon
1 tablespoon grated orange rind
For glaze:
1½ tablespoons water
1½ tablespoons sugar
1½ teaspoons gelatine

Sift flour, spice and salt into a bowl. Rub in butter until mixture resembles coarse breadcrumbs. Combine milk and eggs, and mix into flour with a fork to form a soft dough. (If necessary, add a little more flour).

Form into a ball, then roll out to an oblong shape about 5 mm (¼ in) thick on a lightly floured surface. Spread with softened butter, then sprinkle evenly with brown sugar, fruit, cinnamon and orange rind. Roll up like a Swiss roll, and cut into seven equal slices. Arrange buns, sides touching, in a lightly greased 24 cm (9 in) springform cake tin. Bake in a preheated hot oven (200°C/400°F) for 45 minutes, or until well risen, brown on top and cooked through. Brush with glaze while buns are still hot, then cool and serve split and buttered.

Glaze: Mix water, sugar and gelatine together in a small bowl. Stand in a saucepan of boiling water, and stir until mixture has dissolved.

Wholemeal rounds

(photograph page 90)

This is really a wholemeal scone mixture, but baked in large rounds it looks more interesting. Try it warm, with butter and golden syrup.

2 cups wholemeal self raising flour
1¼ cups white self raising flour
1 teaspoon salt
1 tablespoon sugar
60 g (2 oz) butter, cut in small pieces
About 1½ cups milk soured with 2 teaspoons lemon juice
Melted butter to glaze

Sift flour, sugar and salt into a bowl. Rub in butter until mixture resembles coarse breadcrumbs. Add enough milk to form a soft dough. Knead a few times on a lightly floured surface, then divide dough into two and shape each piece into a ball.

Roll out into two circles a little more than 1 cm (½ in) thick. Prick top of dough with a fork (going about half-way through) into triangle shapes. Brush with melted butter, arrange on greased baking trays and bake in a preheated very hot oven (220°C/440°F) for 12 minutes, or until cooked through. Break into triangles to serve. Slice and spread with butter and golden syrup. Serve with tea or coffee. Serves 8-10.

Mustapha's pitta bread

The small rounds of flat Arab bread called Pitta bread are versatile. Try them in this unusual recipe.

2 rounds Pitta bread
¼ cup oil
Dash cayenne pepper or chilli powder
½ teaspoon salt
1 teaspoon ground cumin
½ cup finely chopped parsley
1 cup grated tasty cheese

Gently pull rounds of bread in half, to make 4 circles. Arrange on a baking tray, and toast on one side under a hot grill. Turn over so that untoasted side is up. In a small saucepan, heat oil with cayenne, salt, cumin and parsley. Pour over bread circles and sprinkle with cheese. Place under the grill until cheese is brown and bubbly. Serves 2.

Rice and vegetable bake has brown rice for nutty flavour and texture.

Cardamom buns
(photograph right)

1½ cups self raising flour, sifted
1½ teaspoons ground cardamom
Dash salt
¼ cup castor sugar
60 g (2 oz) butter, melted
1 egg, beaten
⅓ cup milk
½ teaspoon vanilla

Combine flour, cardamom, salt and sugar. Mix together butter, egg, milk and vanilla and quickly stir into the flour. Do not overmix.

Place 10 mounds of the mixture on greased baking trays. Bake in a preheated hot oven (200°C/400°F) for 12 minutes, or until cooked when tested with a skewer. Serve warm or cold, split and buttered.

Sweet rusks
(photograph right)

These keep well in an airtight jar, and are delicious spread with cream cheese and jam, or butter and honey — or just eaten plain, with a cup of tea.

3 cups plain flour
Pinch salt
3 teaspoons baking powder
⅓ cup sugar
90 g (3 oz) butter, cut in small pieces
¾ cup milk

Sift flour, salt and baking powder into a bowl and stir in sugar. Rub in butter until mixture resembles coarse breadcrumbs. Stir in milk to make a dough, then roll out to 1 cm (½ in) thickness on a lightly floured surface. Cut into circles with a scone cutter. Arrange on a greased baking tray and bake in a preheated hot oven (200°C/400°F) for 12 minutes. Remove from oven, and split each circle into two with a sharp knife. Put them back on the baking tray and return to the turned-off oven to dry out. Makes about 3 dozen.

Easy Quick Breads are made without yeast. They include Wholemeal rounds (at back), Savoury Croissants, Sweet Rusks and Spicy Instant Bread (left) and Cardamon Buns.

Spicy instant bread

(photograph page 90)

A deliciously flavoured bread to enjoy warm for breakfast — nice to make at the weekend. Hot chocolate or milk coffee go very well with it.

4 cups rye flour (from your health food shop)

½ teaspoon salt

1½ teaspoons baking powder

1½ teaspoons bicarbonate of soda

2 cups milk soured with 2 teaspoons lemon juice

1 tablespoon golden syrup

2 tablespoons finely chopped candied peel

1 tablespoon crushed cardamom or fennel seeds

2 teaspoons crushed aniseed

Melted butter to glaze

Grease an oblong bread tin or large loaf tin, and dust lightly with rye flour. Sift flour, salt, baking powder and bicarbonate into a large bowl. Make a well in the centre. Combine remaining ingredients and pour into the well, then gradually incorporate all the flour (use a wooden spoon first, then your hands). If dough seems sticky, just add a little extra flour.

Shape into a loaf, place in the prepared tin and brush top with melted butter. Bake in a preheated moderate oven (180°C/350°F) for 1½ hours, or until cooked when tested with a fine skewer. Cool for 1 minute in the tin, then turn out on to a wire rack.

Serve warm, with butter and your favourite spread. Leftovers are nice toasted. Enough for 6-8 hungry people.

Savoury croissants

(photograph page 91)

These aren't the traditional croissants made with yeast, but a savoury dough formed into croissant shapes. Fun to make!

1 ¾ cups plain flour

½ teaspoon salt

2 ½ teaspoons baking powder

60 g (2 oz) butter, cut in small pieces

¾ cup grated tasty cheese

⅓ cup creamed cottage cheese

About ½ cup milk

1 small can or jar of your favourite savoury spread (e.g. devilled ham, salmon, anchovette etc)

1 egg, beaten

Sift flour, salt and baking powder into a bowl. Rub in butter until mixture resembles coarse breadcrumbs, then work in tasty cheese and cottage cheese. Add enough milk to form a soft dough.

Divide dough in half, and roll each piece out on a lightly floured surface to a square about 5 mm (¼ in) thick. Cut each square into 4 triangles, and spread each triangle with a little savoury spread (don't spread it right to the edges).

Starting with the long edge of the triangle, roll the dough up, and hold the point of the triangle in place with a little beaten egg. Twist into a crescent shape and arrange on greased baking trays. Brush tops with beaten egg and bake in a preheated very hot oven (220°C/440°F) for 10 minutes, or until golden brown and cooked through. Makes 8.

Oatmeal kisses

Crisp little biscuits are sandwiched together with jam when ready to serve, or you can enjoy them plain.

125 g (4 oz) butter or margarine

¾ cup brown sugar, firmly packed

1 egg

1 ½ cups self raising flour

1 teaspoon cinnamon

½ teaspoon salt

1 ½ cups rolled oats

1 tablespoon iced water

Jam for spreading (apricot, raspberry, strawberry, etc.)

Cream butter and sugar until light and fluffy and beat in the egg. Sift flour, cinnamon and salt together and mix into creamed mixture. Work in oatmeal and water. Shape into a roll about 5 cm (2 in) across, wrap in plastic film, and chill for several hours or overnight.

Cut into thin slices and arrange on greased baking trays. Bake in a preheated moderately hot oven (190°C/375°F) for 7 minutes, or until crisp and golden. Cool for a minute on the tins, then remove with a metal spatula to wire racks to finish cooling.

Store in an airtight container, and when ready to serve, sandwich two biscuits together with jam. Makes about 2 dozen "kisses".

Quick fruit and nut loaf

A moist loaf made with oil for easy mixing.

2 ½ cups self raising flour (you may use equal parts of wholemeal and white flour if you wish)

1 teaspoon salt

1 teaspoon mixed spice

¾ cup brown sugar, firmly packed

½ cup chopped walnuts

¾ cup mixed fruit

2 eggs, beaten

¼ cup oil

1 cup milk

1 teaspoon vanilla

Sift flour, salt and spice into a bowl, and stir in the brown sugar, walnuts and fruit. Combine eggs, oil, milk and vanilla. Pour into the dry ingredients and stir with a fork just until moistened. Spoon into a greased loaf tin and bake in a preheated moderate oven (180°C/350°F) for 50-60 minutes, or until cooked when tested with a skewer. Serve warm or cold, sliced and buttered.

Damper

(photograph page 72)

Damper is the original Australian bread, requiring (in its basic form) only flour and water. Damper and billy tea sustained stockmen, squatters and bushrangers alike in our earlier days, and damper has resurfaced as a rather smart thing to serve in restaurants.

A genuine, old-time damper should be baked directly in hot ashes, dusted off, and consumed along with its charred crust. Meanwhile, here is a "citified" version for home cooks. Add the herbs if you are serving damper just with butter, leave them out if you want to enjoy it with honey or jam.

3 cups self raising flour

1 ½ teaspoons salt

60 g (2 oz) butter, cut in small pieces

2 tablespoons chopped fresh herbs (optional)

½ cup milk

½ cup water

Sift flour and salt into a bowl and rub in butter until mixture resembles breadcrumbs (add herbs if using). Make a well in the centre, add milk and water mixed together, and stir lightly with a knife until mixture leaves side of the bowl.

Knead a few times on a lightly floured surface, then shape into a ball. Pat into a circle that will fit into a greased 20 cm (8 in) cake tin.

Cut two slits in the top, about 1 cm (½ in) deep. Brush top with a little milk, then dust with sifted flour. Bake in a preheated hot oven (200°/400°F) for 30 minutes, or until cooked when tested with a fine skewer. Serve warm, sliced and buttered.

Pull-apart bread

Golden-brown slices just pull apart for easy serving — and the method is streamlined, too, using an electric mixer.

| 5 ½ cups sifted plain flour |
| 1 sachet dry yeast |
| 3 tablespoons sugar |
| 2 teaspoons salt |
| 1 ½ cups water |
| ½ cup milk |
| 3 tablespoons oil |
| 60 g (2 oz) butter |

Place 2 cups of the flour in a mixing bowl and combine with yeast, sugar and salt. Heat water, milk and oil together until hot but not boiling. Add to flour-yeast mixture and beat with electric mixer at medium speed for 2 minutes, scraping the bowl several times.

Blend in another ¾ cup of flour at low speed, then beat at high speed for 3 minutes. Work in remaining flour with your hands to make a soft dough.

Turn out on a lightly floured surface and knead until smooth and elastic, about 5 minutes. Place in a warmed, oiled bowl and turn over to cover lightly with oil on all sides. Cover with a tea towel and leave in a warm place for 1 ½ hours, or until doubled in bulk.

Punch dough down with your fist, turn out on a lightly floured board, and cover with the bowl. Let stand for 10 minutes. Divide dough in half and knead a few times. Roll each half out to a rectangle about 40 × 20 cm (16 × 8 in). Roll up firmly from the short side, like a Swiss roll, and cut each roll into 12 slices. Brush each slice with melted butter and stack together again in two greased loaf tins, to form two loaves with 12 slices

each. Let rise again in a warm place until doubled in bulk.

Bake in a preheated very hot oven (220°/440°F) for 30 minutes, or until bread is golden and sounds hollow when tapped. Cool on wire racks, and pull slices apart to serve. Makes 2 loaves.

Banana muesli loaf

There's a delicious combination of flavours and textures in this healthy loaf.

| 90 g (3 oz) butter, softened |
| 2 teaspoons grated lemon rind |
| 1 tablespoon grated orange rind |
| ½ cup raw sugar |
| 2 eggs |
| ½ cup chopped dates or raisins |
| 3 medium-size ripe bananas, mashed |
| ¼ cup chopped walnuts |
| 2 cups wholemeal self raising flour |
| ½ teaspoon bicarbonate of soda |
| Dash salt |
| ½ cup muesli, plain or toasted |
| ⅓ cup orange juice |

Cream butter with fruit rinds and sugar until light and fluffy. Beat in eggs one at a time, then dates, bananas and walnuts.

Sift the flour with bicarbonate and salt and stir in the muesli. Add to butter mixture alternately with orange juice. Spoon into a loaf tin that has been greased and lined on the bottom with greased paper.

Bake in a preheated moderate oven (180°C/350°F) for 1 hour, or until cooked when tested with a fine skewer. Turn out and cool on a wire rack. Serve plain, or sliced and buttered.

Honey-bran muffins

Serve hot from the oven, with butter and a little extra honey. Deep muffin tins are available in Australia now, or you can use deep patty tins.

| 1 ½ cups self raising flour |
| ½ teaspoon salt |
| ¾ cup processed bran |
| ½ cup sultanas |
| 1 egg, beaten with ¾ cup milk |
| ¼ cup hot water |
| ¼ teaspoon bicarbonate of soda |
| 3 tablespoons honey |
| 45 g (1 ½ oz) butter, melted |

Sift flour and salt into a bowl and mix with bran and sultanas. Place egg and milk in a bowl. Mix together hot water, bicarb, honey and butter, then combine with egg and milk.

Tip the liquid ingredients into the flour and mix together just until combined. Don't overmix — batter will still be a little lumpy. Spoon into greased muffin tins, filling them 2/3rds full, and bake in a preheated hot oven (200°C/400°F) for 15 minutes, or until golden brown and cooked through when tested with a skewer. Eat while hot, pulling them apart with the fingers (don't cut with a knife). Makes 12.

Mixed flour bread

1 cup rye flour
3½ cups plain wholemeal flour
1½ cups plain white flour
2½ teaspoons salt
2 teaspoons brown sugar
2 sachets dry yeast
2¼ cups lukewarm water
45g (1½oz) butter, melted
2 tablespoons poppy or sesame seeds

Sift flours and salt into a large bowl, and mix in sugar and yeast. Make a well in the centre. Mix warm water with melted butter, pour into the well, and mix to a soft dough. (Use a wooden spoon first, then your hand).

Knead well on a lightly floured surface until dough is smooth and elastic. Place in a warm, greased bowl and brush top with a little warm water. Cover with a tea towel and leave in a warm place until doubled in bulk, about 1 hour.

Punch dough down with your fist, draw edges to the centre to form a ball, then knead for a minute on a floured surface.

Divide dough in halves, shape into loaves, and fit into two greased 500g (1 lb) bread loaf tins. Moisten tops with a little warm water and allow to rise in a warm place until doubled in bulk. Brush tops again with warm water and bake in a preheated very hot oven (220°C/440°F) for 35 minutes, or until golden brown on base and sides and hollow when tapped. Makes 2 loaves.

Wholemeal bread, photographed below is delicious warm from the oven with butter and honey or your favourite cheese. Like all breads it freezes well, so you can make a double batch and thaw the extra loaves when required.

Wholemeal bread

(photograph left)

4 cups wholemeal plain flour
2 cups white plain flour
2½ teaspoons salt
2 teaspoons brown sugar
2 sachets dry yeast
2¼ cups lukewarm water
2 tablespoons oil
A little warm water

Place flours, salt, sugar and yeast in a large bowl and make a well in the centre. Pour water and oil into the well, then gradually mix in the flour, using a wooden spoon first and then your hand.

Knead on a lightly floured surface for 5 minutes, or until dough is smooth. Wash the mixing bowl in warm water, dry, and grease lightly. Put the dough in the bowl and cover with a tea towel. Leave in a warm place until dough is doubled in bulk — a very slow oven (100°C/200°F) with the door open is suitable.

Punch dough down with your fist, draw edges together to form a ball, then knead for a minute or two on a floured surface. Divide dough in half, shape each half into a loaf and fit into two greased 500g (1 lb) bread loaf tins. Brush tops with a little warm water and leave in a warm place again until dough has risen about 5 mm (¼ in) above the edges of the tins.

Brush again with a little warm water, and bake in a preheated very hot oven (220°C/440°F) for 35-40 minutes. To test if bread is cooked, turn out of tin. If sides and base are golden brown and crusty, and sound hollow when tapped, bread is done. If not, return to oven for 5-10 minutes. Makes 2 × 500g (1 lb) loaves.

Wholemeal raisin loaf

Economical and so easy to make. Unlike most breads, this should be wrapped in foil and allowed to mature for a day before cutting.

1 cup raisins, cut in half
1 cup raw sugar
1 tablespoon honey
15 g (½ oz) butter

½ teaspoon each cinnamon, nutmeg, cloves and ginger

1 cup water
2 teaspoons grated lemon rind
2¼ cups plain wholemeal flour
¼ teaspoon salt
2 teaspoons bicarbonate of soda

Place raisins, sugar, honey, butter and spices in a saucepan with 1 cup of water and bring to the boil. Remove from stove and allow to cool. Stir in lemon rind, then flour sifted with salt and bicarb.

Spoon into a loaf tin that has been greased and lined with greased paper. Bake in a preheated moderate oven (180°C/350°F) for 1¼ hours, or until cooked when tested with a fine skewer. Cool on a wire rack, then wrap in foil and store in a cake tin for 1 day before serving. Serve sliced and buttered for morning or afternoon tea, or packed in lunch boxes.

Hot cross buns

2 cups plain flour
1 teaspoon salt
1 teaspoon mixed spice
½ cup castor sugar
1 sachet dry yeast
1⅓ cups milk
60g (2 oz) butter
1 egg
¼ cup chopped mixed peel
¼ cup currants
¼ cup sultanas
2 extra cups plain flour
Glaze and icing (see below)

Sift the 2 cups of flour, salt and spice into a large bowl. Mix in sugar and yeast. Place milk and butter in a saucepan, and stir just until butter dissolves. Remove from heat and cool to lukewarm. Whisk in the egg.

Add liquid mixture to dry ingredients and beat for 2 minutes with a wooden spoon. Add peel and fruits, then work in the remaining 2 cups of flour (easiest to do by hand). Turn out on a lightly floured

surface and knead until smooth and elastic.

Place dough in a greased bowl, cover with a tea towel and allow to rise in a warm place for 30 minutes. Turn dough out, divide into 12 pieces, and shape each piece into a ball. Place on greased baking trays and allow to rise in a warm place for 20 minutes.

Bake in a preheated very hot oven (220°C/440°F) for 15-20 minutes, or until golden brown and cooked through. Brush with glaze while hot, allow to set, then pipe a cross on top of each bun with icing. Makes 12.

Glaze: Place 2 tablespoons sugar, ½ teaspoon mixed spice and 2 tablespoons water in a small saucepan and boil until mixture is syrupy.

Icing: Mix ¼ cup of icing sugar with a few drops of lemon juice, just enough to give a firm spreading consistency. Use a toothpick to draw crosses if you haven't a piping bag.

Wholemeal hot cakes

We were introduced to these in Canada, where they were served for breakfast with pats of butter, maple syrup, grilled bacon and small grilled sausages! If you don't want to go the whole way, try them just with butter and honey and a cup of good coffee.

1 cup wholemeal self raising flour
1½ cups white self raising flour
1 teaspoon salt
1 tablespoon sugar
2 eggs, beaten with 2 cups milk
90g (3 oz) melted butter
Extra butter for cooking and serving

Sift flour and salt into a bowl and mix with sugar. Add egg mixture and butter, and stir with a wooden spoon until the ingredients are well blended.

Heat enough butter in a heavy frying pan to give a thin film on the bottom, and drop batter in pan in large spoonfuls. Cook until the underneath is golden brown and the top shows small bubbles. Turn and cook the other side. Serve in stacks of 4, with a pat of butter in between. Makes about 20.

COASTAL BOUNTY

As an island continent, Australia has a superb variety of fish and shellfish from which to choose — there are over 70 varieties of fish alone. But it is only quite recently that we have begun to make the most of this bounty of our seas.

Many of our grandmothers and mothers would have flinched from preparing squid, much less eating it! Today, squid and octopus have moved from the menus of little Italian restaurants to more and more home dining tables. We even call squid by its Italian name of calamari, and know three or four delicious ways of cooking it.

Fish shops, where sure favourites such as oysters, bream, snapper, garfish, flake and flathead were mainly sold, have now begun stocking a wider and more exciting range of seafood. Now we are tempted by fresh sardines, mussels, Spanish mackerel, jewfish, trevally, redfish, gemfish and more.

Is there a scallop as luscious and delicate as the Tasmanian scallop? Oysters as delicious as Sydney rock oysters? Fish as sweet, firm and white as Queensland's barramundi? Or seafood as tempting as Western Australia's rock lobsters, abalone from our Southern waters, and the sweet-fleshed prawns found in so many places off the coast?

Not many overseas visitors will disagree that our coastal bounty is among the finest in the world.

The beautiful picture introducing this chapter was taken at Doyle's, a restaurant that symbolises seafood for Sydneysiders and tourists alike.

We are delighted to give you some of Alice Doyle's own recipes, taken from her book, The Doyle's Fish Cookbook.

Captions to preceding 6 pages.

Page 96/97   Alec Campbell, Seal Rocks, New South Wales. (photography: Colin Beard)

Page 98/99   Australian seafood is beautiful and abundant, and can often be enjoyed in a seashore setting, cooked in a variety of ways. (photography: Andrew Elton)

Page 100/101   Beach scene, Queensland.

Facing Page: Scallops, Huskisson, New South Wales. (photography: Colin Beard)

Hearty smoked fish soup

Once our smoked fish was almost all imported. Now we have very good smoked fish of our own — gemfish is particularly good value. Try this economical soup on a winter's night, with lots of hot buttered toast.

60g (2oz) butter
2 cloves garlic, crushed
2 medium onions, finely chopped
1 large potato, peeled and finely chopped
2 medium carrots, finely chopped
750g (1½ lb) smoked gemfish
½ cup finely chopped parsley
1 bay leaf
1 cup tomato puree
5 cups water
½ cup cream
Salt and freshly ground pepper
Freshly grated nutmeg

Heat the butter in a heavy saucepan and gently fry the garlic, onions, potato and carrots until soft, about 10 minutes. (Stir to prevent sticking). Add remaining ingredients except cream, salt and pepper and nutmeg. Bring to the boil, then cover the pan and simmer for 20 minutes, or until fish and vegetables are tender. Remove fish with a slotted spoon, take out bones, and flake the flesh. Also remove bay leaf.

Return fish to the pot with cream. Reheat just to boiling point and add salt and pepper to taste. Serve in deep bowls, sprinkled with a tiny dash of nutmeg. Serves 6-8.

Last-minute salmon soup

Keep this recipe in mind when six hungry people demand something hot and filling in 10 minutes. It can happen!

60g (2oz) butter
2 tablespoons plain flour
2 cups evaporated milk
2 cups water
1½ cups flaked, drained salmon
Salt and freshly ground pepper
1 teaspoon Worcestershire sauce
1 tablespoon lemon juice
Finely chopped parsley to garnish

Melt butter in a heavy saucepan. Stir in flour and blend well. Gradually stir in milk and water mixed together, and continue stirring over low heat until smooth and creamy. Add salmon, season with salt and pepper to taste, and stir in Worcestershire and lemon juice. Simmer for 3 minutes, and serve sprinkled with chopped parsley. With crusty bread and butter, it's almost a meal in itself! Serves 6.

Creamy prawn soup

A very special soup.
1kg (2lb) raw prawns
90g (3oz) butter
1 small carrot, finely chopped
1 small onion, finely chopped
2 sticks celery, finely chopped
2 cups stock made with prawn shells
Salt and freshly ground pepper
1 cup dry white wine
1 cup cream

Peel and de-vein the prawns, and chop finely. Place prawn heads and shells in a saucepan with 3 cups water. Bring to the boil, and simmer until reduced to about 2 cups. Strain and put aside. Discard shells.

Heat the butter in a clean saucepan and gently fry the onion, carrot and celery until soft, about 6 minutes. Add the prawn meat and stock, and simmer for 15 minutes. Season with salt and pepper.

Puree the mixture in a blender or food processor, or push through a sieve. Return to saucepan with the wine, and heat through. Add the cream and stir just until simmering point. Taste for seasoning, and serve at once in heated bowls. Serves 4-6.

Oysters the natural way
(photograph right)

Allow from 6 to 12 oysters per person, if you are using them for an entree. If the oysters have not been opened, open them and see that the shells are cleaned and that no pieces of shell are penetrating the oysters.

Wash carefully, but please do not wash and wash the oysters under a running tap. Retain as much of the oysters' natural juice as you can. If you have bought the oysters already opened, they will probably be OK and not need washing. Do not leave open oysters uncovered in the refrigerator, as this tends to dry them out and a dry film forms over the oyster flesh. Cover oysters with wet greaseproof paper if not intending to use for a while. Be careful not to make the oysters too cold. The flavour is gone if you do.

Serve on special oyster plates (these have a recess or fixed cup in the centre for sauce) or on ordinary dinner plates with small containers to hold sauces etc. in the centre. Vinegar, horseradish sauce, tartare sauce and cocktail sauce are just a few of the many sauces you can use. Serve the oysters with lemon wedges, freshly-ground pepper and salt and thin brown bread and butter. *An Alice Doyle recipe.*

Oysters Kilpatrick
(photograph right)

Here's another dish we can claim as Australian — though unfortunately, we haven't been able to unearth the identity of the "Kilpatrick" who worked out that oysters, bacon and Worcestershire sauce are made for each other.

2 dozen oysters on the shell
Freshly ground pepper
Juice of 1 lemon
Worcestershire sauce
4 rashers streaky bacon, rind removed and finely chopped

Preheat the grill to hot. Arrange oysters on the shell in the grill pan. Grind a little black pepper over, then a squeeze of lemon juice. Carefully spoon ½ teaspoon of Worcestershire sauce over each, then top with about ½ teaspoon of chopped bacon. Grill just until bacon is crisp, and serve at once. Serves 4 as a first course (6 oysters each).

Angels on horseback, oysters Kilpatrick and oysters the natural way . . . three favourite Australian ways with oysters.

Angels on horseback

(photograph page 105)

A charming name for a simple yet distinguished course of grilled oysters wrapped in bacon.

24 oysters

6 rashers streaky bacon, rind removed

Freshly ground pepper

4 slices hot, buttered toast

Lemon wedges to garnish

Remove oysters from shell, or drain well if bottled. Cut bacon into 24 squares, and wrap each one around an oyster.

Thread 6 bacon-wrapped oysters on each of 4 metal skewers. Season with a little freshly ground pepper.

Place under a preheated hot grill, and grill for 3 minutes each side, or until bacon is crisp. Serve on toast, garnished with lemon wedges. Serves 6.

Oyster patties

As children, oyster patties seemed the ultimate in sophisticated "adult" food. In those days, the little patty shells were made from scratch — and naturally, the white sauce too. Let's take some short cuts today!

20 small vol-au-vent cases (puff pastry shells)

20 oysters, on the shell or bottled

1 can cream of oyster soup

2 teaspoons lemon juice

Salt and freshly ground white pepper

1 tablespoon grated Parmesan cheese

½ cup thickened cream

Paprika to garnish

Arrange the vol-au-vent cases on a baking tray and place in a preheated hot oven (200°C/400°F) for 3-4 minutes to heat through and crisp. Drain the oysters, and reserve 2 tablespoons of juice.

Combine oyster liquid, undiluted soup and lemon juice in a saucepan and bring to the boil, stirring. Add salt and pepper to taste. Gently stir in cheese, thickened cream and oysters, and simmer together for 2 minutes.

Spoon filling into pastry cases, making sure one oyster is included in each. Sprinkle tops with a tiny dash of paprika for colour, and serve at once. Serves 10 as part of an appetiser tray (2 each).

Prawn cocktail

(photograph below)

Its success depends on using crisp lettuce, the freshest prawns, and a sauce that's well-flavoured but does not overwhelm the delicate taste of the prawns themselves.

500g (1 lb) cooked prawns, peeled

2-3 teaspoons lemon juice

Salt and freshly ground white pepper

8 slices brown bread

Butter for spreading

Crisp lettuce leaves

Cocktail sauce:

½ cup thickened cream

2 tablespoons tomato sauce

1 teaspoon prepared horseradish

1 teaspoon sugar

1 teaspoon white vinegar

Salt and freshly ground white pepper

Dash Worcestershire sauce (optional)

If the prawns have been refrigerated, let them come to room temperature before serving. If they have prominent dark veins in the back, carefully remove them — small to medium size shouldn't need de-veining. Toss in a bowl with lemon juice and a little salt and white pepper.

Make 4 sandwiches of the brown bread and butter, trim the crusts, and cut each sandwich into 4 triangles. Line 4 pretty glass dishes with lettuce leaves or shredded lettuce. Pile prawns on top. Add a spoonful of sauce, or pass sauce separately, and serve with triangles of bread and butter. Serves 4.

Sauce: Mix all ingredients together until well blended. Taste for seasoning, and add a little extra vinegar or sugar, or a dash of Worcestershire sauce to suit your own taste.

Photograph right:
Grilled lemon mussels make a simple, but unusual first course.

Crumbed scallops

One of the simplest ways to serve scallops, and one everybody enjoys.

750 g (1½ lb) scallops

Plain flour seasoned with salt and pepper

2 eggs, beaten with 2 tablespoons water

Cornflake or cracker crumbs to coat

90 g (3 oz) butter

3 tablespoons oil

Lemon wedges and tartare sauce to serve

Pat scallops dry with paper towels. Roll in seasoned flour and shake off excess. Dip in egg mixture, and then in crumbs. Chill for 10-15 minutes to firm the crumbs. Heat butter and oil in a large, heavy frying pan. Add scallops without crowding the pan — you will probably need to cook them in batches.

Fry over moderate heat for 2 minutes each side, or just until crumbs are crisp and golden. Be careful not to overcook. Drain each batch on paper towels, and keep warm on a baking try in a slow oven. Serve with lemon wedges and tartare sauce. A crisp, green salad is the only accompaniment needed. Serves 4.

Balmain avocado salad
(photograph left)

Use the pretty shells to present the salad!

5-6 Balmain bugs

½ avocado, peeled and cubed

½ tomato, finely chopped

½ teaspoon finely chopped chives

½ teaspoon chopped fresh dill

2-3 teaspoons mayonnaise (preferably home-made)

Salt and freshly ground pepper

Dill sprig to garnish

Cook Balmain bugs for approximately 5 minutes in salted water. Cool, remove meat from tails and cube. Gently toss together all ingredients and chill. To serve, pile salad into the centre of a platter and arrange Balmain bugs around outer edge. Garnish with a fresh dill sprig. Serves 1.

Mussels a la Portuguese
(photograph page 98)

I don't know why we call this dish "Portuguese" — we get the mussels in Sydney. In fact, in my day mussels were exclusive to us Watsons Bay locals. Anyway, it's a smart name and a dish cooked to perfection by Peter and Joe at Doyles on the Beach. Alice Doyle.

1-1.5 kg (2-3 lb) mussels

4 shallots, finely chopped

1 clove garlic, chopped

2 tablespoons olive oil

3 teaspoons butter

⅔ cup dry white wine

⅓ cup water

3 teaspoons finely chopped parsley

2 fresh thyme sprigs or pinch dried thyme

1 or 2 bay leaves

½ teaspoon ground black pepper

125 ml (4 oz) fresh cream

Extra chopped parsley

Lemon quarters

Wash mussels under running water, remove all traces of mud, seaweed and barnacles with brush or knife; remove beards (the rough, furry part around the mussel). If mussel shells are cracked or broken, discard them. If any mussels are slightly open, tap sharply and if they do not close, discard.

Gently fry shallots and garlic in olive oil and butter until transparent but not coloured. Add wine, water, parsley, thyme, bay leaf, pepper and mussels.

Pour cream over the top. Cover pan, bring to the boil and steam over a high heat for about 4 minutes, shaking pan constantly. The shells will open as the mussels cook.

Serve as soon as the shells open. Serve in deep bowls like mixing bowls, garnished with chopped parsley and lemon quarters. Mmmmmm — delicious.

Don't forget a large spoon to scoop up the juice. Serves 2-3.
An Alice Doyle recipe.

Grilled lemon mussels
(photograph page 107)

Most fish shops sell jars of mussels — here's something quick and interesting to do with them.

1 jar mussels

60 g (2 oz) butter, softened

2 cloves garlic, crushed

1 teaspoon grated lemon rind

¼ cup finely chopped parsley

½ cup fine breadcrumbs

Salt and freshly ground pepper

A little extra grated lemon rind or parsley

Drain the mussels (you can save the liquid for soup, or another fish dish). Arrange mussels in small ramekins, scallop shells, or mussel shells you have saved from cooking fresh mussels. Place on a baking tray. Combine remaining ingredients and spoon over mussels. Leave under a preheated hot grill for 3-4 minutes, or until mussels are heated through and topping is crisp and bubbly. Sprinkle with a little grated lemon rind or parsley to serve. Serves 4.

Mussel and potato salad

This wonderful salad is based on a recipe given by Alexandre Dumas junior in a play performed at the Comedie Francaise in Paris, and quoted by Alice B. Toklas in her cookbook. The method has been condensed to save space.

1 kg (2 lb) potatoes, boiled until just tender in beef stock
¾ cup best-quality olive oil
3 tablespoons white wine vinegar
Salt and freshly ground pepper
1 tablespoon finely chopped fresh tarragon, or 1 teaspoon dried
3 tender sticks celery, finely chopped
2 tablespoons finely chopped parsley
1 kg (2 lb) freshly cooked mussels, removed from their shells
125 g (4 oz) button mushrooms, sliced and marinated in a little extra oil and vinegar

Drain and peel the potatoes, and cut into thickish slices while still warm. Beat together oil, vinegar, salt and pepper to taste and tarragon. Gently combine with potatoes. Fold in the mussels, celery and parsley. Garnish with a circle of sliced button mushrooms, cover, and leave in a cool place for an hour or so to mellow the flavours. Serve with a crisp green salad. Serves 6.

Note: In the original Dumas recipe the salad was garnished with truffles cooked in champagne!

Mussels with cheese and rice

An Italian friend taught us this one. It's easy to add your own touch, with herbs, a touch of curry powder or garlic.

3 kg (6 lb) mussels in the shell
30 g (1 oz) butter
1 large onion, finely chopped
½ cup water or dry white wine
Pepper to taste
1 cup raw long grain rice
2 cups mussel cooking liquid
An extra 60 g (2 oz) butter
½ cup freshly grated Parmesan cheese
½ cup finely chopped parsley

Scrub the mussels under running water with a brush, then rinse in several changes of cold water. Discard any mussels with an open shell.

Heat the 30 g of butter and fry the onion until soft. Add mussels, wine, and pepper to taste and bring liquid to the boil. Cover tightly and steam for about 5 minutes, or until mussels open. Discard any that do not open.

Remove mussels from their shells. Strain cooking liquid and reserve 2 cups (you will be surprised how much liquid the mussels have released, so save any over for another seafood dish). Keep mussels handy in a warm place, covered.

Heat the extra 60 g of butter in a clean saucepan and gently fry the rice until it looks translucent. Add cooking liquid, bring to the boil, and cover with a lid. Simmer very gently for 20 minutes, or until tender. Fold the mussels through the hot rice, and spoon into a heated serving bowl. Sprinkle with cheese and parsley and serve at once. Serve 4-6.

Stir-fried abalone

Fresh abalone must be tenderised before cooking. It can be sliced, then pounded vigorously with a mallet; or the whole abalone can be simmered for a couple of hours, then sliced. As a final precaution against toughness, some cooks also like to marinate it in lemon juice before cooking. Canned abalone — you may be pleased to know! — is ready to use in recipes as it is.

(It's also interesting to note that the delicate ear-shaped shell of the abalone is the one that supplies mother-of-pearl for buttons and jewellery).

3 tablespoons oil
1 teaspoon finely chopped fresh ginger
1 clove garlic, crushed
4 shallots, finely chopped
500 g (1 lb) sliced abalone, fresh, or canned and drained
1 tablespoon light soy sauce
1 tablespoon dry sherry
1 teaspoon sugar
½ cup chicken stock

Heat oil and fry ginger, garlic and shallots for a few minutes over moderate heat. Add abalone, raise heat a little, and toss for a minute. Add remaining ingredients and toss another minute. Be careful not to overcook! Taste for seasoning and serve at once, with boiled rice. Serves 4 as a first course, 2 as a main course.

Scallop-bacon kebabs

500 g (1 lb) scallops
¼ cup olive oil
2 tablespoons lemon juice
2 teaspoons Dijon mustard
Salt and freshly ground pepper
6 rashers streaky bacon, rind removed
Finely chopped parsley to garnish

Place scallops in a bowl with oil, lemon juice, mustard and salt and pepper to taste. Toss lightly, cover and allow to stand for 30 minutes. Cut bacon into pieces long enough to wrap around scallops. Thread bacon-wrapped scallops on to 4 flat metal skewers (the skewers will hold the bacon in place). Grill under a preheated medium grill, turning until bacon is crisp — about 3 minutes each side. By this time, the scallops will be cooked through. Sprinkle generously with parsley and serve with buttered rice that has been tossed with toasted, slivered almonds. Serves 4 as a first course, 2 as a main course.

Lobster Newburg

(*photograph page 98*)

1 cooked crayfish (lobster) cut in half
½ cup dry white wine
¼ cup Madeira
1¼ cups thick cream
1 small can champignons, drained
Salt
Dash Tabasco
Yolks of 2 eggs
Lemon slices

Remove flesh from crayfish, place shells in oven to heat.

Place wine and Madeira in saucepan, heat, and simmer about 3 minutes. Add lobster, heat through.

Add cream, champignons, salt and Tabasco, stirring. Cook for a few minutes until all is combined and hot. When ready to serve, stir through egg yolks. Heat, but careful, do not boil.

Fill hot crayfish or lobster shells and serve with plain, boiled, seasoned fluffy rice, sprinkled over with paprika. Garnish with lemon slices, and of course, all fish dishes must be served on hot plates. Serves 2. An Alice Doyle recipe.

Whole baked fish with herbed stuffing makes a satisfying main course, served with a crisp salad or freshly cooked vegetables.

Lobster salad

(photograph page 98)

1 cooked crayfish (lobster)
Lettuce
Mayonnaise or tartare sauce or potato salad, parsley and orange slices
Stuffed olives (optional)
Salad ingredients to taste

Place the crayfish on cutting board, pull tail out and flatten. Take a sharp knife and starting from the bottom of the tail, cut evenly in two. Alternatively, ask your fishmonger to split the crayfish. Clean inside of head and take out the long "vein" extending to the tail. Some people like the coral of the crayfish in the head section and eat that. If it is very fresh, and bright yellow, why not? Rinse the crayfish carefully for a few minutes only under running water until head is clean. Place each half on a plate.

Loosen meat from shell, starting from tail and chopping or cutting the flesh a little. I always do this because sometimes the flesh is hard to cut in the shell when you are eating it with the salad.

Place a small piece of lettuce in the empty head sections and fill with tartare sauce, mayonnaise, or if liked, potato salad, fresh, crisp parsley and orange slices. I like to cut stuffed olives in half and place on the white flesh of the tail, as an extra decoration. Surround the lobster with cupped lettuce leaves filled with a selection of your own favourites — such as radishes, pineapple, cucumbers, onions, tomatoes, grated carrots and celery. Serves 1-2. *An Alice Doyle recipe.*

Delicious grilled green lobster

(photograph page 98)

Make sure your uncooked lobster is fresh and has been cleaned correctly after being cut in two. If using a frozen crayfish, be sure to defrost naturally.

1 green crayfish (lobster) split in half or 2 frozen lobster tails
Dash Tabasco
Liberal amount of butter
Sprinkle paprika
Little salt (optional)
Lemon juice
Hot melted butter
Freshly ground black pepper

Chop flesh of crayfish while still in shell. Sprinkle dash of Tabasco over each half. Add generous dabs of butter, both over and under flesh. Sprinkle over paprika, a little salt if liked (not really necessary) and a squeeze of lemon juice.

Thus prepared, place the two halves on a tin plate or griller, and put under a medium griller, basting frequently and turning over the flesh. It should be cooked in 20 minutes.

Serve your grilled green lobsters with a small container of hot, melted butter and on the table, your pepper grinder for fresh pepper.

I think this dish is very good served with whole potatoes, which have been carefully boiled, strained, split at top as though making chips but not cut through, and then brushed over with melted butter and put under a hot griller to brown and dry out. In fact, this is a delicious way of doing potatoes with any dish, meat or fish. Serves 3.
An Alice Doyle recipe.

Baked scalloped prawns

Fresh prawns are baked in layers with buttery, herbed breadcrumbs in between. It's a good way of making a kilo of prawns stretch to a main course for 6 people. (You could use cooked crabmeat the same way).

1 kg (2 lb) green prawns
125 g (4 oz) unsalted butter, melted
2 tablespoons finely chopped parsley
1 tablespoon finely chopped chives or shallots
1 tablespoon chopped fresh tarragon, or 1 teaspoon dried
1½ cups fresh breadcrumbs, rubbed through a sieve
2 tablespoons lemon juice
2 tablespoons dry sherry
Salt and freshly ground pepper
Freshly grated nutmeg

Shell and de-vein the prawns, and chop them finely. Mix the melted butter with remaining ingredients, seasoning generously with salt, pepper and nutmeg.

Sprinkle a layer of the breadcrumb mixture in 6 buttered ovenproof ramekins or souffle dishes. Add a layer of chopped prawns, then more crumbs, and so on, finishing with breadcrumbs. Place in a preheated hot oven (200°C/400°F) and bake for 15 minutes, or until prawns are cooked and topping is crisp and golden. Serve with green salad. Serves 6.

Doyle's deep-frying batter

There are so many different recipes for making batter for coating fish, croquettes, fish cakes, shellfish, etc. Once you find the one you like I suggest you stick with it, as we have.

Anyway, as requested so many times and told so many times to people from all parts of the world, here is the Doyle's batter recipe. It is so simple. The "secret" is in the beating.

Say, 1 cup plain flour
1 cup cold water gradually increasing to about 2 cups

Place the flour in basin with 1 cup of water, then with a rotary hand held beater start beating. Gradually add your extra cup of water and beat until you get plenty of "body" into that batter. You may have to add more water. The result has to be a thin, smooth, well-bodied batter that adheres to a wooden spoon. Keep testing by dipping spoon in and letting the batter drop slowly back into the mixture. If it drops slowly it's O.K. and ready to use.

Our only other "secrets" are plenty of beautiful, fresh, clean oil and the fish to go with it. *An Alice Doyle recipe.*

Peter Doyle's prawn cutlets

(photograph page 98)

Delicious, airy-fairy prawn cutlets are a favourite dish in seafood restaurants throughout Australia.

1 kg (2 lb) green prawns
Pepper and salt
Flour
Water
Oil for deep-frying
Lemon wedges or Cocktail sauce

The time-consuming part of making prawn cutlets is the preparation beforehand. Cut or pull off heads. Shell, being careful not to remove tail. Split prawn down back and de-vein. Wash and pat dry.

Open prawns out and flatten, using the flat side of a cleaver, a rolling pin or a broad-bladed knife. Season the prawns with pepper and salt and refrigerate, covered, until ready to cook.

Make a very fresh batter of just plain flour, adding cold water slowly and beating until you have a thin, runny batter, just like pancake batter.

Heat oil in a deep saucepan or fryer which should be at least half full. Dip the prawns in the batter and add to oil, a few at a time. The prawns come straight up to the surface and in a couple of minutes they are cooked. Drain well.

Serve straight away with lemon wedges or, as we do, a creamy, freshly-made cocktail sauce.

Nothing to it — no secret batters, just very fresh batter, good prawns, the best of cooking oil and cooked to order, not reheated. Serves 4 as an entree, 2 as a main course. *An Alice Doyle recipe.*

Editor's Note: Use the recipe for Doyle's deep-frying batter for the prawns.

Curried prawns

One of the original old favourites we always used to order in Chinese restaurants. Of course, now we know there are dozens of ways of making curried prawns, and they've become a favourite among home cooks.
This version is fairly mild
— but spicy.

2 tablespoons ghee (clarified butter) or oil)
1 medium onion, finely chopped
1 clove garlic, crushed
1 teaspoon finely chopped fresh ginger
1 teaspoon turmeric
1 teaspoon ground cumin
1 teaspoon ground coriander
¼ teaspoon chilli powder
1 teaspoon sugar
2 cups canned coconut milk
Salt to taste
750 (1 ½ lb) green prawns, shelled and de-veined
1 tablespoon lemon juice

Heat the ghee in a large frying pan and fry the onion, garlic and ginger over medium heat until softened, about 4 minutes. Stir in the turmeric, cumin, coriander, chilli and sugar and cook for 1 minute.

Add the coconut milk, bring to the boil, and add salt to taste. Add the prawns (cut into pieces if very large) and simmer for 4 minutes, or until they turn pink. Stir in the lemon juice, taste for seasoning, and serve with boiled rice. Serves 4.

Note: If green prawns aren't available, you may use cooked prawns. Simmer just until heated through.

Noodles with fennel and prawns

This is one of our favourite recipes — as pretty as it's delicious.

500g (1lb) green or white fettucine (ribbon noodles) or better still, a mixture of both colours
1 bulb fennel, trimmed
2 cloves garlic, crushed
Salt and freshly ground pepper
90g (3oz) butter
16 large green prawns
½ cup freshly grated Parmesan cheese
½ cup finely chopped parsley

Bring a large saucepan of lightly salted water to the boil. Add the fettucine, the whole bulb of fennel, and the garlic.

Cook rapidly for 8 minutes, or until fettucine is tender but still firm. Drain.

Place fettucine in a heated bowl. Cut the fennel into thin slices and mix through the fettucine. Season with salt and freshly ground pepper. Meanwhile, peel and de-vein the prawns. Heat the butter in a heavy frying pan and cook the prawns over medium heat until they turn pink, about 4 minutes.

Arrange the prawns over the fettucine and fennel, and pour the buttery pan juices over. Sprinkle with cheese and parsley and serve at once with crusty bread, a green salad and a glass of chilled dry white wine. Serves 4.

Whole baked fish with herbed stuffing

(photograph page 111)

1 large snapper or other whole fish
125g (4oz) butter
2 cups bread cubes
4 rashers of bacon, chopped
1 small clove garlic, crushed
1 stick of celery, sliced
3 shallots, finely chopped
2 tablespoons chopped fresh herbs, or 2 teaspoons dried
Salt and freshly ground pepper
A little melted butter
Sliced limes or lemons to garnish

Wipe cavity of fish and place fish on an oiled baking dish. Heat butter in a large pan, add bread cubes and fry until crisp and golden. Remove from pan and set aside to cool. Place bacon in the same pan, and fry until the fat runs. Add garlic, celery and shallots and cook until soft, about 5 minutes. Combine with bread cubes, herbs, salt and pepper.

Spoon filling into the fish and brush fish with melted butter. Bake in a pre-heated moderate oven (180°C/350°F) for about one hour, or until flesh is white and opaque and flakes easily when tested with a fork. To serve, cut fish into slices and serve each with a spoonful of herbed bread stuffing. Garnish with lime or lemon slices. Serves 4-6, depending on size of fish.

Garnished steamed fish
(photograph above)

A slimmer's special — steamed fish garnished with julienne vegetables.

4 thick fillets white fish (gemfish is excellent)
A little butter
Salt and freshly ground pepper
Squeeze lemon juice
2 medium carrots
4 sticks celery

Arrange fish on a buttered, heatproof plate. Dot with a little butter and season with salt, pepper and lemon juice. Cover with another plate or aluminium foil, and place on top of a saucepan of boiling water. Steam for 10 minutes, or until fish is white and opaque and flakes easily.

Meanwhile, cut carrots and celery into matchstick strips (julienne). Cover with boiling, salted water and boil just until tender-crisp, about 3 minutes. Drain and season. Serve fish on a hot plate, with the juices that have collected in the plate poured over, and a garnish of the vegetables. A boiled or baked potato is a lovely accompaniment, and acceptable in a slimming routine if you eat it plain or with a little natural yoghurt. Serves 4.

Spiced cold fish

Fish steaks are cooked in an aromatic liquid, which forms a jellied sauce when cold. An unusual first course or luncheon dish.

6 fish steaks about 2.5 cm (1 in) thick
¼ cup olive oil
4 shallots, finely chopped
2 cloves garlic, crushed
2 cups water
2 tablespoons lemon juice
1 teaspoon grated lemon rind
1 teaspoon ground cumin
1 teaspoon curry powder
Salt and freshly ground pepper
2 teaspoons sugar

Remove any skin and bones from fish. Heat the oil, and fry the shallots and garlic until softened, about 3 minutes. Add remaining ingredients, bring to the boil and simmer for 3 minutes.

Add fish steaks and simmer for 25 minutes, or until fish is cooked. Arrange fish in a shallow serving dish. Taste liquid for seasoning, strain over fish, and chill. Delicious with a cucumber salad. Serves 4.

Crisp-skin ginger fish

*Double frying gives fish a really
crunchy surface. It's a method
the Chinese have perfected, and not
too difficult to manage at home.*

4 medium-size whole bream
2 teaspoons finely chopped fresh ginger
1 tablespoon salt
¼ teaspoon Chinese 5-spice powder
Plain flour
Oil for deep frying
1 tablespoon light sesame oil
Finely shredded shallots to garnish

Make sure fish are thoroughly cleaned
and scaled. Make 3 diagonal slashes
through the skin on each side of fish.

Mix together ginger, salt and 5-spice
powder and brush over inside and outside
of fish. Cover, and leave for several hours.

Dip fish on both sides in flour, and
gently shake off excess. Leave another
15 minutes to dry out.

Heat enough oil in a deep fryer or
heavy saucepan to cover fish completely.
Lower fish into hot oil in a frying basket,
and fry until golden and crisp, about
4 minutes. Remove and drain on paper
towels. (You will probably need to cook
fish in 2 batches).

Reheat oil, and fry again for 3 minutes,
or until brown and very crisp. Drain well,
arrange on a hot platter, and sprinkle
with sesame oil and shredded shallots.
Serve with boiled rice. Serves 4.

Note: Light sesame oil is available at
Asian grocery shops. If you can't find it,
use ordinary oil flavoured with a little
extra grated ginger.

Fish souffle

*If you have some leftover, cooked fish
(fresh, smoked or canned) here is
an exciting thing to do with it.*

1 cup cooked, flaked fish
60g (2oz) butter
3 tablespoons plain flour
1 cup milk
3 egg yolks, beaten
Salt and freshly ground pepper
2 tablespoons grated Parmesan cheese
4 egg whites
Butter and fine, dry breadcrumbs

Chop fish very finely. Melt the butter
over low heat, add flour, and stir for 1
minute. Add milk and stir constantly
until sauce boils and thickens. Mix a
little of the hot sauce into the beaten egg
yolks, then tip this mixture back into the
pan and stir just until the sauce returns to
the boil.

Remove from heat and stir in fish, salt
and pepper to taste and grated cheese.
Beat egg whites to a firm snow and fold
in. Spoon into a souffle dish or other
straight-sided dish that has been buttered
and sprinkled with breadcrumbs. Place
in a preheated hot oven (220°C/450°F)
and bake for 20 minutes, or until puffed
and golden. Serve at once. Serves 4.

Marinated fried mullet

*Mullet is a good-looking fish that
enjoys cruising under wharves and
around pylons — or it did when we
were children holidaying in the
Woy Woy district of New South
Wales. The job of "jagging" a mullet
seems a bit barbaric in retrospect,
but Dad always welcomed the catch,
and had his special way of cooking it.
Buy mullet (if you don't jag your
own) from fish markets, or fish shops
with a good turnover. It must be fresh.*

4 medium-size mullet
Salt
1 onion, finely chopped
Juice of 1 lemon
1 tablespoon sugar
1 teaspoon crushed peppercorns
Cornflour for coating
Oil for frying
Lemon wedges to serve

Clean the mullet thoroughly, remove
heads, and rub inside with salt to remove
the black membrane. Cut into thick slices. Place in a shallow dish with onion,
lemon juice, sugar and peppercorns.
Cover, and marinate for 1-2 hours, turning pieces over now and again.

Drain fish and pat dry with paper
towels. Dip both sides in cornflour and
shake off excess.

Heat enough oil in two heavy frying
pans to give a depth of about 2.5 cm
(1 in). Add fish, and fry over moderate
heat until crisp and golden underneath,
about 3 minutes. Turn and cook the other
side, until flesh is white and opaque all
through, and flakes easily. Serve with
lemon wedges, chips, and a green salad.
Serves 4.

Baked fish parcels

*This easy cooking method is suitable
for fish steaks, thick fillets,
or small whole fish.*

4 thick pieces fish
60g (2oz) butter, melted
4 small bay leaves
4 slices onion
4 thin slices lemon
4 tablespoons finely chopped parsley
125g (4oz) mushrooms, sliced
Salt and freshly ground pepper

Cut 4 pieces of aluminium foil big enough
to wrap around fish.

Butter the foil, and place a piece of fish
in the centre of each. Drizzle melted butter over, then top with the remaining
ingredients.

Fold the foil around fish to seal it
securely, arrange parcels on a baking
tray, and place in a preheated moderate
oven (180°C/350°F). Bake for 20 minutes, or until fish flakes easily when tested
with a fork. Serve parcels unopened, so
diners can open their own at the table.
Serves 4.

Barbecued whole fish

*A lovely way to cook trout,
bream, or any firm-fleshed fish. A
hinged, double-sided griller makes
it easy to turn the fish without
breaking them.*

4 whole fish, each weighing about 500g (1lb)
Oil
4 thick slices onion
4 sprigs parsley
4 thin slices lemon
Salt and freshly ground pepper
Lemon wedges to garnish

Make sure fish are thoroughly cleaned
and scaled. Make 3 diagonal slashes on
each side and brush inside and out with
oil. Season generously with salt and pepper, and place an onion slice, a sprig of
parsley and a slice of lemon in the cavity
of each.

Brush 2 hinged grillers generously with
oil, and place fish inside. Grill over glowing coals for about 5 minutes each side,
or until flesh is white and opaque and
flakes easily. Serve with lemon wedges.
Serves 4.

Fish in prawn sauce

(photograph right)

| 750 g (1 ½ lb) firm white fish fillets |
| ¼ cup dry white wine |
| Few sprigs parsley |
| 1 bay leaf |
| Salt and freshly ground pepper |
| Water to cover |
| 60 g (2 oz) butter |
| 2 tablespoons plain flour |
| 1 cup stock from cooking fish |
| ½ cup milk |
| ¼ cup cream |
| 1 small bunch spinach, cooked and finely chopped |
| 500 g (1 lb) old potatoes, boiled and mashed |
| 250 g (8 oz) prawns, peeled |

Remove any skin and bones from fish and cut into serving pieces. Place in a large frying pan with wine, parsley, bay leaf, salt and pepper to taste and just enough water to cover.

Bring to the simmer, and cook for 15 minutes, or until fish is white and opaque and flakes easily when tested with a fork. Drain fish, reserving 1 cup of stock. Melt the butter in a heavy saucepan, stir in the flour and cook for 1 minute. Slowly stir in the fish stock, then the milk. Stir until mixture boils, then remove from heat, stir in cream and season with salt and pepper. Add prawns and fold through.

Place a layer of spinach in a casserole dish. Arrange fish on top, and spoon prawn sauce over. Pipe or spoon the potatoes around the edge of the dish. Place in a preheated hot oven (200°C/400°F) for 15 minutes, or until heated through. Serves 4-6.

Pipis in wine and mushrooms

Pipis are small molluscs found on surf beaches from Queensland to Western Australia. The smooth shells with their shiny purple lining are familiar to everyone who has ever gone shell-gathering. Once used only as bait, pipis are now appearing on restaurant menus and are usually available at fish markets — or if you are quick off the mark, you can gather them yourself along the shorelines. This is an easy and delicious recipe.

| 1 kg (2 lb) pipis in the shell |
| 60 g (2 oz) butter |
| 1 tablespoon oil |
| 1 medium onion, finely chopped |
| 1 fat clove garlic, crushed |
| 2 medium tomatoes, peeled and chopped |
| 1 tablespoon chopped fresh basil, or 1 teaspoon dried |
| 1 cup dry white wine |
| 125 g (4 oz) mushrooms, finely chopped |
| Salt and freshly ground pepper |
| 1 teaspoon sugar |
| ¼ cup finely chopped parsley |

Soak pipis in cold, salted water for 1 hour, then drain. Heat butter and oil in a wide, deep saucepan or frying pan. Add pipis, onion and garlic and toss over moderate heat until pipis open, about 5 minutes. Add remaining ingredients, cover the pan, and simmer for 10 minutes. Taste for seasoning, ladle into heated bowls, and serve with plenty of crusty bread. Serves 4 as a first course, 2 as a main course.

Note: Our Australian pipis are equivalent to what Americans call clams, so are interchangeable in any clam recipes you find.

Garlic squid

Three varieties of squid are fished commercially in Australia, the most common one being found from northern Queensland right around the coast to Western Australia.
The preparation is a little fiddly, but 80% of the squid is edible and the flesh succulent and delicate. If in doubt about how to clean, ask your fishmonger for a practical demonstration.

| 12 small squid |
| ¼ cup olive oil |
| 2 fat cloves garlic, crushed |
| Salt and freshly ground pepper |
| ¼ cup dry white wine |
| 2 tablespoons finely chopped parsley |
| Lemon wedges to serve |

With a good tug, pull away the head and tentacles from the body pouch. Discard the internal organs, which will also come away. Cut off the head near the base of the tentacles and discard. Rinse the body pouch well under running water, and slide out the cellophane-like backbone. Peel the skin from the body and tentacles (or rub skin off with salt). Cut the tentacles into rings, and the body into slices.

Heat the oil in a heavy frying pan, add garlic, and fry for a minute over moderate heat. Add squid and salt and pepper to taste and toss for 5 minutes.

Add wine, and bring to the simmer. Taste for seasoning, and stir in parsley. Serve at once, with crusty bread, fried bread, or boiled rice. Serves 3-4.

Note: With a little bit of luck, the ink sac will remain intact when you pull off the head of the squid. If it bursts, you will have to rub stains with salt and rinse well to remove.

Deep fried squid

(photograph page 98)

| 1 kg (2 lb) squid, thoroughly cleaned and skinned |
| 1 large clove garlic, bruised |
| 1 cup sauterne |
| Pepper and salt |
| Plain flour |
| Batter (see Doyle's deep-frying batter) |
| Olive oil for deep frying |
| Lemon wedges |

Wash squid and pat dry. Cut into rings, place in saucepan. Add water to cover, garlic, sauterne and freshly ground pepper and salt to taste.

Boil squid gently for 1 hour. Drain, discarding garlic, and cool.

When squid is cool and dry, roll in flour seasoned with salt and pepper, dip in batter and deep fry in hot oil until golden. Remove and drain. Serve hot with bread and lemon wedges. Serves 4-6. An Alice Doyle recipe.

Fish in prawn sauce is a delicious combination of fish fillets and prawns in a subtle, wine-flavoured sauce, on a bed of spinach, garnished with creamed potatoes and baked in the oven.

Little fish parcels
(photograph below)

Smoked fish makes a tasty filling, or you could use salmon or prawns.

| 4 sheets ready-rolled puff pastry |
| 1 egg, beaten |

For filling:

| 1 medium-size can creamed sweet corn |
| 500 g (1 lb) smoked fish, cooked and flaked |
| 1 small green pepper, finely diced |
| ½ cup sour cream |
| 2 tablespoons chopped parsley |
| Salt and freshly ground pepper to taste |

Prepare filling by mixing all ingredients together. Cut each pastry sheet in half and divide filling among the 8 pieces of pastry. Moisten edges with water and fold pastry over the filling, pressing edges together firmly. Place the parcels on a baking tray. Brush with beaten egg and bake in a preheated hot oven (200°C/400°F) for 20-30 minutes, until golden brown. Serves 8.

Pan-fried fish
(photograph page 98)

Pan frying is often the best cooking method when you have small fillets of fine-textured fish such as whiting, John Dory or silver bream. For something extra special, may I suggest you fry in pure olive oil. You can then enjoy your fish hot or cold, served with freshly ground pepper and salt and lashings of lemon. Then of course it is also delicious fried in butter or your favourite frying oil. I think margarine, especially polyunsaturated, tends to stick to the pan.

For 6 large fillets beat 2 eggs in 1 cup of milk, and put aside. Dip each fillet into plain flour seasoned with salt and pepper. Shake off excess. Dip floured fillets into egg mixture and place in a pan containing a little oil heated almost to boiling point. (If liked, you can roll fillets in breadcrumbs as a final step before placing in the pan). Cook until golden — about 10 minutes if the fillets are thin, 15 minutes if thick — please don't overcook. Serve with lemon wedges dipped in finely chopped parsley.

Note: Put extra milk with the egg mixture to make it go further.
An Alice Doyle recipe.

Fish roll

Another money-stretching idea, using leftover fish or canned fish.

| 2 cups sifted self raising flour |
| ½ teaspoon salt |
| 90 g (3 oz) butter, cut into small pieces |
| About ¾ cup of milk |

For filling:

| 2 cups drained, flaked salmon or other cooked fish |
| 1 cup cooked green peas |
| 4 sticks celery, finely chopped |
| 1 small onion, grated |
| 1 cup thick white sauce |
| 2 tablespoons grated tasty cheese |
| 1 tablespoon lemon juice |
| Salt and freshly ground pepper |

Sift flour and salt into a bowl. Rub in butter until mixture resembles coarse breadcrumbs. Add enough milk to make a soft dough — you may not need the whole ¾ cup. Turn out on to a lightly floured surface, and knead into a ball. Roll out into an oblong shape 5 mm (¼ in) thick.

Mix together filling ingredients and spread evenly over dough within 2.5 cm (1 in) of the edges. Roll up gently and carefully like a Swiss roll, tucking in ends so filling won't ooze out. Brush with a little milk, make a few slits in top for steam to escape, and place on a greased baking tray.

Bake in a preheated very hot oven (220°C/440°F) for 10 minutes, then reduce heat to moderate (180°C/350°F) and bake a further 35 minutes, or until pastry is crisp and golden. Let stand for 5 minutes, then cut in thick slices to serve. Serves 6.

Note: You can make the white sauce with a packet mix if time is short.

Pickled cold fish

*A piquant, cold first course for
a summer dinner party.*

*750g (1½ lb) thick fish fillets
(snapper, gemfish or barramundi)*

½ cup olive oil

2 large onions, thinly sliced

2 cloves garlic, crushed

*1 teaspoon coarsely crushed black
peppercorns*

8 whole allspice

½ cup white vinegar

¼ cup water

1 tablespoon sugar

2 bay leaves, crumbled

1 teaspoon salt

Pinch cayenne pepper

Cut fish into 2.5 cm (1 in) squares. Heat the oil in a heavy frying pan, and fry the fish on both sides over moderate heat until golden and cooked through, about 3 minutes each side. Remove with a slotted spoon and drain on paper towels.

Add onions and garlic to the saucepan, and cook until softened, about 3 minutes. Add remaining ingredients, bring to the boil, and simmer for 3 minutes. Taste for seasoning.

Remove any skin and bones from fish and place in a shallow glass or pottery dish. Pour hot liquid over, and cool. Cover tightly with plastic film or aluminium foil, and chill for several hours before serving. Serve fish in small bowls, with the onion slices arranged on top and the strained liquid spooned over. Serves 6 as a first course.

Old-fashioned fish pie

*Fish fillets are sandwiched together
with stuffing, then baked and topped
with tomatoes and mashed potatoes.*

8 thin fish fillets (such as bream)

Salt and freshly ground pepper

1 cup soft white breadcrumbs

1 clove garlic, crushed

2 tablespoons finely chopped parsley

60g (2 oz) butter, melted

½ teaspoon dried mixed herbs

1 teaspoon grated lemon rind

½ cup cream

*2 medium tomatoes, peeled and
thinly sliced*

*2 cups seasoned mashed potatoes
(instant will do)*

1 egg, beaten

Carefully pick over fish fillets and remove any skin and bones. Arrange 4 fillets side by side in a buttered, shallow casserole dish, and season with salt and pepper. Combine breadcrumbs, garlic, parsley, melted butter, herbs, lemon rind and salt and pepper to taste. Spread over fish.

Arrange remaining fillets on top, and season. Spoon cream over, cover dish with foil, and bake in a preheated moderate oven (180°C/350°F) for 20 minutes, or until fish flakes easily when tested with a fork.

Remove from oven, arrange tomato slices on top and season with salt and pepper. Combine mashed potato and egg and spread over all. Return dish to the oven for 5 minutes or until potato topping is lightly browned. Serve from the casserole with a green vegetable. Serves 4.

Crunchy fillets

*Coat fillets in cornmeal
for extra crunchiness.*

6 medium fish fillets

*Plain flour seasoned with salt
and pepper*

1 cup evaporated milk

About 1 cup cornmeal (polenta)

60g (2 oz) butter

2 tablespoons oil

Lemon wedges to serve

Pat fillets dry, roll in flour and shake off excess. Dip in evaporated milk, then in cornmeal. Chill for 15 minutes to firm the crumbs.

Heat butter and oil in a heavy frying pan, and fry fillets on both sides over medium heat until brown and crisp, about 3 minutes each side. Drain on paper towels and serve piping hot with lemon wedges. Serves 4-6.

Note: For a change, use equal amounts of polenta and wheatgerm.

Lazy Lil's fish stew

It's ready in 30 minutes.

¼ cup olive oil

1 small carrot, finely chopped

1 medium onion, finely chopped

*4 sticks celery (with leaves)
finely chopped*

1 fat clove garlic, chopped

1 bay leaf

1 tablespoon tomato paste

1 cup dry white wine

Salt and freshly ground pepper

*1 kg (2 lb) firm fish fillets,
cut in 5 cm (2 in) pieces*

2 tablespoons finely chopped parsley

Buttered rice or noodles to serve

Heat the oil in a large, heavy saucepan and fry the vegetables until tender, about 6 minutes. Add bay leaf, tomato paste and wine and simmer for 5 minutes. Season with salt and pepper to taste, add fish pieces, and cover the pan. Simmer until fish is cooked through, 6-8 minutes. Taste for seasoning, and sprinkle with chopped parsley. Serve with buttered rice or noodles. Serve 6.

Note: This is also a good way to dress up fish fingers. Cut in 2 or 3 pieces, and simmer just until heated through.

Smoked fish supreme

This is a "pantry cupboard" recipe — for that occasion we all face now and again, the need to produce a tasty main course in a big hurry.

| 3 cups freshly cooked rice (about 1 cup raw) |
| 500 g (1 lb) smoked fish |
| 60 g (2 oz) butter |
| Salt and freshly ground pepper |
| Milk to cover |
| 1 packet white sauce mix |
| 2 tablespoons chopped dill or parsley |
| 2 × 200 g cans prawns |

Toss the hot rice with butter and salt and pepper to taste. Spread in the bottom of a greased, shallow casserole dish. Place the fish in a frying pan with enough milk to cover it, and simmer for 8 minutes, or until fish is white and flakes easily. Drain, reserving milk. When cool enough to handle, remove skin and bones from fish and separate into large flakes. Make up the white sauce to medium thickness, according to packet directions, and using the milk from the fish. (If necessary, add more milk).

Drain the prawns and rinse in a sieve under cold running water. Pat dry, and combine with the white sauce and chopped dill or parsley.

Arrange fish over the rice and cover with sauce. Place in a preheated very hot oven (220°C/440°F) for 5 minutes, or until heated through and bubbly. Serve with crustry bread and a green salad. Serves 4-6.

Fried tiny fish

Fish shops often have a display of tiny fish in the window. They may be called anchovies, pilchards or sardines, but by any name are sweet and delicious. We like them crisply fried, and served as an appetiser with lemon wedges, tartare sauce, and brown bread and butter.
The preparation is the longest part of this recipe — the rest is easy!

| 500 g (1 lb) tiny fish |
| Salt and freshly ground pepper |
| Lemon juice |
| Cornflour |
| Oil for frying |

Wash the fish and drain well. Grasp each fish by the body and squeeze with the thumb to flatten it. Grasp the head with the other hand, and pull off and downward at the same time (sounds complicated, but you'll be fine with a little bit of practice). The head will come away attached to the backbone, giving you a perfect little filleted fish.

When all are prepared, season them with salt and pepper and sprinkle with lemon juice. Roll in cornflour, shake off excess, and spread out on a tray to dry off for 10 minutes.

You can then deep-fry the fish in hot oil until crisp and golden, or shallow-fry in about 1 cm (½ in) of oil in a frying pan. Either way, they will only take a minute.

Serve piping hot. Serves 2-3 as an appetiser.

Salmon rissoles

These were once a Sunday night favourite in every second Australian home. Made with Australian canned salmon or tuna, they're economical as well as tasty.

| 1 × 450 g can salmon or tuna |
| 2 cups hot, mashed potato (instant will do) |
| 1 medium onion, grated |
| 1 tablespoon lemon juice |
| 2 teaspoons anchovy paste |
| 1 egg, beaten |
| Salt and freshly ground pepper |
| Fine, dry breadcrumbs |
| 60 g (2 oz) butter |
| 2 tablespoons oil |
| Lemon wedges or sauce for serving (see note) |

If using salmon, remove any skin and bones. Flake fish and place fish and juice from can in a large bowl. Mix in hot potato, onion, lemon juice, anchovy paste and egg.

Season with salt and pepper and shape into 8 balls. Roll in dry breadcrumbs, then pat into 8 cakes.

Heat oil and butter in a heavy frying pan, and fry cakes on both sides until crisp and golden, about 3 minutes each side. Serve with lemon wedges or sauce. Serves 4.

Note: Tartare sauce or mayonnaise flavoured with chopped fresh dill is nice with salmon rissoles. Or you can use white sauce flavoured with anchovy paste, or with a chopped, hard-boiled egg folded through.

Buffet fish pie
(photograph right)

Here's a striking centrepiece for your next buffet party, a spinach and tuna filling enclosed in pastry cut in the shape of a fish.

| 2 × 375 g pkts. puff pastry |
| 1 large bunch spinach |
| 60 g (2 oz) butter, cut in small pieces |
| Salt and freshly ground pepper |
| Freshly grated nutmeg |
| 4 hard-boiled eggs, chopped |
| 2 tablespoons chopped fresh dill, or 1 teaspoon dried |
| 2 large cans (440 g) tuna packed in oil |
| 1 cup thickened cream |
| 1 egg, beaten |

Roll out one packet of pastry to a rectangle about 40 × 20 cm (16 × 8 in). Cut into a fish shape with a sharp knife. Trim stalks from spinach, wash leaves well, and cook until tender. Drain, chop very finely and cool.

Spread spinach on fish shape, leaving a 2.5 cm (1 in) border of pastry all around. Season with salt, pepper and nutmeg, and dot with butter.

Sprinkle chopped eggs and dill over spinach, then tuna, broken into flakes. Spoon thickened cream evenly over tuna. Roll out second packet of pastry and cut into a fish shape. Brush edges of bottom crust with beaten egg, and press top crust firmly into place. Using a sharp knife, mark gills, fins and tail. With the points of a pair of scissors, snip rows of scales, and use a raisin or olive for the eye. Make a couple of slits in the top for steam to escape, and brush with beaten egg.

Bake in a preheated hot oven (200°C/400°F) for 10 minutes. Reduce heat to moderate (180°C/350°F) and bake a further 20 minutes or until crisp and golden. Serve hot or cold, with tartare sauce or mayonnaise and a green salad. Serves 6-8.

At grand banquets in colonial days the pastry cooks would present splendid dishes in extravagant ways to impress the guests and show off their skills. Dishes like our buffet fish pie were served after hours of patient preparation. Our fish pie looks spectacular but is easy as pie to make with ready-made pastry!

A LITTLE BIT OF ENGLAND

In this chapter we wish to pay tribute not only to the English, but the whole of Britain, to the Scots, the Welsh and the Irish – all those good cooks among our early colonists who brought their traditional recipes and skills with them when they landed on our shores.

The hot southern climate was mighty different from that of their colder homelands, nevertheless they persevered with the presentation of the warming, filling dishes they knew. Incongruous though some of them may be, most are still happily with us and have become an important part of the Australian cuisine.

Thick soups, stews, roasts, grills, pies and puddings have never lost their appeal in Australia. Mum still cooks them when the family comes to dinner, and they are still the main attractions on the menus of many country hotels and boarding houses.

In fact, there is an increasing revival of restaurants serving English-style food in the appropriate atmosphere all over Australia. From Western Australia to Tasmania, we find converted old stone houses and inns with roses around the door. They're as popular with locals as they are with weekend travellers and tourists, who welcome the nostalgia they impart. Lace cloths and doyleys grace the tables and tea is served with proper ceremony.

Even among gourmets and the well-travelled, there can be as much discussion about the merits of perfect bread-and-butter pudding as there is about the latest creative triumph of a fashionable young chef.

Here is a selection of lovely traditional foods from the lands of our British forefathers, for you to cook and enjoy in your own homes.

Captions to preceding 6 pages.

Page 122/123   The stables of Entally House, near Launceston, Tasmania, established in 1819. The smaller, brown stone building on the left is a chapel. (photography: Colin Beard)

Page 124/125   Turkey, plum pudding, fruit cake and mince pies; a typical Australian Christmas dinner in the British tradition, photographed at Lazar Restaurant, Melbourne, Victoria. (photography: Phil Wymant)

Page 126/127   Old stone bridge, Hadspen, Tasmania. (photography: Colin Beard)

Facing Page: Inverness, Moss Vale, New South Wales. (photography: Colin Beard)

Creamy tomato soup

750 g (1½ lb) ripe tomatoes, roughly chopped
4 shallots, chopped
2 teaspoons sugar
1 cup water
Salt and freshly ground pepper
45 g (1½ oz) butter
2 tablespoons plain flour
2 cups milk
½ cup pouring cream
2 tablespoons each finely chopped parsley, mint and fresh basil

Place tomatoes, shallots, sugar, water and salt and pepper to taste in a saucepan. Cover, and cook over low heat for 30 minutes, or until tomatoes are very soft. Rub mixture through a sieve to make a puree, and wash and dry saucepan.

Melt butter in the saucepan, add flour, and stir over very low heat until well blended. Gradually stir in milk, then the tomato puree. Continue stirring until soup comes to the boil, then stir in cream and herbs. Taste for seasoning, and serve in heated bowls. Serves 4-6.

Cream of barley soup

A Victorian favourite with a subtle flavour you will enjoy today.

125 g (4 oz) pearl barley
4 cups chicken or veal stock
½ cup milk
½ cup pouring cream
60 g (2 oz) butter
Salt and freshly ground pepper
Finely chopped parsley to garnish

Place the barley in a saucepan, cover with cold water, and bring to the boil. Simmer for one minute, then drain. Return to the saucepan with the stock, and simmer covered for 2 hours or until very tender.

Whirl the soup in a food processor or blender, or rub through a sieve, pressing through as much solids as possible. Return to the saucepan with the milk and cream and stir gently until piping hot. Add the butter cut into small pieces and season to taste with salt and pepper.

Serve in heated bowls, and sprinkle generously with parsley. Serves 4-6.

Three Scottish soups

(photograph right)

Here are 3 famous soups that have become part of our Australian culinary tradition.

Scotch broth

500 g (1 lb) neck of lamb
⅓ cup barley
6 cups lightly salted water
1 small turnip, cut into small pieces
2 sticks celery, chopped
2 medium carrots, chopped
1 leek, cleaned and chopped
1 medium onion, chopped
1 wedge of cabbage, sliced
Salt and freshly ground pepper
2 tablespoons finely chopped parsley

Trim as much fat as possible from meat and put in a saucepan with lightly salted water and barley. Bring to the boil, then simmer covered for 1 hour. Skim any froth from the top and add vegetables except cabbage and parsley. Simmer covered for another 30 minutes. Remove bones from soup, cut off the meat, chop into small pieces, and return to the pot. Add cabbage and season to taste with salt and pepper. Simmer for another 15 minutes, or until cabbage is tender. Taste for seasoning, ladle into heated bowls, and sprinkle with parsley. Serves 6.

Note: Some recipes add parsnip to the broth, others leave out the cabbage or leek. We hope you enjoy this version, passed on by a Scottish friend's grandmother.

Beef and vegetable soup

(photograph right)

A hearty, economical soup!
A few beef bones
8 cups water
2 large onions, chopped
4 carrots, chopped
Salt and freshly ground pepper
1 small head cauliflower
1 cup shelled green peas, fresh or frozen
1 small firm lettuce

Place the beef bones in a greased baking dish, and bake in a moderate oven (180°C/350°F) until nicely browned, about 30 minutes. Place bones in a large saucepan with water, onions, carrots, and salt and pepper to taste. Bring to the boil, cover, and simmer for one hour. Remove bones and skim any froth from the surface. Break cauliflower into small florets and add them to the pot with the peas. Simmer for another 15 minutes, until cauliflower and peas are tender. Cut lettuce into strips (as for coleslaw) and add to the pot. Reheat just to boiling point, taste for seasoning, and ladle into heated bowls. Serves 8.

Cock-a-leekie soup

(photograph right)

This is traditionally made with a boiling fowl, but in Australia we are lucky enough to have chicken available at a reasonable price. It is even nicer prepared a day ahead, and reheated.

90 g (3 oz) butter
750 g (1½ lb) chicken pieces such as thighs, drumsticks
3 leeks, trimmed and sliced
8 cups chicken stock or water
Few sprigs of thyme and parsley, tied together with a bay leaf
2 tablespoons raw rice
Salt and freshly ground pepper
Chopped parsley to garnish

Heat the butter in a deep, heavy saucepan and fry the chicken pieces gently on all sides, until golden but not brown. Add leeks and fry another minute or two, stirring. Add stock, bring to the boil, and skim any froth from the surface. Add bundle of herbs, cover the pan, and simmer for 1½ hours. Remove chicken pieces and herbs from pot. When cool enough to handle, take chicken meat from bones, chop into small pieces, and return to the pot with rice. Simmer for another 30 minutes and add salt and pepper to taste. Serve in deep, heated bowls, sprinkled with parsley. Serves 6-8.

These three soups originally came to us from Scotland and are now staples in many Australian homes. Scotch broth is made with economical lamb neck. Beef soup is rich in vegetables, and Cock-a-leekie soup is made with chicken and vegetables, as the name suggests.

Kidney soup

Just as it used to be served in the gentlemen's clubs of London!

6 lamb kidneys or 250g (8oz) ox kidney
60g (2oz) butter
1 small onion, finely chopped
1 small carrot, finely chopped
5 cups beef stock
1 tablespoon cornflour mixed to a paste with cold water
Salt and freshly ground pepper
4 tablespoons dry sherry
Croutons (small squares of fried bread) to garnish

Remove skin and fatty core from kidneys, and cut kidneys into thin slices.

Heat the butter in a heavy saucepan, add kidneys and onion, and stir until kidneys are a rich brown. Add carrot and stock, cover, and simmer for 1 hour or until kidneys are very tender. Strain stock into a clean saucepan, discarding vegetables. Cut kidney slices into small dice and keep ready.

Heat the stock to boiling point, and stir a little into the cornflour mixture. Return this to the saucepan and stir over medium heat until smooth. Taste for seasoning, add chopped kidneys and sherry, and simmer for a minute. Serve in heated bowls, sprinkled with croutons. Serves 4-6.

Mulligatawny soup

English merchants trading in India soon spread the news of this delicious curry soup to other parts of the English-speaking world. It used to appear on the menus of smart Australian restaurants — and has remained a favourite among many home cooks.

1 kg (2 lb) chicken pieces, such as thighs, drumsticks, breasts
2 tablespoons plain flour
2 teaspoons curry powder
1 teaspoon turmeric
½ teaspoon ground ginger
60g (2oz) butter
6 cloves
12 peppercorns
1 large apple, peeled and diced
6 cups chicken stock
Salt to taste
2 tablespoons lemon juice
½ cup pouring cream
Boiled rice and chutney to serve

Wipe chicken pieces with paper towels. Combine flour, curry powder, turmeric and ginger and rub well into chicken. Heat the butter in a heavy saucepan, and lightly brown the chicken on all sides. Add cloves, peppercorns, apple and stock, bring to the boil, and simmer covered for 1 hour. Remove chicken pieces, and discard peppercorns and cloves.

Skin chicken, and cut flesh into small dice. Return to soup with lemon juice and cream, gently reheat, and add salt to taste. Serve in heated bowls, with hot boiled rice and chutney offered separately to stir into the soup. Serves 6.

Note: If you wish, the soup can be whirled in a blender or food processor for a smoother texture. You might also like to add other curry accompaniments such as coconut, sultanas, chopped peanuts etc. as well as the rice and chutney.

Shepherd's pie

This began its life as a way of coping with tough mutton. The shepherd's wife would cook the mutton, then chop it into small pieces and pound it in a mortar. Mixed with gravy and baked with a potato topping, it was transformed.

In Australia, it has been a favourite way to use up the remains of the Sunday roast. Our mothers often made extra gravy especially, and the sturdy iron mincer clamped on the kitchen table on Monday was a sure sign that "Shepherd's Pie" was in the offing.

500g (1 lb) cold cooked lamb or beef
30g (1oz) butter
1 medium onion, finely chopped
1 cup leftover gravy (or gravy mix made according to packet directions)
750g (1½ lb) old potatoes
An extra 60g (2oz) butter
Salt and freshly ground pepper
A little hot milk
½ cup grated cheese (optional)

Mince the meat, after removing all fat and gristle, or chop it as finely as possible by hand.

Heat the 30g of butter in a small frying pan, and fry the onion until soft and golden. Stir into the meat with the cold gravy, taste for seasoning, then spoon mixture into a greased pie dish. (The dish should not be too shallow; the meat mixture should be at least about 5cm (2 in) deep).

Peel the potatoes, boil until tender, then mash with the butter, pepper and salt, and enough hot milk to give a spreading consistency. Allow to cool.

Spread the potatoes over the meat, working lightly with a fork and roughing up the surface. If liked, sprinkle with grated cheese. Place in a preheated moderate oven (180°/350°F), and bake for 25 minutes, or until meat is piping hot and potato topping golden. Serves 4.

Tripe and onions
(photograph right)

750g (1½ lb) tripe
2½ cups milk
1 cup water
3 large onions, thinly sliced
Salt and freshly ground pepper
2 tablespoons plain flour blended to a smooth paste with a little milk
2 tablespoons finely chopped parsley

Cut the tripe into bite-size squares, place in a saucepan and cover with cold water. Bring to the boil, simmer for 1 minute, then drain.

Return tripe to the saucepan with the milk, water, onions, and salt and pepper to taste. Simmer for 3 hours, covered.

Pour about half a cup of the hot liquid into the flour paste, stirring constantly. Tip this back into the saucepan and stir until sauce is smooth and thickened. (If you like a thicker sauce, add more flour-and-water paste).

Stir in the chopped parsley, taste for seasoning, and serve piping hot. Excellent with creamy mashed potatoes. Serves 6.

There are many elaborate tripe dishes, particularly those from France and Italy, but this old-fashioned version, which is the original English one, is Australia's favourite. Delicious for a Sunday night supper in winter!

Cornish pasties

(photograph left)

For pastry:

(Same as for Apple dumplings, page 138 but without sugar)

For filling:

250 g (8 oz) rump steak
250 g (8 oz) old potatoes
1 small onion, chopped
1 small turnip, chopped
Salt and freshly ground pepper
2 tablespoons finely chopped parsley
2 tablespoons water

To glaze:

Beaten egg

Remove any fat and gristle from steak and cut meat into 1 cm (½ in) cubes. Mix with onion, turnip, salt and pepper to taste, parsley and water. Divide pastry into 6 pieces. Roll out each piece on a floured surface into a circle the size of a saucer. Divide the filling among the pastry rounds, and moisten edges of pastry. Fold circles over into a half-moon shape, and press edges firmly together. Brush tops with egg, arrange on a greased baking tray, and place in a preheated very hot oven (220°C/440°F). Bake for 20 minutes, then lower heat to moderate (180°C/350°F) and bake for another 25 minutes. Serve pasties hot, with tomato sauce. Serves 6.

Note: As with many traditional dishes, there are many recipes for pasties. In Cornwall itself, we tasted one version made mostly of potatoes and parsley, with no meat. What is not open to discussion in Australia is the essential touch we have added ourselves, a good dollop of tomato sauce!

Love in disguise

Our forefathers made great use of offal. This intriguing (if disconcerting) name describes a dish of lamb hearts, stuffed and baked, then rolled in breadcrumbs and lightly browned.

3 lamb hearts
3 long rashers streaky bacon
60 g (2 oz) butter, melted
1 egg yolk, beaten
1 cup fine, dry breadcrumbs

Stuffing:

1 cup soft breadcrumbs
2 tablespoons shredded suet or butter
1 small onion, very finely chopped
2 tablespoons finely chopped parsley
2 teaspoon chopped fresh sage, or ¼ teaspoon dried
2 teaspoons grated lemon rind
Salt and freshly ground pepper
A little water

Wash hearts and cut away all gristle and membrane. Make a cavity in the centre of each, and soak hearts in lightly salted cold water for 30 minutes. Drain and pat dry with paper towels.

Combine stuffing ingredients, adding enough water to moisten. Fill hearts with stuffing and wrap each in a rasher of bacon, securing it in place with toothpicks. Arrange hearts upright in a small baking dish, and pour melted butter over. Cover tightly with a lid or aluminium foil, and bake in a preheated moderate oven (180°C/350°F) for 1½ hours, or until tender. Carefully remove hearts and when cool enough to handle, roll in beaten egg yolk and then dry breadcrumbs. Return to the dish but do not cover, and bake for a further 10 minutes or until coating is crisp and lightly browned. Nice with red currant jelly and creamy mashed potatoes. Serves 6.

Dungog rabbit stew

Simple ingredients make a nourishing, homely stew — just the way it was made 100 years ago.

1 rabbit, cut into joints
4 rashers bacon, rind removed
2 sticks celery, finely chopped
1 large onion, finely chopped
2 large carrots, finely chopped
Salt and freshly ground pepper
1 cup water
2 cups milk
1 tablespoon cornflour blended to a paste with a little extra milk
¼ cup finely chopped parsley

Place rabbit in a deep, heavy saucepan. Chop bacon into small pieces and sprinkle over rabbit with vegetables. Season generously with salt and pepper, and pour over water and milk. Bring to the boil, then cover tightly and simmer for 2 hours, or until rabbit is very tender (turning pieces in liquid once or twice).

Transfer rabbit to a heated platter. Stir a little of the hot liquid into cornflour paste, then stir this back into the pan and simmer until sauce is smooth and thickened. Stir in parsley, taste for seasoning, and spoon sauce over rabbit. Serves 4.

Oxtail stew

Kangaroo tail can be used instead of oxtail in this simple but richly-flavoured stew.

1 oxtail, cut into slices
30g (1oz) butter
2 large onions, finely chopped
1 large carrot, sliced
1 medium turnip, cut into dice
2 tablespoons chopped, fresh mixed herbs or 2 teaspoons dried mixed herbs
3 cups beef stock
Salt and freshly ground pepper
1 tablespoon plain flour mixed to a smooth paste with a little extra stock
Chopped parsley to garnish

Trim as much fat as possible from oxtail. Heat the butter in a large, heavy saucepan and fry the onion until starting to soften. Add oxtail, carrot and turnip and stir over high heat until oxtail starts to brown. Add remaining ingredients except flour paste and bring to the boil, stirring. Lower heat, cover, and simmer for 3 hours, or until oxtail is tender.

Stir a little hot liquid into the flour paste, then stir this back into the stew. Simmer until sauce is smooth and thickened and taste for seasoning. Sprinkle with chopped parsley to serve and have lots of crusty bread to dip in the gravy. Serves 4.

Corned beef patties

Ingenuity has produced dozens of ways to bring variety to corned beef (that staple of early Australian cuisine). Here is an old favourite, good for any meal — including breakfast.

1 cup self raising flour
Good pinch salt
1 egg, beaten with 2/3 cup milk
2-3 shallots, finely chopped
1½ cups finely chopped, cooked corned beef
Oil for frying

Place flour, salt and egg mixture in a large bowl, and beat until well blended. Stir in shallots and corned beef.

Heat enough oil in a heavy pan to give a depth of about 5 mm (¼ in) and drop in large spoonfuls of the mixture. Flatten them out a little with a spatula. Cook over moderate heat until patties are brown and crispy on the bottom and bubbles appear on the surface. Turn over and cook the other side until crisp and brown. Serve piping hot, with tomato sauce or chutney. Serves 4.

Double-celery chicken
(photograph below)

Celery is used in the stuffing and also served with the chicken in this old English recipe, slightly adapted for today's cooks

1 chicken weighing about 2kg (4lb)
60g (2oz) butter
1 small onion, finely chopped
4 sticks celery, finely chopped
1½ cups soft breadcrumbs
2 teaspoons grated lemon rind
2 tablespoons finely chopped parsley
1 tablespoon currants
1 egg, beaten
Salt and freshly ground pepper
An extra 60g (2oz) butter, softened
2 cups chicken stock
½ bunch celery, cleaned and cut into short lengths

Wipe chicken inside and out with damp paper towels. Heat 60g of butter in a frying pan and fry onion and celery until soft. Remove from heat and stir in breadcrumbs, lemon rind, parsley, currants, egg and salt and pepper to taste. Stuff chicken with the mixture and truss into shape. Rub chicken all over with softened butter and place breast side up on a greased rack set in a greased baking dish. Pour stock into the dish.

Roast in a preheated moderate oven (180°C/350°F) for 1 hour, basting occasionally with pan juices. Turn chicken over on to its breast and add celery to juices in pan. Continue cooking for another 40 minutes, or until chicken and celery are tender. (Add extra stock at any time if liquid in pan is drying up).

Remove chicken to a warm platter and allow to rest for 10 minutes before carving. Remove celery with a slotted spoon and arrange around chicken. Adjust seasoning of pan juices, reheat, and serve as gravy. Serves 4-6.

Potted beef

A spicy spread that keeps well in the refrigerator (in the old days, it would have been stored in the meat safe, of course).
Serve as a snack on hot buttered toast, or spread on rounds of fried bread or French bread to enjoy with drinks.

500g (1lb) good quality beef steak such as rump or topside
60g (2oz) butter
¼ cup water
1 small onion, finely chopped
1 teaspoon salt
1 tablespoon anchovy paste
Pinch cayenne pepper
1 teaspoon freshly grated nutmeg
¼ teaspoon allspice
2 tablespoons ghee (clarified butter)

Remove any fat and gristle from beef and chop meat into very small pieces.

Place in a saucepan with remaining ingredients except ghee, bring to the boil, then simmer, covered, for 3 hours, stirring often. Cool a little, then beat with a wooden spoon until everything is well blended. Taste for seasoning, spoon into small glass or earthenware pots, and cover with a layer of melted ghee. Store in the refrigerator.

Note: If mixture seems to be drying out too much as it cooks, add a little extra butter and water.

Roast beef and Yorkshire pudding

Good roasting cuts of beef include sirloin on the bone, rolled sirloin, rump and a corner cut of topside. The method of roasting given here (which is called "quick roasting" because of the initial high temperature) gives a crisp, brown crust on the outside. Lovely!

| 2-3 kg (4-6 lb) beef roast |
| Softened butter (if meat is lean) |

| 1 tablespoon plain flour |
| 1½ cups beef stock or vegetable water |
| Salt and freshly ground pepper |
| Yorkshire pudding |

Arrange meat fat-side up on a greased rack set in a greased baking tin. If meat is lean, rub all over with a little butter.

Place in a preheated very hot oven (220°C/425°F) for 20 minutes, then reduce heat to moderate (180°C/350°F). Start timing now. For rare beef, allow 16-17 minutes for every 500 g (1 lb). For medium beef, allow 20 minutes.

When beef is cooked to your liking, remove to a platter and allow to rest for 30 minutes before carving, or while you bake the pudding. (The juices settle in the tissues, making the meat juicier and easier to carve).

Meanwhile, make gravy: Pour off all but 2 tablespoons of drippings in the baking tin, sprinkle in the flour and stir over moderate heat until blended. Stir in the stock or vegetable water and continue stirring until gravy is smooth and thickened. Season with salt and pepper to taste, and serve in a gravy boat with the beef. Serves 6-8.

Yorkshire pudding

This is a light, airy pudding with a crisp coating and spongy base which falls when it is cut. Prepare it 10-15 minutes before roast is removed from oven, and allow to stand.

| 2 eggs |
| 1 cup milk |
| 1 cup plain flour, sifted |
| ½ teaspoon salt |
| ¼ cup fat from roasting pan |

Beat eggs in a deep bowl or a food processor fitted with the steel blade. Add milk and beat in. Gradually beat in flour and salt and continue beating until batter is very smooth. Pour fat into a loaf tin about 20 × 20 cm (8 in × 8 in). Turn oven temperature up to hot (200°C/400°F) and place tin in oven until fat is smoking hot. Pour in batter and bake for 35-40 minutes, or until well risen, crisp and brown on top. Serve cut in squares with roast beef, gravy and vegetables.

Apple dumplings

(photograph below)

Whole apples are stuffed with nuts and baked inside a pastry crust. For a change, you can use sultanas or dates in the filling.

| 2 cups plain flour |
| Pinch salt |
| 1 tablespoon sugar |
| 125 g (4 oz) firm margarine or butter, cut into pieces |
| 3-4 tablespoons iced water |

| 4 medium Granny Smith apples |
| 3 tablespoons golden syrup |
| 1 cup chopped hazelnuts or walnuts |
| 1 egg, beaten |
| Sugar |

Sift flour and salt into a bowl and stir in sugar. Rub in margarine with the fingertips until mixture resembles coarse breadcrumbs. Sprinkle three tablespoons of water over the top, and mix with a knife to a firm dough. (If too dry, add a little extra water). Wrap in plastic film and chill for 30 minutes.

Divide dough into four pieces and shape each piece into a ball. Roll out on a lightly floured surface to a circle large enough to wrap around apples. Peel and core apples. Mix golden syrup and nuts together and use to stuff apples. Place an apple on each pastry square, dampen the edges of the pastry, and wrap firmly around the apple.

Place dumplings seam-side down on a greased baking tray. Brush with beaten egg and sprinkle with sugar. Bake in a preheated hot oven (200°C/400°F) for 20 minutes.

Reduce heat to moderate (180°C/350°F) and bake for a further 30 minutes, or until apples are soft when tested with a fine skewer. Serve dumplings warm with cream or custard. Serves 4.

Rhubarb crumble

The touch of ginger is a trick learned from a great-grandmother. It seems to mellow the tartness of the rhubarb, and not as much sugar is needed.

1 bunch rhubarb
½ cup sugar
½ teaspoon ground ginger
1½ cups plain flour
Pinch salt
90 g (3 oz) butter
½ cup brown sugar, firmly packed

Wash and trim rhubarb and cut into 1 cm (½ in) pieces. Toss with sugar and ginger and place in a buttered pie dish.

Sift flour and salt into a bowl and rub in butter with the fingertips until mixture resembles fine breadcrumbs. Stir in brown sugar, and sprinkle the mixture over rhubarb.

Bake in a preheated moderately hot oven (190°C/375°F) for 35 minutes, or until rhubarb is soft and topping crisp. Serve warm with custard or cream. Serves 6.

Lovely apple pie

Pastry:
2 cups plain flour
Pinch salt
¼ teaspoon baking powder
1 tablespoon sugar
125 g (4 oz) butter
2 egg yolks
3-4 tablespoons iced water
Squeeze lemon juice
A little milk and sugar to glaze

For filling:
5 large, tart apples, peeled and finely sliced
¾ cup sugar
Grated rind and juice 1 medium lemon
1 tablespoon cornflour
1 teaspoon mixed spice
¼ teaspoon ground cloves

Sift flour, salt, baking powder and sugar into a bowl. Cut butter into small pieces and rub into flour with fingertips until mixture resembles breadcrumbs. Beat egg yolks lightly with 3 tablespoons of water and lemon juice, and stir into mixture with a knife to form a dough. (If necessary, add a little extra water.) Knead lightly, wrap in plastic film, and chill for 30 minutes before rolling out.

Divide dough into two pieces, one a little larger than the other. Roll out larger piece to line a 23 cm (9 in) pie tin. Roll out second piece to form a lid.

Meanwhile, make filling by mixing together all ingredients. (If apples are very tart, you may need to add a little extra sugar.)

Spoon filling into pastry case, and brush rim of pastry with a little milk. Press pastry lid into place, and crimp or flute the edges for a pretty effect.

Make a small slit in the top for steam to escape, brush with milk and sprinkle with sugar. Bake in a preheated hot oven, (200°C/400°F), for 15 minutes, then reduce heat to moderate (180°C/350°F). Bake for a further 20 minutes, or until pastry is crisp and golden and filling soft. Serve pie warm, with cream or custard. Serves 6.

Steamed jam pudding

On cold winter evenings, our mothers could be relied upon to produce all sorts of lovely hot puddings. A special favourite was this light steamed pudding, with its pretty coat of jam.

125 g (4 oz) soft margarine or butter
½ cup castor sugar
1½ cups self raising flour
Pinch of salt
2 eggs
2 tablespoons milk
1 teaspoon vanilla
¾ cup tart jam (raspberry, plum, etc.)

Cream margarine and sugar until light and fluffy. Sift flour and salt together, and beat eggs with milk and vanilla.

Add flour to butter and sugar mixture alternately with eggs, beginning and ending with flour.

Grease a 4-5 cup pudding basin, and place jam in the bottom. Carefully spoon in the pudding mixture. Tie down with a double thickness of buttered greaseproof paper or aluminium foil, or cover with a snap-on lid.

Steam the pudding in the top half of a double boiler for 2 hours. If you don't have a steamer, place the pudding basin on an upturned saucer in a saucepan, and add enough boiling water to come halfway up the sides of the basin. Cover the saucepan and boil steadily for 2 hours, topping up the water level as necessary with more boiling water.

To serve, remove paper or lid and invert the pudding on to a heated dish. The hot jam will run down the sides to form a delicious sauce. Nice with custard, cream or icecream. Serves 4-6.

Note: Golden syrup or honey make a delicious change from jam.

Jam roly poly

Puddings made with suet are warming, filling, economical reminders of our early days. This basic recipe can be varied by using golden syrup instead of jam, or a filling of mixed fruit mixed with brown sugar and grated lemon rind.

1 cup plain flour
1 cup self raising flour
Good pinch salt
125 g (4 oz) shredded suet
Water for mixing
1 cup tart jam (raspberry, plum, etc.)

Sift flours and salt into a bowl and mix in suet. Gradually stir in enough water to make a firm dough, and shape into a ball.

Roll out on a lightly floured surface to a rectangle about 1 cm (½ in) thick. Spread jam over surface to within 2.5 cm (1 in) of edges.

Dampen edges of dough with water, and roll pudding up lightly, pressing ends together so jam won't ooze out.

Scald a pudding cloth, wrap the roly poly in it, and tie the ends of the cloth with string. Lower into a large pan of rapidly boiling water and boil steadily for 2 hours, replenishing the water as necessary to keep the pudding covered.

Drain pudding in a colander, then unwrap and slide on to a heated serving dish. Serve cut in slices, with custard. Serves 6-8.

Apple Charlotte

There's a tart-sweet stewed apple filling layered between buttery, crisp crumbs. Brown sugar and cinnamon add the classic finishing touch.

| 4 large, tart apples (eg. Granny Smith) |
| ½ cup sugar |
| Grated rind and juice of 1 large lemon |
| 90 g (3 oz) butter, softened |
| 3 cups soft white breadcrumbs |
| ½ cup brown sugar |
| 2 teaspoons cinnamon |

Peel and core apples and cut into thin slices. Place in a saucepan with sugar, lemon juice and rind. Stir over moderate heat until sugar dissolves, then cover tightly and simmer until apples are tender. Allow to cool.

Grease a 23 cm (9 in) round pie plate generously with butter, and press 1 cup of breadcrumbs around sides and base. Spoon in half the apples. Cover with another cup of crumbs, and dot with small pieces of butter. Add remaining apple and top with remaining crumbs. Mix brown sugar and cinnamon together, sprinkle over crumbs, and dot with rest of butter.

Place in a preheated moderate oven (180°C/350°F) and bake for 40 minutes, or until crumbs on top and the pudding base are crisp and golden. Serve warm or cold, with cream or custard. Serves 6-8.

Lemon sago

Once, it seemed, no house could be without sago. It's time to discover it again, in this delightfully light, summery pudding.

| ½ cup sago |
| 2¼ cups water |
| 1 large, juicy lemon |
| 3 tablespoons golden syrup |
| 3 tablespoons brown sugar |

Place sago and water in a saucepan. Grate the rind of the lemon and squeeze the juice. Add rind to the sago, bring to the boil, and simmer until sago is soft and transparent, stirring often.

Remove from heat and stir in lemon juice, syrup and brown sugar. Pour into a mould, cool, then chill until set. Serve with cream or custard. Serves 6.

Blancmange

Despite the French name, it was once Queen of the British puddings — suitable for guests, as well as excellent food for children and invalids. Smart restaurants are reviving it today, and adding a sauce of tart, pureed fruit such as raspberries or plums.

| 2¼ cups milk |
| 3 tablespoons cornflour |
| Tiny pinch salt |
| 2 tablespoons sugar |
| 1 teaspoon rosewater or vanilla, or a few drops almond or lemon essence |
| 1 cup fruit puree (optional) |

Blend cornflour to a smooth paste with a little of the milk. Heat remaining milk with salt and sugar until nearly boiling. Pour hot milk slowly on to cornflour, stirring constantly. Return to the pan, bring to the boil, and simmer for 2 minutes, stirring all the while. Add flavouring and pour into a mould that has been rinsed in cold water. Cool, then chill. Turn out on to a serving plate and coat with fruit puree if desired. Serves 4-6.

Bread and butter pudding

(photograph right)

| Some people remove the crusts from the bread, but we like the crispy edges! |
| 4 slices white sandwich bread |
| Butter for spreading |
| ½ cup sultanas or raisins |
| 2 tablespoons candied peel |
| 2 eggs |
| 1½ cups milk |
| 2 tablespoons sugar |
| Pinch salt |
| 1 teaspoon vanilla |
| Freshly grated nutmeg |
| A little extra sugar |

Butter the bread fairly generously, and cut into small squares.

Arrange half the bread in a buttered, 4-cup casserole or pie dish, and sprinkle with the fruit and peel. Cover with remaining bread.

Beat the eggs with the milk, sugar, salt and vanilla and pour into the dish. Allow to soak for 30 minutes. Sprinkle the pudding with nutmeg and a little sugar and bake in a preheated moderate oven (180°C/350°F) for 40 minutes, or until golden-brown and set. Serve warm, either by itself or with stewed fruit or cream or both. Serves 4-6.

Fruit fool

The early "fools" contained only fruit puree and cream. Thrifty Victorian housewives replaced the cream with custard to cut costs. We like to combine the two!

| 2 cups sweetened fruit puree (apple, rhubarb, apricot or gooseberry) |
| 1 cup custard sauce |
| 1½ cups cream, whipped |
| Slivered, toasted almonds to garnish |

Combine fruit puree and custard. Fold in the whipped cream, and chill. Spoon into pretty bowls or glasses, and garnish with toasted almonds. Serves 6-8.

Note: For convenience, you may use prepared Dairy Custard if you wish.

Rice pudding

Possibly the simplest version of this dear old pudding, and still one of the best.

| ⅓ cup raw, short-grain rice |
| Tiny pinch salt |
| ¼ cup sugar |
| 2½ cups milk |
| ½ teaspoon vanilla |
| ½ cup raisins (optional) |
| Freshly grated nutmeg |
| Large pat butter |

Place rice, salt and sugar in a greased pie dish or casserole and pour milk over. Stir in vanilla and raisins if using. Sprinkle with grated nutmeg, dot with butter, place in a preheated cool oven (160°C/325°F) and bake for 2 hours, stirring now and again. Sprinkle with a little extra grated nutmeg and serve hot. Serves 4.

Bread and butter pudding can be made in many tempting variations. Why not use stale sponge cake or fruit bread instead of white bread? And you can add the flavour of a dash of brandy or sherry instead of vanilla.

Christmas pudding

It is traditionally made with suet, but you may substitute the same quantity of butter or margarine if you wish. In this case, rub butter into the flour until mixture resembles breadcrumbs before adding remaining ingredients.

1 cup self raising flour
½ teaspoon salt
1½ teaspoon mixed spice
3 cups soft white breadcrumbs
185 g (6 oz) shredded suet
1⅓ cups brown sugar
1 kg (2 lb) mixed fruit
125 g (4 oz) dates, chopped
125 g (4 oz) blanched almonds, chopped
Grated rind and juice 1 small lemon
1 large tart apple, peeled and grated
Grated rind and juice 1 small orange
4 large eggs
⅓ cup brandy or rum
Extra brandy to serve

Sift flour, salt and spices into a bowl. Add breadcrumbs, suet, sugar, mixed fruit, dates, almonds, apple and lemon and orange rinds. Beat eggs with orange and lemon juice and brandy, stir into dry ingredients and combine them all well.

Spoon into a greased, 8-cup pudding basin and cover with greased greaseproof paper, then tie down with greased aluminium foil or use a snap-on lid.

Steam pudding steadily for 6 hours, replenishing boiling water as necessary.

When pudding is cool, cover with a fresh piece of greaseproof paper and clean foil or a snap-on lid. Store in a cool, dry place and steam for 3 hours on Christmas Day to reheat.

Turn out on to a heated serving platter, pour a little warmed brandy over, and set alight at the table or bring flaming from the kitchen. Serve with Hard sauce and cream or custard. Serves 8-10.

Note: The pudding can be steamed in two 4-cup basins if desired. In this case, steam for 4 hours to cook, and allow 2 hours to reheat.

Sago plum pudding

If you've never tasted this economical favourite from the past, be prepared for a surprise. It has rich, traditional plum pudding flavour and marvellous texture.

2 tablespoons sago
¾ cup milk
¼ cup brandy or sherry
60 g (2 oz) butter
½ cup sugar
1 teaspoon bicarbonate of soda
Pinch of salt
1 cup soft white breadcrumbs
1 cup mixed fruit
2 teaspoons grated lemon rind
½ teaspoon mixed spice
½ teaspoon ground ginger

Place sago in a bowl with milk and brandy, cover, and stand overnight. Cream butter and sugar until light and fluffy, then stir in sago and remaining ingredients.

Spoon into a buttered 4-cup pudding basin, cover with a double thickness of aluminium foil or a snap-on lid, and steam for 2 hours. Turn out on to a serving dish, and serve hot with Hard sauce, custard or cream. Serves 4-6.

Hard sauce for plum pudding

When the "hard" sauce meets the hot plum pudding, it quickly melts to give a delicious creamy texture.

125 g (4 oz) unsalted butter
1½ cups icing sugar, sifted
2-3 tablespoons brandy or rum

Cream the butter until white and fluffy, then gradually beat in the icing sugar. Add brandy or rum little by little to suit your taste, beating well between each addition. Pile into a serving dish, cover, and chill until firm. Serve in a generous spoonful on hot plum pudding or other steamed puddings. Serves 8.

Custard sauce

The touch of cornflour is not strictly "proper" in custard, but a grandmother taught us the trick — and it gives foolproof, creamy results each time.

1½ cups milk
2 eggs
Tiny pinch salt
1½ tablespoons sugar
2 teaspoons cornflour
½ teaspoon vanilla

Heat 1 cup of the milk to just below boiling point. Meanwhile, beat the eggs with remaining milk, salt, sugar and cornflour.

Tip the hot milk into the eggs, and beat thoroughly. Return to the saucepan and continue beating with a rotary beater over very low heat until the custard is thickened and increased in volume.

Remove from heat and beat in vanilla. Pour into a bowl, cover top with a circle of dampened greaseproof paper (to prevent a skin forming) and allow to cool. Beat again before serving. Serves 6.

Note: The custard may also be served hot, or warm. Excellent with stewed fruits, steamed pudding, for trifles etc.

Brandy sauce

Another traditional sauce for plum pudding and steamed puddings. In fact, some luxury-loving people like to serve Brandy sauce, Hard sauce, custard or cream with the Christmas pudding!

1 cup milk
Tiny pinch salt
1 small piece cinnamon stick
1 tablespoon sugar
3 teaspoons cornflour mixed to a paste with a little extra milk
2-3 tablespoons brandy

Place milk, sugar, salt and cinnamon in a small saucepan and bring slowly to the boil, stirring.

Pour some of the hot milk on to the cornflour paste, stirring until smooth. Return this to the saucepan and simmer, stirring, until sauce is smooth and thickened. Remove from heat, take out cinnamon stick, and stir in brandy to suit your taste. Serve hot. Serves 4.

Christmas cake

Make 4-6 weeks before Christmas so that the flavour can mature.

250g (8oz) butter, softened.
1⅓ cups brown sugar
4 large eggs, beaten
Grated rind and juice of 1 medium lemon
1 tablespoon treacle or golden syrup
3 tablespoons brandy or rum
1½ cups plain flour
1½ cups full of self raising flour
Pinch salt
½ teaspoon each cinnamon, nutmeg, ground cloves and ginger
500g (1 lb) sultanas
375g (12oz) currants
375g (12oz) raisins
250g (8oz) glace cherries, chopped
250g (8oz) blanched almonds, chopped
Extra blanched almonds to decorate (if not icing)
Extra brandy for sprinkling over cake

Cream butter and sugar until light and fluffy, then gradually beat in the eggs. Stir in lemon juice and rind, treacle and brandy. Sift flours with salt and spices and fold in. Combine dried fruits, cherries and almonds and stir into the mixture.

Meanwhile, preheat oven to slow (150°C/300°F) and line a deep, greased 23 cm (9 in) cake tin with two layers of greased greaseproof paper or aluminium foil.

Spoon in the mixture, hollow out centre a little to give an even, flat surface and decorate top with almonds if you don't intend to ice the cake. Bake for 4 hours on the centre shelf of the oven, or until a skewer inserted in the middle comes out clean.

Remove cake from oven and sprinkle with 2-3 tablespoons extra brandy. Wrap in a teatowel and leave until cool. Store in an airtight container, but do not remove paper.

Note: If you wish to ice the cake, see recipes for Almond paste and Royal icing.

Almond paste

185g (6oz) ground almonds
500g (1 lb) icing sugar, sifted
1 egg yolk, beaten
2 tablespoons sherry
1 teaspoon lemon juice
Few drops almond essence

Combine ground almonds and sugar. Mix egg yolk with sherry, lemon juice and essence and stir in. Mixture should be firm enough to roll out — if necessary, add a little more sifted icing sugar.

Roll out to fit cake on a surface dusted with icing sugar. This amount is enough for a round or square cake about 23 cm (9 in) in diameter.

To apply to cake: First brush the cake with apricot jam that has been sieved, then warmed. Place almond paste in position and press gently with a rolling pin, so it adheres to jam. Trim the edges if necessary and allow it to set for 48 hours before coating with Royal icing.

Royal icing

This is the traditional white icing that goes over almond paste on a Christmas cake.

2 egg whites
500g (1 lb) pure icing sugar, sifted
1 teaspoon strained lemon juice

Beat egg whites until frothy, then beat in icing sugar, one tablespoon at a time. Add lemon juice and continue beating until soft peaks form.

Icing can be smoothed over almond paste for a flat surface, or roughed up to look like snowy peaks. Add your own decorations (eg. a little Santa, holly leaves, cherries, tiny silver balls) and leave for 1 day to set.

Mince pies

Pastry:
3 cups plain flour
½ teaspoon baking powder
Pinch salt
185g (6oz) butter
2 egg yolks
3-4 tablespoons iced water
Good squeeze lemon juice
Milk and sugar to glaze

Mincemeat:
500g (1 lb) raisins
125g (4oz) sultanas
125g (4oz) candied peel
4 tablespoons dark, chunky marmalade
2 large, tart apples, peeled and grated
1 cup sugar
Grated rind and juice 1 medium lemon
500g (1 lb) shredded suet
1 teaspoon freshly grated nutmeg
½ teaspoon each cinnamon and ground ginger
1 cup brandy

Pastry: Sift flour, baking powder and salt into a bowl. Cut butter into small pieces and rub into flour until mixture resembles breadcrumbs. Beat egg yolks with 3 tablespoons of water and lemon juice, sprinkle over flour, and mix with a knife to form a dough. If necessary, add a little more water. Knead lightly, wrap in plastic film and chill for 30 minutes.

Divide pastry into thirds. Roll out two thirds thinly, and cut into circles big enough to line patty tins about 5 cm (2 in) in diameter. (Make the pies smaller or larger if you wish).

Roll out remaining pastry and cut into circles for lids.

Fill each pastry case two-thirds full with mincemeat (see below), and moisten rims of pastry with a little milk.

Press lids into position, crimping the edges together. Make a small slit in the top of each for steam to escape, brush with milk and sprinkle with sugar. Bake in a preheated hot oven (200°C/400°F) for 20 minutes, or until pastry is crisp and golden. Serve pies warm. Makes 20-30, depending on size of patty tins.

Note: Pies can be made beforehand, and frozen, then reheated.

Mincemeat: Make this at least 2 weeks before using, so that the flavour will mature. Stored in airtight jars in a cool, dry place, it keeps well for months.

Chop dried fruits and marmalade finely by hand, or use a food processor fitted with the steel blade, or a hand mincer. Mix in remaining ingredients, cover and leave overnight. Stir well, spoon into jars and cover tightly.

Rock cakes

They're part of all our childhoods, and still found in cake shops throughout the country. This extra-fruity version is quick, easy, and freezes well, so you can make an extra batch for school lunches.

| 2 cups self raising flour |
| ¼ teaspoon salt |
| 125 g (4 oz) butter or margarine |
| ½ cup sugar |
| 1 cup mixed fruit |
| 1 egg |
| ½ teaspoon vanilla |
| 2 tablespoons milk |
| Extra sugar for sprinkling on top |

Sift the flour and salt into a bowl. Cut butter or margarine into small pieces and rub through flour until mixture resembles coarse breadcrumbs. Stir in sugar and fruit.

Beat egg with vanilla and milk and combine with flour mixture, stirring just until dry ingredients are moistened.

Using two forks dipped in water, place heaps of mixture on greased baking trays, leaving a space between each. Sprinkle tops with sugar, and bake in a preheated hot oven (200°C/400°F) for 15 minutes, or until golden and cooked through when tested with a skewer. Cool on wire racks, and serve freshly made, split and buttered. Makes 18-20.

Queen of puddings

(photograph left)

A crumb custard is topped with jam, and then a "crown" of snowy meringue . . . it's the sort of nursery pudding most of us never outgrow.

| 2 cups milk |
| 30 g (1 oz) butter |
| 2 teaspoons grated lemon rind |
| ½ cup castor sugar |
| 1½ cup soft white breadcrumbs |
| 3 eggs |
| 2 tablespoons raspberry or other berry jam |

Heat the milk just to boiling point and stir in butter, lemon rind, and 2 tablespoons of the sugar. Pour this over the breadcrumbs and allow to stand for 15 minutes.

Separate the eggs, beat the yolks, and stir into the breadcrumb mixture. Spoon into a greased 4-5 cup casserole or pie dish, and bake in a preheated moderate oven (180°C/350°F) for 30 minutes, or until set.

Remove from oven and spread jam over the top of the pudding. Whip the egg whites until they hold firm peaks, then beat in the remaining sugar little by little to form a stiff, glossy meringue.

Spread the meringue over the pudding, swirling it into peaks on top. Return to the oven for 10 minutes, or until tipped with gold. Serve pudding warm or cold, plain or with cream. Serves 4-6.

Treacle tart

Sweet crisp pastry:

| 90 g (3 oz) butter, softened |
| 2 tablespoons sugar |
| 1 cup plain flour |
| ½ cup self raising flour |
| Pinch of salt |
| About 4 tablespoons iced water |

For filling:

| ¾ cup golden syrup or treacle |
| 1½ cups soft white breadcrumbs |
| 1 teaspoon cinnamon |
| ½ teaspoon ground ginger |
| ½ teaspoon allspice |
| Grated rind of one small lemon |
| 2 tablespoons lemon juice |

Pastry: Cream butter and sugar. Sift flours with salt, and work into butter mixture. Add enough iced water to form a firm dough, wrap in plastic film and chill for 30 minutes. Roll out on a lightly floured surface to fit a greased, 20 cm (8 in) tart plate. Press into sides and bottom of plate, trim any overhang, and save the scraps for decoration. Mix filling ingredients together, spoon into pastry, and spread evenly. Roll out pastry scraps, cut into thin strips, and arrange over filling in a lattice design. (Dampen ends of strips and press firmly against rim of pastry to hold them in place).

Bake the tart in a preheated, moderately hot oven (190°C/375°F) for 25 minutes, or until pastry is crisp and filling firm. Serve warm, with cream or custard. Serves 6-8.

Syllabub

One kind of syllabub is traditionally made by milking a cow directly into a bowl containing port or sherry. This method may not be so exciting — but the results are still delicious, and possibly more predictable!

| 1 large, juicy lemon |
| ½ cup castor sugar |
| 2 tablespoons brandy |
| 1 tablespoon sweet sherry |
| 1 cup pouring cream |

Grate the lemon rind, being careful not to get any white pith, and squeeze the juice. Allow rind and juice to soak together for an hour or two, then strain juice into a bowl with the sugar. Add brandy, sherry and cream and beat until mixture forms soft peaks.

Spoon into small glasses and chill several hours or overnight. Serve with a crisp, sweet biscuit. Serves 6.

Note: Don't worry if the liquid separates from the cream — it looks even prettier and tastes just as nice.

Lemon pudding

This early favourite has remained a favourite — sometimes under the name of "Lemon Delicious Pudding". As it cooks, a light sponge mixture forms on top of a tangy lemon sauce.

| 60 g (2 oz) butter |
| ½ cup sugar |
| Pinch salt |
| ½ cup self raising flour |
| Grated rind and juice of 1 large lemon |
| 2 large eggs, separated |
| 1¼ cups milk |

Cream butter and sugar. Sift salt and flour and mix in, then add grated rind and juice. Beat egg yolks with the milk and fold into the pudding, then fold in stiffly-beaten egg whites.

Spoon into a greased 4-cup ovenproof dish, and stand this in a baking tin. Add enough hot water to come half-way up the sides of the dish, and bake in a preheated moderate oven (180°C/350°F) for 45 minutes, or until sponge is set and golden on top. Serve warm, with cream. Serves 4-6.

Roast turkey with two stuffings

It is traditional (and delicious) to use two kinds of stuffings, one for the breast and one for the body cavity.

| One 4 kg (8 lb) turkey |
| 90 g (3 oz) butter, softened |
| Salt and freshly ground pepper |
| 2 tablespoons plain flour |
| 3 cups chicken or turkey stock (made with giblets) |

Orange-Apple Stuffing:

| 60 g (2 oz) butter |
| 1 medium onion, finely chopped |
| 2 sticks celery, finely chopped |
| 1 medium apple, peeled and chopped |
| 3 cups soft white breadcrumbs |
| Grated rind and juice of 1 large orange |
| 1 teaspoon each dried sage and thyme |
| Salt and freshly ground pepper |
| 1 tablespoon sugar |

Sausage-Chestnut Stuffing:

| 30 g (1 oz) butter |
| 1 small onion, finely chopped |
| 500 g (1 lb) sausage mince |
| 2 cups soft white breadcrumbs |
| 2 teaspoons grated lemon rind |
| ½ cup finely chopped parsley |
| 1 cup unsweetened chestnut puree (fresh or canned) |
| Salt and freshly ground pepper |

Make the stuffings first. For orange-apple stuffing, melt butter and fry onion, celery and apple until soft. Remove from heat, stir in remaining ingredients and allow to cool.

For sausage stuffing, melt butter, add onion and sausage mince, and stir until mince loses its pink colour. Combine well with remaining ingredients and allow to cool.

If turkey was frozen, make sure it has thawed completely. Stuff the neck with orange-apple stuffing, smoothing the breast into a nice, plump shape. Use the sausage stuffing for filling the body cavity. Truss the turkey, place on a rack in a large roasting tin, rub all over with softened butter and season with salt and pepper. Cover the turkey and rack loosely with a "tent" of buttered aluminium foil, and roast in a preheated, moderately slow oven (170°C/325°F) for 3 hours, or until juices run clear when the thickest part of the thigh is pierced with a fine skewer.

Baste turkey with pan drippings every 30 minutes as it cooks, and remove foil for the last 30 minutes so it will brown well. Transfer turkey to a board or serving platter, and rest in a warm place for 20 minutes before carving.

To make gravy, pour off all but 4 tablespoons of drippings, sprinkle in flour, and stir over moderate heat until blended. Add stock, season to taste, and stir until smooth and thickened. Serves 8-10.

Note: You will not need to rub the turkey with butter if it is the self-basting type. Bacon rolls and small sausages may be cooked separately in the oven and used to garnish the turkey.

Macaroni cheese

Many a family has been nourished on this filling dish. Keep it in mind for an economical Sunday supper on a chilly night.

| 185 g (6 oz) macaroni, any shape |
| 45 g (1 ½ oz) butter |
| 2 tablespoons plain flour |
| 2 teaspoons prepared mustard |
| Salt and freshly ground pepper |
| 1 ½ cups milk |
| 185 g (6 oz) tasty cheese, grated |

Cook macaroni until tender in boiling, salted water, according to packet directions. Drain well. Melt butter over low heat, add flour, and stir until smooth. Add mustard and stir in milk very gradually. Continue stirring until sauce boils and is smooth and thick. Season with salt and pepper, remove from heat, and stir in half the cheese.

Fold macaroni through sauce and spoon into a greased baking dish. Sprinkle with remaining cheese and bake in a preheated moderately hot oven (190°C/375°F) for 20 minutes, or until browned on top and bubbly. Serves 4-6.

Welsh rarebit

In Britain, this was often served as a savoury course at the end of the meal. We like it also for breakfast, or as a light lunch or supper. The breadcrumbs aren't found in every recipe for rarebit, but add interesting texture.

| 60 g (2 oz) butter |
| 1 teaspoon prepared English mustard |
| ½ teaspoon salt |
| Freshly ground pepper |
| 2 tablespoons soft white breadcrumbs |
| 1 egg yolk, beaten |
| 1 teaspoon Worcestershire sauce |
| 125 g (4 oz) tasty cheese, grated |
| 3 tablespoons beer (flat beer will do) |
| 4 slices hot, buttered toast |

Melt the butter in a saucepan over low heat, and stir in mustard, salt and pepper to taste. Add breadcrumbs and stir until coated with butter, then stir in egg yolk, sauce and cheese. Continue stirring until cheese melts, then stir in beer and heat through. (Do not allow to boil).

Taste for seasoning, and serve at once over hot buttered toast. For lunch, you might like to add pickled onions and a green salad. Serves 4.

Note: If you wish, the rarebit can be browned quickly under a hot grill after it is spread on toast.

Rhubarb tart

(photograph above)

1 bunch rhubarb weighing about 500g (1lb)
½ cup sugar
Pinch ground ginger
1 tablespoon cornflour
For pastry:
1½ cups plain flour
Pinch salt
60g (2oz) butter, softened
2 tablespoons castor sugar
2 egg yolks, beaten
1 teaspoon lemon juice
Milk to glaze

Trim rhubarb and cut into 2.5 cm (1 in) pieces. Mix with sugar, ginger and cornflour. Sift flour and salt into a shallow bowl. Make a well in the centre and add remaining ingredients. Work these together into a paste, using the fingertips, then gradually work in the flour from the sides. Knead lightly to form a dough, shape into a ball and wrap in plastic film.

Chill for 1 hour before rolling out.

Put about ¼ of the pastry aside. Roll the rest out to fit a greased 20 cm (8 in) flan tin, pressing it well into the bottom and sides. Roll the rest of the pastry out and cut into strips to make a lattice topping for the tart. Spoon filling into the tart shell, dampen edges of the pastry strips, and arrange over the top. (Press them firmly against the edges of the pastry shell, so they won't shrink away during baking). Brush strips with milk and bake in a preheated hot oven (200°C/400°F) for 30 minutes, or until rhubarb is soft and pastry crisp and golden. Serve warm, with whipped cream.

An afternoon tea party

(photograph right)

Delicious scones, pretty sandwiches, and a chocolate sponge filled with cream and strawberries add up to a perfect afternoon tea for sweet tooths.

Caramel scone pinwheels:
2 cups self raising flour
Pinch salt
30g (1oz) butter, cut in pieces
1 tablespoon lemon juice
1 cup milk
185g (6oz) cream cheese, softened
½ cup brown sugar
3 teaspoons cinnamon
Melted butter to glaze

Sift flour and salt into a bowl and rub in butter until mixture resembles fine breadcrumbs. Add lemon juice to the milk and allow to thicken slightly. Add milk to flour and mix to a soft dough. Roll out on a lightly floured surface to a rectangle about 37 × 30cm (14 × 12 in).

Spread cream cheese evenly over dough and sprinkle with brown sugar mixed with cinnamon. Starting from the long end of dough, roll it up like a Swiss roll. Cut into 5cm (2 in) slices, and place in well-buttered deep patty tins. Bake in a preheated hot oven, (200°C/400°F) for 20-25 minutes, until cooked through. Glaze tops with melted butter and serve hot or cold. Makes about 2 dozen.

Note: The same dough can be used to make plain scones. Pat out to about 2cm (¾ in) thickness, and cut into rounds with a floured scone cutter. Arrange on a greased scone tray, and bake in a preheated very hot oven (225°C/450°F) for 12-15 minutes, until well risen and golden brown. Serve hot, split and buttered, or with jam and cream.

Barley water

Said to be one of Queen Victoria's favourite drinks — and still a refreshingly different thirst-quencher for today's tastes.

4 tablespoons pearl barley
5 cups water
2 medium lemons
Sugar to taste

Rinse the barley in cold water and drain.

Grate the rind from the lemons and squeeze the juice. Place barley, the 5 cups of water and lemon rind in a saucepan. Bring to the boil, then simmer, covered, for 2 hours. Strain into a tall jug or container, add lemon juice and sugar to suit your own taste. Stir until sugar dissolves, then cool and chill. Makes 6 tall glasses.

Cheese straws

¾ cup plain flour
¼ teaspoon dry mustard
½ teaspoon salt
Pinch cayenne pepper
60g (2oz) firm butter
¾ cup grated, tasty cheese
1 egg yolk
1 teaspoon water or lemon juice

Sift flour, mustard, salt and cayenne into a bowl. Cut butter into small pieces and rub through flour until mixture resembles coarse breadcrumbs.

Beat the egg yolk with water and stir into the mixture to form a soft dough. Wrap in plastic film and chill for 30 minutes.

Roll out on a lightly floured surface to about 5mm (¼ in) thickness, and cut into strips 5mm × 7.5cm (¼ in × 3 in). Arrange straws on a lightly greased baking tray and bake in a preheated hot oven (200°C/400°F) for 6 minutes, or until crisp and golden. Cool on a wire rack and serve at once, or store in an airtight container. Makes about 30.

Chocolate sponge

3 eggs
½ teaspoon vanilla
¾ cup castor sugar
¾ cup self raising flour
¼ cup cocoa
Pinch salt
1 teaspoon butter
2 tablespoons hot water
1 punnet strawberries, sliced
1 cup cream, whipped with 1 tablespoon sugar
Sifted icing sugar to decorate

Beat eggs, vanilla and sugar together until thick and creamy. Sift together, flour, salt and cocoa, sprinkle over top of the egg mixture, and fold in. Melt the butter in the hot water, and fold through quickly and lightly.

Spoon the butter into two 18cm (7 in) sandwich tins that have been greased and lightly floured. Place on the centre shelf of a preheated moderately hot oven (190°C/375°F) and bake for 20 minutes or until cakes spring back when touched lightly with a fingertip. Remove cakes from the oven, leave a minute in the tins, then turn out on wire trays to cool.

When ready to serve, fold strawberries into whipped cream and use to sandwich cakes together. Decorate top of sponge with sifted icing sugar. Serves 6-8.

Ribbon sandwiches

6 slices brown sandwich bread, crusts removed
3 slices white sandwich bread, crusts removed
125g (4oz) cream cheese, softened
½ cup sliced strawberries
1 cup drained, finely chopped canned apricots, pineapple or peaches

Spread 3 slices of brown bread with softened cream cheese and top with strawberries. Press 3 more slices of brown bread on top, spread them with cream cheese and top with chopped apricots, pineapple or peaches. Spread the 3 slices of white bread with remaining cream cheese and press on top, cheese-side down. This will give you 3 three-decker sandwiches. Wrap each one separately in plastic film and chill for 30 minutes. To serve, cut each sandwich in half, then cut each half into three fingers. Serves 6.

Apricot pinwheel sandwiches

8 slices white sandwich bread, crusts removed
90g (3oz) cream cheese, softened
Apricot jam for spreading

Spread bread with softened cream cheese and then apricot jam. Roll each slice up like a Swiss Roll, wrap in plastic film and chill for 30 minutes. Cut in 1cm (½ in) slices to serve. Serves 6.

The English used to have four meals a day, including "tea" at five in the afternoon before a late dinner or supper. In Australia this has become "afternoon tea", a light meal of treats such as the cake, scones and sandwiches in our picture.

IT'S SHOW TIME

Whether they are called shows, fairs or fetes, one of their most important functions is to show off delicious home-made treats from local helpers. On any weekend, somewhere in Australia there's bound to be a competition for the best sponge cake, or a stall selling home-made lamingtons, coconut ice, pickles and marmalade to raise money for a good cause.

"I have to cook something for the fete" is a cry heard from both the city career woman and the outback housewife-jillaroo-shearer's cook. (We will pause here for a moment to pay tribute to the countrywomen of Australia, many of whom combine more jobs in one day than city women have even heard of – and most of them superb cooks into the bargain!)

At the big annual shows which are held in capital cities and country towns, standards are extraordinarily high and artistic skills combine with cookery to create works of art. Preserved fruits glisten like jewels in crystal syrups, and the dexterity required to arrange peas or carrot slices in precise rows is one that takes years of practice and an incredibly steady hand with a pair of tweezers.

There is no doubt about the achievement and thrill of receiving a prize at a big show. But on a smaller scale, the rewards are equally great when a small boy brings his friends back to your modest stall at the school fete for some more of your coconut ice!

We hope you enjoy our collection of Show Time recipes – many of them gathered from industrious friends, and many based on years of practical experience.

Captions to preceding 6 pages.

Page 150/151   Display of vegetables and fruit at Easter Show, Sydney Show Ground, New South Wales. (photography: Colin Beard)

Page 152/153   Good amateur cooks all over Australia have a chance to show off their skills at local fetes and fairs — and the big city shows. (photography: Andrew Elton)

Page 154/155   Grand parade, Easter Show, Sydney Show Ground, New South Wales. (photography: Colin Beard)

Facing Page: Easter Show, Sydney Show Ground, New South Wales. (photography: Colin Beard)

157

Mango chutney

Don't save this superb chutney for curries — serve with corned beef, pickled pork, meat loaf, kebabs and spicy chicken dishes.

3 large, ripe mangos, peeled and chopped
1 small onion, finely chopped
1 small red chilli, seeds removed and finely chopped
2 cloves garlic, crushed
1 teaspoon celery seeds
½ cup chopped raisins
¼ cup currants
2 teaspoons finely chopped fresh ginger
2 teaspoons salt
½ teaspoon each nutmeg, cinnamon and allspice
½ cup brown sugar
⅔ cup malt vinegar

Combine all ingredients in a large bowl, cover and stand overnight.

Next day, place in a saucepan and bring to the boil. Simmer until thick, about 1½ hours, stirring often. Spoon into hot, sterilized jars, seal tightly and store in a cool place.

Green tomato chutney

Do you live alone, or perhaps there are just two of you? Here's a recipe that makes only a few jars of delicious chutney.

1 kg (2 lb) green tomatoes, chopped
250 g (8 oz) onions, finely chopped
250 g (8 oz) cooking apples, peeled and chopped
2 small, fresh red chillies
2 teaspoons chopped fresh ginger
1¼ cups brown sugar
1 cup raisins, chopped
1 teaspoon cinnamon
1½ teaspoons salt
1¼ cups malt vinegar

Place chopped tomatoes, onions and apples in a saucepan. Crush the chillies with a rolling pin, and tie in a muslin bag (or disposable cloth) with the ginger. Add to the pan with remaining ingredients.

Bring to the boil, stirring to dissolve sugar. Simmer for about 2 hours, stirring occasionally, until thick. Remove muslin bag and spoon into hot, sterilized jars. Seal tightly and store in a cool place.

Jill's tomato sauce
(photograph right)

A sweet and spicy tomato sauce that goes with just about everything.

2 kg (4 lb) tomatoes, peeled and chopped
375 g (12 oz) cooking apples, peeled, cored and chopped
1 cup malt vinegar
1½ cups sugar
¼ teaspoon each ground cloves and ginger
1 tablespoon salt
Pinch cayenne pepper

Place all ingredients in a large heavy saucepan. Bring to the boil, stirring to dissolve sugar. Simmer for 1¼ hours, covered. Puree mixture in batches in a blender, or a food processor fitted with the steel blade (or press through a sieve).

Return to the saucepan, bring to the boil and simmer uncovered for 20 minutes or until a sauce consistency. Pour into hot, sterilized jars and seal tightly. Store in the refrigerator.

Choko-ginger chutney

If you still have a choko vine on your back fence, this chutney will have special appeal. (Incidentally, did you know that the choko is called "chayote" in Latin America, and North Americans regard it as a rare and exotic vegetable?)

6 large chokos
250 g (8 oz) dates, stoned and chopped
250 g (8 oz) raisins, chopped
1 large onion, finely chopped
1 large cooking apple, peeled and chopped
½ cup chopped, preserved ginger in syrup
250 g (8 oz) sultanas, chopped
1½ cups sugar
1½ tablespoons salt
½ teaspoon cayenne pepper
3 cups malt vinegar

Peel chokos, cut in half and remove stones. Chop flesh into very small pieces and put in a large, heavy saucepan with remaining ingredients.

Bring to the boil, stirring until sugar dissolves. Simmer until thick, about 1½ hours, stirring often. Spoon into hot, sterilized jars, seal and label. Store in a cool place.

Mint sauce

If you have a thriving mint patch, make extra quantities of this favourite sauce to give to friends.

½ cup tightly packed mint leaves
2 tablespoons sugar
4 tablespoons boiling water
2 tablespoons vinegar
½ teaspoon salt
Dash white pepper

Wash mint leaves, place on a chopping board and sprinkle with sugar. Chop very finely with a heavy knife (the sugar will make it easy). Place in a small jug or bowl, pour boiling water over and cover. Allow to steep for 15 minutes, then stir in vinegar, salt and pepper. Taste for seasoning, and add a little extra vinegar or sugar if desired to suit your own taste. Serve sauce with roast lamb, or in potato salad or with sliced cucumbers.

Fruit chutney

1 teaspoon mustard seed, lightly crushed
3¾ cups malt vinegar
1 teaspoon whole cloves
2 bay leaves
1 teaspoon whole allspice
1 × 2.5 cm (1 in) cinnamon stick
125 g (4 oz) dried apricots, chopped and soaked in a little boiling water
1.5 kg (3 lb) cooking apples, peeled and chopped
750 g (1½ lb) onions, peeled and chopped
750 g (1½ lb) tomatoes, peeled and chopped
1½ cups sultanas
1½ cups raisins
1 tablespoon salt
2¼ cups brown sugar

Place mustard seed, vinegar, cloves, bay leaves, allspice and cinnamon in a saucepan. Bring slowly to the boil, and simmer for 3-4 minutes. Remove from heat, allow to steep for 4 hours, then strain into a large saucepan.

Drain apricots and add to saucepan with remaining ingredients. Bring to the boil, stirring to dissolve sugar. Cook gently, stirring often, until thick — about 1½ hours. Ladle into hot, sterilized jars, and seal tightly. Store in a cool, dark place.

Tomato relish

Marvellous with cold meats, hamburgers, meat loaf, corned beef — almost anything. Or even by itself on bread and butter.

3 kg (6 lb) ripe tomatoes, peeled and chopped
4 tablespoons salt
250 g (8 oz) onions, peeled and sliced
6 fat cloves garlic, crushed
1¾ cups malt vinegar
750 g (1½ lb) sugar
2 tablespoons dry mustard
2 tablespoons mild curry powder
2 tablespoons cornflour, if necessary

Place tomatoes in a bowl. Sprinkle with 2 tablespoons of salt and stand overnight. Place onions and garlic in another bowl, sprinkle with remaining 2 tablespoons of salt and stand overnight. Next day, drain all liquid from tomatoes and onions and discard liquid.

Place vegetables in a saucepan with vinegar, bring to the boil and simmer for 45 minutes. Add sugar, mustard and curry powder and stir until dissolved. Boil for another 30 minutes, stirring occasionally. If mixture is not thick enough, thicken with cornflour blended to a paste with a little water.

Pour into hot sterilized jars, seal and label when cool. Store in the refrigerator.

Harlequin pepper relish
(photograph right)

If you can't find peppers in three different colours, the relish will still taste great — but won't look quite as dashing.

2 medium size red peppers
2 medium green peppers
2 medium yellow peppers
2 medium white onions
¾ cup malt vinegar
1 cup water
¾ cup sugar
1 tablespoon salt
½ teaspoon freshly ground nutmeg

Remove seeds and ribs from peppers and cut flesh into small dice. Chop onions very finely. Place in a saucepan with cold water to cover and bring to the boil. Cook 30 seconds, then drain.

Combine vinegar, 1 cup water, sugar, salt and nutmeg in a saucepan and boil for 10 minutes. Add drained vegetables and cook for 5 minutes. Spoon into hot, sterilized jars, seal and label. Delicious as part of an antipasti, or with cold meats.

Note: This same basic approach can be used with other vegetables. Follow the recipe for Harlequin Pepper Relish, but instead of peppers use tiny florets of cauliflower, chopped green beans, cubes of peeled eggplant, chopped onions or a mixture of vegetables.

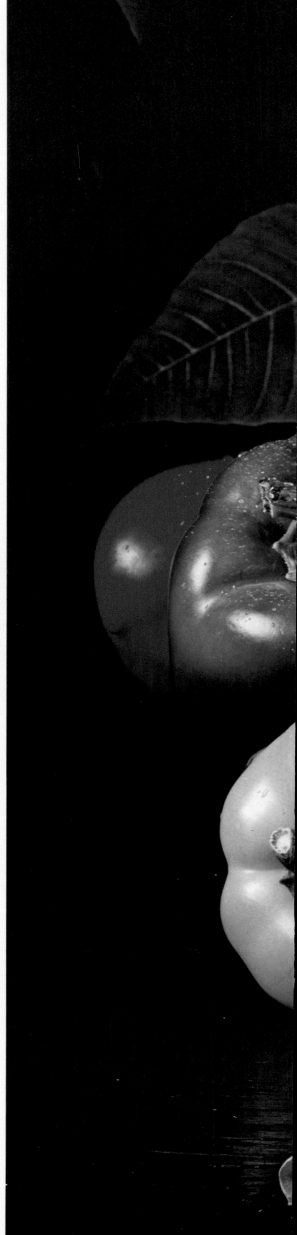

Plum sauce

Many Chinese dishes are served with plum sauce for dipping. Here's a short-cut way to make your own.

| 30g (1 oz) butter |
| 4 shallots, finely chopped |
| 1 clove garlic, crushed |
| 1 teaspoon finely chopped fresh ginger |
| ¾ cup plum jam |
| 1 tablespoon soy sauce |
| 1 tablespoon brown sugar |
| Salt and freshly ground pepper |

Heat the butter in a saucepan and gently fry the shallots, garlic and ginger until very soft, about 6 minutes. Stir in remaining ingredients, seasoning to taste with salt and pepper. (You may also like to add a little extra vinegar or sugar, depending on the sweetness of the jam.) Simmer for 3 minutes, then push through a fine sieve. Serve hot or cold. This sauce keeps well in a screwtop jar in the refrigerator.

Crunchy pickled onions

Crusty bread, firm butter, tasty cheese and pickled onions — can you think of a more satisfying lunch?

| 1 kg (2 lb) tiny white onions, peeled |
| 8 cups cold water |
| 1 cup salt |
| ½ cup sugar |
| 4 cups white vinegar |
| 12 peppercorns |
| 6 cloves |
| 1 × 5 cm (2 in) cinnamon stick |
| 2 teaspoons whole allspice |
| 3-4 small, fresh red chillies |

Place onions in a large bowl. Stir water and salt together until salt dissolves and pour over onions. Cover with a lid or aluminium foil and leave for 2 days, stirring now and again.

Place remaining ingredients except chillies in a saucepan. Bring slowly to the boil, stirring until sugar dissolves. Remove from heat, cover, and allow to steep for 2 hours.

Drain onions. Pack into sterilized jars, with a chilli in each jar. Strain pickling liquid over and seal tightly. Leave in a cool place for 3-4 days before serving.

Apple jelly
(photograph below)

Clear and sparkling — perfect as a glaze for fruit tarts, as well as a delicious spread.

| 2 kg (4 lb) crisp, tart apples |
| Water to cover |
| Sugar |
| Juice of 1 large lemon |

Wash apples (do not peel or core) and chop roughly. Place in a saucepan and add enough water to cover. Bring to the boil, then simmer gently until apples are tender, about 1 hour, stirring occasionally with a wooden spoon.

Make a bag out of cheesecloth, disposable cloth or other porous material, large enough to hold apples. (Or you can buy jelly bags from health food stores). Pour apples and liquid into the bag and suspend it over a bowl. Allow to drip overnight. Measure juice carefully and place in saucepan. Add 1 cup of sugar for each cup of juice to the pan, with the lemon juice. Bring to the boil and boil rapidly until liquid reaches jelly stage *(see note after Orange-Port marmalade)*.

Pour into hot, sterilized jars, seal and label and store in a cool place.

Note: Follow the same method for making quince jelly.

Orange-port marmalade

(photograph below)

5 medium-size sweet oranges
4 cups water
3 cups sugar
1 teaspoon citric acid (from chemist or health food store)
½ cup port wine

Wash and dry oranges. Peel rind thinly from 2 oranges and cut into thin strips about 4 cm (1½ in) long. Peel remaining oranges, making sure to remove all white pith, and chop flesh into small pieces. Save the pips and soak in cold water to cover. (The pips are rich in pectin, which helps to make jams and marmalades jell).

Cover strips of rind and flesh with the 4 cups of water and soak overnight. Next day, add water from pips to oranges and soaking water and simmer until strips of rind are soft — about 45 minutes. Add sugar and citric acid and stir until sugar dissolves. Boil rapidly until marmalade jells, about 20 minutes. Stir in port and cool slightly before spooning into hot, sterilized jars.

Note: To test for jelling, pour 1 teaspoon of hot syrup into 1 tablespoon of methylated spirits. If syrup remains liquid, further cooking is required. *Do not taste jam and be sure to discard methylated spirits at once.*

Plum-madeira jam

(photograph above)

1 kg (2 lb) ripe plums
1 cup water
3 cups sugar
1½ teaspoons ground cinnamon
½ cup Madeira wine

Wash plums, halve and remove stones. Place water and 1½ cups of the sugar in a heavy saucepan and stir until sugar dissolves. Boil for 5 minutes without stirring. Add plums, return to the boil and cook for 20 minutes, or until plums are soft and pulpy. Add rest of sugar and cinnamon, stir until mixture returns to the boil then cook without stirring for another 10 minutes (or until jam jells). Stir Madeira, cool slightly and spoon into hot, sterilized jars. Seal at once, label, and store in a cool place.

Note: See note at end of Orange-port marmalade for jell test.

Grape jam

(photograph page 152)

1.75 kg (3¼ lb) muscatel grapes, washed and stems removed
7 cups sugar

Cover grapes with 2 cups of the sugar and allow to stand overnight.

Bring grapes and any juices that have formed to the boil, then simmer for 40 minutes, stirring occasionally.

Add remaining sugar, stir until dissolved, then boil steadily for 25-30 minutes, skimming off seeds as they rise to the surface. Pour jam into hot, sterilized jars. Seal, label, and store in a cool place.

Tropical conserve

An Australian jam to delight your overseas visitors, with its combination of pawpaw, pineapple and ginger.

| 1 medium-size pawpaw |
| 1 medium-size ripe pineapple |
| 2 tablespoons finely chopped preserved ginger in syrup |
| 2 cups sugar |
| 4 tablespoons lemon juice |

Peel and seed pawpaw and chop coarsely. Peel, core and chop pineapple (pieces should be about the size of a thumbnail).

Place chopped fruits, ginger and sugar in a large saucepan and stir over low heat until sugar dissolves. Add lemon juice, bring to the boil, then simmer for 35 minutes, or until thickened. Spoon into hot, sterilized jars. Seal, label, and store in a cool place.

Citrus marmalade
(photograph page 152)

| 1 medium-size grapefruit |
| 3 medium oranges |
| 6 medium lemons |
| 12 cups water |
| 10 cups sugar |

Peel rind very thinly from fruit, being careful not to get any of the white pith. Cut rind into matchstick strips (julienne). Remove pith from fruit and chop flesh over a bowl to catch the juices. Retain seeds, and place in a separate bowl.

Add strips of rind to fruit and juices in bowl, and soak for 24 hours in the 12 cups of water. Cover seeds with water and soak separately.

Place fruit rind and water in a saucepan. Drain water from seeds and add this water to the saucepan. Bring to the boil, then simmer for 35 minutes. Add sugar, stir until dissolved, then boil for another 40 minutes, or until marmalade jells (*see note*).

Remove any scum that comes to the surface while marmalade is cooking, and pour into hot, sterilized jars. Seal and label. Store in a cool place.

Note: A professional jam-maker says the easiest way to test for jelling is to pour 1 teaspoon of the hot jam into 1 tablespoon of methylated spirits. If the jam is ready, it will form a jelly. If it is still runny, it needs further cooking. *Do not taste jam and be sure to discard methylated spirits at once.*

Pear and rum jam
(photograph below)

| 1 kg (2 lb) ripe pears |
| ¾ cup water |
| 3 cups sugar |
| 1 teaspoon citric acid |
| ½ cup dark rum |

Peel, core and chop pears in small pieces. Place water and 1½ cups of sugar in a saucepan and stir over low heat until sugar dissolves. Boil without stirring for 5 minutes. Add pears and cook until soft and pulpy, about 20 minutes. Stir in remaining sugar and citric acid. Return mixture to the boil and cook a further 15 minutes, or until jam jells (*see note after Orange-Port Marmalade*). Stir in rum, cool slightly and spoon into hot, sterilized jars. Seal jars at once, label, and store in a cool place.

Note: A dash of spirits adds interest to almost any jam. You can also make a delicious topping for icecream or pancakes by warming jam with a splash of rum or brandy.

Liqueur oranges
(photograph right)

Serve with icecream for dessert.

| 8 small, sweet oranges |
| 1 cup water |
| ½ cup sugar |
| 4 cloves |
| Grated rind and juice of 1 medium lemon |
| ½ cup Grand Marnier, Cointreau, or brandy |

Peel the rind from the oranges and cut into very thin strips. Remove all white pith from the oranges and cut through the membranes to separate into segments.

Place strips of rind in a saucepan with water, sugar, cloves, rind and juice of lemon. Bring to the boil and simmer for 5 minutes, or until syrupy.

Pour syrup over the orange segments and stir in the liqueur. Ladle into a jar or bowl, cover and cool. Chill before serving. This keeps well in the refrigerator.

Cumquat marmalade

This is our favourite marmalade, and one pretty little cumquat tree provides enough fruit to brighten breakfast the whole year round.

375 g (12 oz) cumquats
3 cups water
Juice ½ large lemon
2½ cups sugar

Wash cumquats and cut into very thin slices without peeling. Reserve the pips and place in a small bowl with just enough water to cover. Allow to soak overnight. Cover the sliced fruit with 3 cups of water and soak overnight.

Next day, strain water from pips and place in a saucepan with sliced fruit and soaking water. Cook gently until liquid is reduced by half. Add lemon juice and sugar and stir until sugar dissolves.

Bring to the boil and boil rapidly until marmalade jells (*see note after Orange-Port Marmalade*). Remove from heat and leave in the saucepan for 10 minutes. Stir gently, then spoon into hot, sterilized jars. Seal tightly and store in a cool place.

Lemon butter

3 medium-size lemons
125 g (4 oz) butter, cut in small pieces
1½ cups sugar
4 eggs, beaten

Grate the rind from the lemons (being careful not to get any white pith) and squeeze the juice.

Strain the juice, and place with rind, butter and sugar in a basin set over simmering water. Stir until sugar dissolves.

Pour a little hot lemon mixture on to beaten eggs and mix well. Tip this back into the basin and continue stirring until mixture coats the back of a spoon. Pour into hot, sterilized jars and seal. When cool, store in the refrigerator.

Note: Lemon butter is versatile. It makes a lovely filling for sponges or small tarts, and is delicious on hot buttered toast or scones. Orange butter is made the same way, but add a dash of lemon juice to sharpen the flavour.

Coconut ice

Always a money-spinner at fetes. The pretty pink and white colour scheme is part of its appeal.

4 cups sugar
1 cup milk
1 cup desiccated coconut
½ teaspoon vanilla
¼ teaspoon pink food colouring

Place 2 cups of the sugar and half a cup of milk in a saucepan. Stir until mixture comes to the boil and sugar dissolves, then simmer gently for 4 minutes. Add half a cup of the coconut and the vanilla. Pour into an 18 × 28 cm (7 × 11 in) lamington tin that has been greased and lined with greased aluminium foil.

Repeat the process with remaining sugar, milk and coconut, adding pink colouring instead of vanilla. Pour pink layer over white layer and leave in a cool place until set. Cut into squares or bars to serve. (For a fete, coconut ice looks attractive arranged in little boxes, or wrapped in clear cellophane paper).

Toffee apples
(*photograph below*)

8-10 small crisp apples
Wooden skewers (Your butcher has them)
2 cups sugar
2 tablespoons honey
½ cup water
Few drops red food colouring

Wash and dry apples thoroughly and insert a wooden skewer in each one at the stalk end.

Place sugar, honey and water in a heavy saucepan and stir over low heat until sugar dissolves. Bring to the boil, then boil briskly without stirring until a little syrup dropped into cold water forms a crisp ball. (This will take about 15 minutes). Stir in a few drops of food colouring.

Reduce heat to very low — just enough to keep toffee warm — and dip apples, turning them around till they are completely coated. Place on a greased tray until set and wrap in clear cellophane to take to fetes or picnics.

Peanut brittle

2 cups sugar
½ cup water
2 tablespoons liquid glucose
15 g (½ oz) butter, melted
1 teaspoon bicarbonate of soda
1 cup chopped, roasted peanuts

Place sugar, water and glucose in a saucepan and stir over low heat until sugar dissolves. Increase heat to moderate, and bring mixture to the boil. Boil rapidly without stirring until toffee turns a deep yellow, and a little dropped in cold water is brittle enough to snap in two.

Remove from heat and stir in butter, bicarbonate and peanuts (mixture should froth up a little).

Pour on to a flat, greased surface — a slab of marble or a stainless steel tray. Leave until cool enough to handle, then pull between the hands until toffee is very thin.

When quite cold, break into small pieces and store in an airtight jar.

Toasted marshmallows

(photograph page 152)

1 tablespoon gelatine
¼ cup cold water
1 cup boiling water
1 cup liquid honey
2 teaspoons lemon juice
2 cups desiccated coconut

Sprinkle gelatine over cold water to soften. Place boiling water and honey in a saucepan over medium heat and stir until honey dissolves. Add softened gelatine, bring to the boil and boil steadily without stirring for 15 minutes. Remove from stove and leave until mixture is lukewarm.

Transfer to the small bowl of an electric mixer, add lemon juice, and beat at high speed until white and very thick. Pour into a deep 20 cm (8 in) square cake tin that has been rinsed in cold water. Chill until set.

Using a wet knife, cut marshmallow into squares. Place coconut in a heavy frying pan, stir with a wooden spoon until a golden colour, and put aside to cool.

Roll marshmallow squares in coconut until well coated, and store in a covered container in the refrigerator.

Chocolate crunchies

250 g (8 oz) dark chocolate, broken into small pieces
½ teaspoon vanilla
2 tablespoons golden syrup
60 g (2 oz) butter
2 cups cornflakes

Melt the chocolate in a basin set over simmering water, then stir in vanilla, syrup and butter. Stir until butter melts and mixture is smooth. Remove from heat and stir in the cornflakes. Spoon the mixture into paper patty cases, and chill until set. Makes about 15.

Orange date creams

30 large dates, pitted
1 small egg white
3 teaspoons grated orange rind
1 teaspoon orange flower water (from the chemist)
About 2 cups sifted icing sugar
Candied orange peel, walnut pieces, glace cherries etc. to decorate

Flatten each date out a little with your finger to make a cavity for the filling. Beat the egg white lightly and mix in the orange rind and orange flower water. Stir in enough icing sugar to give a firm consistency. (You may need more than 2 cups sugar).

Make little balls of the icing sugar mixture and stuff dates. Decorate each one with peel, nuts, cherries, etc. and chill until serving time. For fetes, place in tiny paper patty cases and arrange in small boxes, covered with clear cellophane.

Note: You may use lemon juice instead of orange flower water, if you wish.

Walnut fudge

A creamy, easy-to-make fudge. For a fete, you can cut into bars, wrap in cellophane and tie with pretty ribbons. At home, enjoy in small pieces with after-dinner coffee.

1 cup finely chopped walnuts
125 g (4 oz) butter or margarine
1 × 400 g can condensed milk
1 teaspoon liquid glucose
1 cup brown sugar, firmly packed

Line an 18 cm (7 in) shallow square cake tin with greased aluminium foil. Sprinkle half the walnuts over the base.

Place butter, condensed milk, glucose and brown sugar in a saucepan and stir over low heat until well combined. Bring to the simmer. Continue cooking, stirring constantly with a wooden spoon, until fudge turns a rich caramel colour and leaves the sides of the pan.

Pour carefully into the prepared tin, cool a little, and press remaining walnuts on top. Mark into desired shapes with a knife and cut into pieces when cold.

Mint cream delights

Here's a grown-up sweet to nibble after dinner.

1 cup sugar
1 cup thickened cream
2 tablespoons gelatine
2 tablespoons green Creme-de-Menthe liqueur
Sifted icing sugar

Place sugar, cream and gelatine in a saucepan and stir over low heat until sugar dissolves. Continue stirring until mixture comes to the boil, then simmer without stirring for 10 minutes. Remove from heat and stir in the liqueur.

Sprinkle a loaf tin about 25 × 8 cm (10 × 3 in) with sifted icing sugar. Pour in the mixture and leave until set. Remove from the tin, cut into squares, and roll in more icing sugar. Store in the refrigerator.

Honeycomb

Yes, it's the delicious old-fashioned kind that bubbles up like magic when you add bicarbonate of soda.

1 cup sugar
1 cup golden syrup
1 tablespoon white vinegar
1 tablespoon bicarbonate of soda

Place sugar, golden syrup and vinegar in a large saucepan and stir over medium heat until sugar dissolves. Continue cooking, without stirring, until a little of the mixture dropped into cold water separates into hard, brittle threads that snap easily. Remove from heat and stir in the bicarbonate of soda. The mixture will immediately bubble up. Pour into a shallow, greased tin about 23 cm (9 in) square, and place tin on a wire rack to cool.

When quite cold, break into pieces. Store in layers in a tin with a tight fitting lid, putting sheets of foil between each of the layers.

Apricot slices

There are lots of good things in these chewy sweetmeats.

¾ cup chopped dried apricots
½ cup water
½ cup finely chopped walnuts or almonds
2 teaspoons lemon juice
1 teaspoon grated lemon rind
½ cup honey
1 tablespoon wheatgerm
1 cup powdered skim milk
½ cup chopped sultanas
½ cup desiccated coconut
Extra coconut

Place apricots and water in a small saucepan, simmer for 10 minutes, and allow to cool. Mix well with remaining ingredients, then divide mixture into three. Shape each portion into a 2.5 cm (1 in) roll, wrap in plastic film, and chill overnight. Cut in slices to serve.

Little cream meringues

2 large egg whites at room temperature
⅔ cup sugar
Whipped cream to serve

Beat the egg whites until stiff peaks form. Sprinkle 1 tablespoon of sugar over and beat for another 2 minutes, or until meringue is thick and glossy. Carefully fold in the remaining sugar.

Line a baking tray with greased greaseproof paper or non-stick cooking parchment (usually available from kitchen shops and health food shops). Make 12 small mounds of the mixture on the tray or use a piping bag to make little rounds. Place in a preheated very cool oven (120°C/240°F) for about 1¼ hours, or until meringues are crisp and just faintly tinted.

Remove from oven and cool on the tray. Sandwich together with whipped cream to serve. Makes 6 pairs.

Gingerbread men and hearts
(photograph right)

If you wish, you can make your own interesting shapes from this classic gingerbread mixture. We chose little people and fat hearts.

125 g (4 oz) butter
½ cup sugar
1 egg yolk
2½ tablespoons golden syrup
2 cups plain flour
Pinch salt
1 teaspoon cinnamon
1 teaspoon bicarbonate of soda
2 teaspoons ground ginger
Currants, sliced cherries, licorice etc. to decorate

Cream butter and sugar until light and fluffy. Add egg yolk and golden syrup and beat thoroughly. Sift dry ingredients together and work into butter mixture to form a soft dough.

Knead lightly on a floured surface and roll out to about 3 mm (⅛ in) thickness. Cut into gingerbread men and hearts with floured cutters. Use currants, sliced cherries, tiny strips of licorice etc. to make features on men. Arrange on greased baking trays and bake in a preheated moderate oven (180°C/350°F) for 15 minutes. Cool on the trays, then store in airtight containers.

Note: If you are making the gingerbread for adults, there is no need to decorate the gingerbread men. They still look appealing without eyes or noses!

Chocolate chip cookies

| 2 cups self raising flour |
| Pinch salt |
| 150 g (5 oz) butter, cut in small pieces |
| ½ cup castor sugar |
| ¼ cup crushed nuts |
| 1 egg, beaten |
| ½ teaspoon vanilla |
| ½ cup chocolate chips |

Sift flour and salt into a bowl. Rub in the butter until mixture resembles coarse breadcrumbs, then stir in the sugar and nuts. Add the egg and vanilla and mix to a stiff dough. Add the chocolate chips, kneading them into the dough with the fingers. Divide dough in two and form each piece into a cylinder about 5 cm (2 in) in diameter. Wrap in plastic film and chill for 30 minutes.

Using a sharp knife dipped in water, cut the dough in thin slices. Arrange on greased baking trays, spaced well apart. Bake in a preheated moderate oven (180°C/350°F) for 12 minutes, or until golden. Leave for a minute on the trays, then cool on wire racks. Makes about 30.

Ginger Nuts

Remember when you used to dunk these in milk or tea, and rescued them just before they got so soft they dropped off?

| 1 cup self raising flour |
| ½ teaspoon bicarbonate of soda |
| 2 teaspoons ground ginger |
| 1 teaspoon cinnamon |
| ¼ teaspoon ground cloves |
| 2 teaspoons sugar |
| 60 g (2 oz) butter |
| 5 tablespoons golden syrup |

Sift flour, soda and spices into a bowl. Place sugar, butter and syrup in a small saucepan and stir until melted. Cool a little, then stir into the flour mixture. Roll into about 24 small balls, and space well apart on greased baking trays. Flatten slightly with the bottom of a glass. Bake in a preheated moderately hot oven (190°C/375°F) for 17 minutes, or until firm. Remove from oven, cool on the baking trays for a few minutes, then transfer with a metal spatula to wire racks to finish cooling. Store in an airtight container.

Almond macaroons

Delicious with coffee, and also to accompany icecreams, custards and stewed fruits.

| ¾ cup sugar |
| ¾ cup ground almonds |
| 3 egg whites |
| 2 drops almond essence |
| 8 blanched almonds, split in halves |

Combine sugar and ground almonds. Beat egg whites with essence until stiff peaks form. Combine both mixtures to form a soft dough.

Grease a baking tray, and line with cooking parchment or greased aluminium foil. Drop 16 small mounds of the mixture on to the paper, or pipe in 5 cm (2 in) rounds. Press a split almond on top of each macaroon, and bake in a preheated moderately slow oven (160°C/320°F) for 40 minutes, or until firm and pale gold. Cool on a wire rack.

Marble cake

| 125 g (4 oz) butter |
| ¾ cup sugar |
| 1 teaspoon vanilla |
| 2 eggs, beaten |
| 2 cups self raising flour |
| Pinch salt |
| 4 tablespoons milk |
| 2 tablespoons cocoa |
| ½ teaspoon instant coffee |
| 2 tablespoons hot water |

Cream butter, sugar and vanilla until light and fluffy. Gradually beat in the eggs and mix well. Sift flour and salt together and fold in, then stir in milk. Place half the mixture in another bowl. Mix cocoa, instant coffee and water together and stir into one half of mixture.

Spoon the plain mixture into an 18 cm (7 in) round cake tin that has been greased, and lined with greased greaseproof paper. Spoon chocolate mixture on top, then run a knife several times through the two mixtures to give a marbled effect when cut.

Bake the cake in a preheated moderate oven (180°C/350°F) for 50 minutes, or until a skewer inserted in the centre comes out clean. Leave a minute in the tin, then turn out on a wire rack to cool. Serve plain or iced.

Swiss roll
(photograph right)

We give you the basic recipe and ideas for delicious fillings.

| 3 eggs |
| ½ cup castor sugar |
| 2 tablespoons hot water |
| ½ teaspoon vanilla |
| 1 cup self raising flour |
| Extra castor sugar |
| Jam and whipped cream for filling |

Beat eggs and sugar until thick and creamy. Trickle water and vanilla around the sides of the basin, then sift flour over the top. Using a metal tablespoon, fold lightly together, being careful not to overmix.

Grease a Swiss roll tin, then line with greased greaseproof paper. Pour the mixture in and bake in a preheated moderate oven (180°C/350°F) for 12-15 minutes, or until beginning to shrink from the sides of the tin.

While roll is cooking, sprinkle castor sugar evenly over a clean tea towel or kitchen paper. Turn cooked roll directly from the oven on to the castor sugar and peel off greaseproof paper.

If edges are crispy, trim them with a sharp knife. Quickly roll up tea towel and cake together, starting from the long side. Allow to stand until cold, then unroll. Spread with whipped cream and jam and roll up again. (If you wish to use jam only on the cake, you need only leave it rolled for 2 minutes. Unroll, spread with jam, and enjoy it warm).

Chocolate roll: Add 1½ tablespoons of cocoa to the flour and sift together. Increase hot water to 3 tablespoons. Roll up with chocolate filling.

Chocolate filling: Whip together until stiff, 1½ cups cream, 1 tablespoon cocoa, 1 tablespoon sugar and 1 tablespoon rum or brandy.

Apple raspberry filling: Cook 2 peeled, chopped Granny Smith apples until soft in a little water and lemon juice. Mash and cool. Spread roll with raspberry jam, then apples, and roll up.

Strawberry banana filling: Slice a punnet of strawberries and marinate in a dash of brandy. Spread roll with whipped cream, then top with strawberries and 2 sliced bananas. Roll up and serve at once.

Lemon-Passionfruit filling: Spread roll with lemon butter. Whip cream until stiff, fold in pulp of 3 passionfruit, and spread over lemon butter. Roll up and serve.

Chocolate fudge cake

This is absolutely the best chocolate cake we know — like eating chocolate velvet.

125 g (4 oz) butter or margarine
1 cup sugar
2 eggs
1 teaspoon vanilla
⅔ cup cocoa
½ cup hot water
2 teaspoons vinegar
1 cup milk
1 ¾ cups plain flour
1 teaspoon baking powder
1 teaspoon bicarbonate of soda
Pinch salt
Creamy Chocolate Icing (see below)
Grated chocolate to decorate

Cream butter and sugar until light and fluffy, then beat in eggs and vanilla. Blend cocoa with hot water to make a smooth paste and gradually stir in to creamed mixture. Combine vinegar and milk and leave for a minute to sour.

Sift together flour, baking powder, bicarbonate and salt. Add to creamed mixture alternately with sour milk. Stir lightly but thoroughly.

Pour into two greased 20 cm (8 in) sandwich tins and bake in a preheated moderate oven (180°C/350°F) for 30 minutes, or until tops spring back when lightly pressed.

Cool in tins for 10 minutes, then turn out and allow to cool completely. Fill and ice with chocolate icing and decorate with grated chocolate.

Creamy chocolate icing: Beat 125 g (4 oz) butter until creamy. Sift 2½ cups icing sugar and blend 3 tablespoons cocoa with 3 tablespoons hot water until smooth. Add icing sugar to butter alternately with cocoa mixture, using enough cocoa to give a good spreading consistency.

Sue's sponge sandwich
(photograph page 152)

Sponge cakes take pride of place at every show and on every country afternoon tea table. Note that you need large eggs for this recipe.

4 large eggs, separated
¾ cup castor sugar
1 cup self raising flour
¼ cup cornflour
Pinch salt
1 tablespoon butter
4 tablespoons boiling water
1 cup cream, whipped
Passionfruit pulp, lemon cheese, sliced strawberries or jam for filling
Sifted icing sugar to decorate

Beat egg whites until stiff peaks form. Beat in sugar 1 tablespoon at a time, and continue beating for 5 minutes. Beat egg yolks in a separate bowl (you can use same beater) and gently combine with egg whites.

Sift flour, cornflour and salt together, sprinkle over the egg mixture and fold in. Melt butter in the boiling water and combine quickly and lightly.

Grease two 20 cm (8 in) round sandwich tins and dust lightly with cornflour. Divide cake mixture between the tins, and bake in a preheated moderately hot oven (190°C/375°F) for 20 minutes, or until tops spring back when gently touched.

Turn out on to wire racks to cool, then sandwich together with whipped cream and your choice of filling. Dust top with icing sugar, or sift the icing sugar through a paper doyley to make a pretty pattern.

Lamingtons
(photograph page 152)

The story goes that Lord Lamington, an early Governor of Queensland, was so popular that Queenslanders named one of their favourite cakes after him. That still doesn't tell us how the combination of tender cake, chocolate icing and coconut began — but it's certainly an Australian original!

For cake:

3 eggs
¾ cup castor sugar
¾ cup self raising flour
Pinch salt
45 g (1½ oz) butter, melted
3 tablespoons boiling water

For icing:

2 cups icing sugar, sifted
3 tablespoons cocoa
30 g (1 oz) butter, melted
4 tablespoons boiling water
About 2 cups desiccated coconut

Beat eggs and sugar together until thick and pale. Sift flour and salt and fold in, then combine melted butter and boiling water and combine quickly and lightly.

Pour into a greased and floured 18 × 28 cm (7 × 11 in) lamington tin. Bake in a preheated hot oven (200°C/400°F) for 20 minutes, or until cooked when tested with a fine skewer. Cool on a wire rack, then cut into 12 squares.

To make icing, sift icing sugar and cocoa into a bowl. Add melted butter and boiling water and mix well until smooth, then stand the bowl in a saucepan of boiling water.

Using two forks, dip squares of cake in hot icing, let excess drip off, then roll in coconut. Leave in a cool place for icing to firm.

Note: For easy cutting, it's best to make the cake a day before.

Prune cake

If you are looking for a new idea for a cake, you may like to try this one — it's light, moist and spicy!

125 g (4 oz) butter
1 cup brown sugar
2 eggs
2 cups self raising flour
½ teaspoon salt
1 teaspoon each cinnamon, nutmeg, allspice
¼ teaspoon ground cloves and ginger
1 cup milk
1½ cups chopped, soft prunes (ready-to-eat-variety)

For filling:

2 cups sifted icing sugar
2 teaspoons grated lemon rind
30 g (1 oz) butter, softened
About 2 tablespoons lemon juice

Cream butter and sugar until light and fluffy. Add eggs and beat well. Sift flour with salt and spices and fold into creamed mixture, alternately with the milk. Lastly fold in the prunes.

Spoon in to a greased, deep 20 cm (8 in) cake tin that has been lined with greased greaseproof paper. Bake in a preheated moderate oven (180°C/350°F) for 50 minutes, or until cooked when tested with a skewer. Turn out on a wire rack and when cold ice with lemon icing.

Icing: Combine sugar and lemon rind. Stir in butter, then add lemon juice little by little until icing is a good spreading consistency.

Date and nut loaf

2½ cups self raising flour
1 teaspoon mixed spice
½ teaspoon salt
¾ cup brown sugar, firmly packed
½ cup chopped walnuts
½ cup chopped dates
2 eggs
¼ cup oil
1 cup milk
1 teaspoon vanilla

Sift flour, spice and salt into a bowl and stir in sugar, walnuts and dates. Beat the eggs, then beat in oil, milk and vanilla. Pour all at once into the dry ingredients and stir just until moistened. Don't over-mix — the batter will still be lumpy.

Spoon into a loaf tin that has been greased and the base lined with greased greaseproof paper. Bake in a preheated moderate oven (180°C/350°F) for 50 minutes, or until cooked through when tested with a skewer. Turn out on to a wire rack to cool, and serve freshly made, sliced and buttered.

Butter cake

Some of us like our butter cake spread with extra butter! It can also be iced with vanilla or lemon icing.

125 g (4 oz) butter
½ cup castor sugar
2 eggs
1 teaspoon vanilla
1¼ cups self raising flour
¼ cup cornflour
Pinch salt
⅓ cup milk

Beat butter and sugar together until light and creamy. Add eggs and vanilla and beat well. Sift flours and salt together and fold into butter mixture, alternately with milk.

Grease a 23 × 10 cm (9 × 4 in) loaf tin and line the base with greased greaseproof paper. Spoon in the mixture, level the top and bake in a preheated moderately hot oven (190°C/375°F) for 40 minutes, or until cooked when tested with a fine skewer. Cool on a wire rack and serve plain, buttered or iced.

Sultana cake

Another time-honoured show cake that keeps well and is excellent for packed lunches.

185 g (6 oz) butter
⅔ cups castor sugar
3 eggs
½ teaspoon vanilla
1½ cups sultana
1½ cups plain flour
½ cup self raising flour
Pinch salt
2 tablespoons dark rum

Cream butter and sugar until light. Add eggs one at a time and continue beating for 5 minutes. Add vanilla and sultanas. Sift flours and salt and fold in, then fold in rum.

Grease a deep 18 cm (7 in) square cake tin, and line with greased brown paper. Pour in the mixture and smooth the top. Bake in a preheated slow oven (160°C/325°F) for 1½ hours, or until cooked when tested with a fine skewer. Allow to cool in the tin, then remove paper and store cake in an airtight tin.

Passionfruit cheese
(photograph page 152)

A beautifully-flavoured spread for toast, or a filling for tarts and cakes. It will keep for months in the refrigerator.

125 g (4 oz) butter
Pulp of 8 large passionfruit
1 cup sugar
4 egg yolks

Place all ingredients in the top of a double boiler, or a basin that will fit in the top of a saucepan. Stir constantly over simmering water until the mixture thickens — about 20 minutes. Pour into hot, sterilized jars, seal and cool. The mixture will thicken as it cools. Store jars in the refrigerator.

Dundee cake
(photograph page 174)

185 g (6 oz) soft butter
1⅓ cups sugar
6 eggs
¼ cup brandy or fruit juice
2 cups currants
1½ cups raisins, chopped
1 cup chopped mixed peel
2 teaspoons grated lemon rind
1 cup chopped, blanched almonds
3 cups plain flour
1 teaspoon baking powder
½ teaspoon salt
1 teaspoon cinnamon
½ teaspoon nutmeg
¼ cup slivered, blanched almonds to decorate

Cream butter and sugar until light and fluffy. Beat in eggs one at a time, beating well after each addition. Stir in brandy. Combine currants, raisins, mixed peel, lemon rind and chopped almonds in a separate bowl. Sift dry ingredients over the fruit and toss until the fruit is well coated with flour. Add to the creamed mixture and stir to blend. Spoon into a 23 cm (9 in) round or 20 cm (8 in) square tin which has been greased and lined with greased brown paper or foil.

Hollow out the centre a little so the cake will rise evenly and sprinkle slivered almonds over the top. Bake in a preheated moderately slow oven (160°C/325°F) for about 2 hours. (A fine skewer inserted in the centre of the cake should come out clean when the cake is ready). Store in an airtight container for a few days before serving.

173

Two-tone fruit cake
(photograph right)

Here's a fruit cake that looks intriguing when sliced, and has wonderful flavour.

1 cup raisins, chopped
¾ cup stoned prunes, chopped
1 cup coarsely chopped walnuts
½ cup chopped mixed peel
1 teaspoon cinnamon
½ teaspoon ground cloves
½ teaspoon allspice
1 tablespoon treacle or golden syrup
1 cup sultanas
1 cup chopped dried apricots
¾ cup blanched almonds
3 slices glace pineapple, chopped
An extra ½ cup chopped mixed peel
½ teaspoon ground ginger
½ teaspoon ground mace
1 tablespoon lemon juice
250g (8oz) butter
1 cup sugar
4 eggs
2 cups plain flour
1 teaspoon baking powder
1 teaspoon salt

Combine raisins, prunes, walnuts, ½ cup mixed peel, cinnamon, cloves, allspice and treacle. In another bowl, combine sultanas, apricots, almonds, pineapple, the extra ½ cup of mixed peel, ginger, mace and lemon juice.

Cream butter and sugar until light and fluffy. Add eggs one at a time, beating well after each addition. Sift flour, baking powder and salt together and combine well with the creamed mixture. Add half the batter to each bowl of fruit mixture.

Spoon the first mixture (with raisins and prunes) over the base of a 25cm (10in) round tin that has been greased and lined with greased aluminium foil. Spoon the second mixture over the top, so evenly.

Bake in a preheated slow oven (150°C/300°F) for 4 hours, or until a fine skewer inserted in the centre of the cake comes out clean. Leave cake in tin for a few minutes, then turn out to finish cooling. Carefully peel off the paper, wrap cake tightly in fresh foil, and store in an airtight container for several weeks before cutting, so the flavours can mature.

Photograph at right shows an old favourite, Dundee cake, and an exciting new idea — fruitcake in two colours.

PASTURES AND PRODUCE

Visitors to Australia find it delightful that there are still market gardens and dairy cows grazing on the fringes of our capital cities.
Many of these dairy farms and market gardens have been in the same families for generations, and some have roadside stalls where browsers can buy fresh eggs, poultry, honey, and fruit and vegetables that truly are "just picked this morning".

At the same time, the influence of Asian and European settlers has played an important part in the abundance of beautiful foods available in our fruit shops and dairy cases.

Chinese and Vietnamese market gardeners grow the crisp, fresh greens so essential for Asian cookery, and edging more and more into our everyday diet. Italians and Greeks have helped to educate us to the charms of baby vegetables such as tiny squash and zucchini, miniature eggplants, tomatoes and cucumbers.

Many of the cheeses we now produce in Australia – Feta, Brie, Mozarella, Blue Vein and Cheddar – are made by tradesmen who learned their skills in the European countries where these classic cheeses originated.

This chapter is devoted – with appreciation and admiration – to the products of our Australian pastures and small farms and those who operate them.

Captions to preceding 6 pages.

Page 176/177   Cabbage patch, Nowra, New South Wales. (photography: Colin Beard)

Page 178/179   A barn in lush dairy country is the tranquil setting for an array of farm-fresh produce and pork, egg, chicken dishes. (photography: Phil Wymant)

Page 180/181   Melbourne markets, Victoria. (photography: Colin Beard)

Facing page: Potato field, Tasmania.

Garnished cheese soup

(photograph right)

An unusual idea for a family meal or party — creamy cheese soup is accompanied by bowls of delicious "trimmings". Add crusty bread, and the meal is complete.

60 g (2 oz) butter

2 tablespoons plain flour

3 cups chicken stock

1 cup milk

Salt and freshly grated pepper

Dash freshly grated nutmeg

2 egg yolks

1 cup cream

1 cup grated tasty cheese

Garnishes (see below)

Melt the butter in a heavy saucepan, stir in the flour, and cook over low heat for 1 minute. Gradually stir in the stock and milk, and continue stirring over medium heat until mixture boils and thickens. Season with salt and pepper and nutmeg.

Beat the egg yolks with the cream and gradually stir into the hot soup. Reheat, but do not allow to boil. Stir in the cheese until it melts, and taste for seasoning. Serve from a tureen surrounded by garnishes, which each diner adds to his soup to suit his own taste. Serves 4-6.

Garnishes: Peeled prawns, thinly sliced radishes or green peppers, thinly sliced cucumber or celery, chopped ham mixed with chopped leeks, etc.

Fresh pea soup

There couldn't be an easier soup to make, or one which is enjoyed by so many people.

1 kg (2 lb) young peas in the pod

60 g (2 oz) butter

6 shallots, finely chopped

1 clove garlic, crushed

2 tablespoons finely chopped mint

1 teaspoon sugar

Salt and freshly ground white pepper

4 cups water

1 cup cream

A little extra chopped mint

1 cup sippets (tiny squares of fried bread)

Shell the peas, saving 6 or 8 of the most tender pods. Heat the butter in a heavy saucepan and add the peas, pods and garlic. Toss for a minute or two. Add mint, sugar, salt and pepper to taste and water. Bring to the boil, then simmer with the lid on for 20 minutes, or until peas are tender. Puree in batches in a blender, and return to the saucepan. Reheat to boiling point, stir in cream, and taste for seasoning. Serve in heated bowls, sprinkled with mint and sippets. Serves 4.

Stir-fried snow peas

Tender young pea pods, with tiny peas inside, are superb eaten whole. Try them raw, with a creamy dip — or in this easy, Chinese—style recipe.

250 g (8 oz) snow peas

2 tablespoons oil

1 small clove garlic, crushed

1 slice fresh ginger, chopped

2 teaspoons light soy sauce

Freshly ground white pepper

Pinch of sugar

Trim the ends of the snow peas and string if necessary. Rinse pods in cold water and dry.

Heat the oil in a large, heavy frying pan and fry the garlic and ginger for a minute. Add the peas and toss for 3 minutes, or until tender-crisp. Sprinkle with soy sauce, pepper and sugar and toss for another few seconds. Serve at once. Serves 2-3.

Orange cabbage patch

Cabbage takes well to sweet flavours, and is often cooked with apple. In this recipe, orange is the interesting addition.

60 g (2 oz) butter

1 small, firm cabbage, shredded (as for coleslaw)

2 medium onions, finely chopped

Pinch ground cloves

Salt and freshly ground pepper

2 large oranges, peeled and thinly sliced

½ cup orange juice

1 tablespoon brown sugar

⅓ cup sour cream or natural yoghurt

Heat the butter in a large frying pan and toss the cabbage and onion over medium heat for a couple of minutes. Add remaining ingredients except sour cream. Toss for another minute or two, until cabbage is tender-crisp. Taste for seasoning and quickly stir in the sour cream or yoghurt. Serves 6-8.

Garden omelette

4 eggs

2 tablespoons water

Salt and freshly ground pepper

½ cup cooked ham, cut in fine strips

30 g (1 oz) butter

4 asparagus spears, heated in a little butter

¼ cup grated tasty cheese

1 tablespoon finely chopped parsley or chives

Beat the eggs and water with a fork, and stir in salt and pepper to taste and ham. Heat the butter in a medium-size frying pan until it sizzles. Pour in the egg mixture over high heat. As soon as the edges set (almost immediately) draw them towards the centre, and tilt the pan so uncooked egg runs underneath. Repeat until the omelette is set underneath, but the top is still moist. Arrange asparagus spears on one half of the omelette, and sprinkle with cheese and parsley. Fold the other half of the omelette over, and roll on to a heated plate. Serve at once. Serves 2.

Garnished cheese soup will appeal to those who like something nutritious, delicious — and different!

Baked eggs with cream and cheese

Butter
4 eggs
4 tablespoons sour cream
Salt and freshly ground pepper
4 tablespoons grated Gruyere cheese
Hot buttered toast to serve

Butter 4 small ramekins or souffle dishes and break an egg into each. Season with salt and pepper.

Spoon a tablespoon of sour cream over each egg, and sprinkle with cheese. Bake in a preheated moderate oven (180°C/350°F) for 10 minutes, or until whites are firm and yolks still a little runny.

Serve in the ramekins, with hot buttered toast. Serves 4.

Curried eggs and bacon

(photograph below)

Here's a new way of presenting a popular dish — the eggs are cut in half, coated with curry sauce, and sprinkled with crisp bacon. Good for any casual meal.

6 hard-boiled eggs, shelled
45 g (1½ oz) butter
Pinch sugar
1½ teaspoons mild curry powder
2 tablespoons plain flour
1½ cups chicken stock
2 teaspoons lemon juice
4 rashers streaky bacon, rind removed
Finely chopped parsley to garnish

Cut the eggs in half lengthways, and arrange cut-side down in a greased, shallow casserole dish.

Melt the butter in a saucepan, stir in curry powder, sugar and flour, and cook for 1 minute. Remove from heat and stir in stock and lemon juice. Return to the stove, and gradually bring to the boil, stirring constantly. Taste for seasoning (add salt and pepper if required) and spoon over eggs.

Bake in a preheated hot oven (200°C/400°F) for 5 minutes, or until eggs are heated through and sauce is bubbly. Meanwhile, chop bacon and fry until crisp. Sprinkle bacon over eggs and garnish with parsley. Serve with hot buttered toast or boiled rice. Serves 3-4.

Bacon & egg puff

(photograph right)

5 eggs
4 tablespoons plain flour
1½ cups evaporated milk
1 tablespoon finely chopped chives or shallots
Salt and freshly ground pepper
15 g (½ oz) butter
4-6 rashers streaky bacon, rind removed
125 g (4 oz) button mushrooms
Chopped chives to garnish

Beat eggs and flour together until smooth, then stir in evaporated milk, chives and salt and pepper to taste. (Don't over-mix). Allow batter to stand for 20 minutes or so.

Put butter in a souffle dish or straight-sided casserole, and place dish in a pre-heated hot oven (200°C/400°F) for 3-4 minutes or until butter is sizzling. Pour batter into dish and bake for 15-20 minutes, until well puffed and golden brown. Meanwhile, fry bacon until crisp, remove from pan and toss mushrooms in bacon fat until tender. Season with salt and pepper. Place bacon and mushrooms in centre of puff and serve immediately. Serves 3-4.

Cheese souffle omelette

This is the very fluffy omelette, in which yolks and whites are beaten separately.

4 eggs, separated
2 tablespoons cream
Salt and freshly ground pepper
½ cup Mozarella cheese, cut into tiny cubes
2 teaspoons chopped chives
30 g (1 oz) butter

Beat the egg yolks with cream and salt and pepper. Beat the whites until they hold soft peaks, and fold into the yolks with the cheese and chives.

Heat the butter in a heavy frying pan, and pour in the mixture. Cook over medium heat, without stirring, until set on the bottom.

Place the pan under a preheated medium grill, and cook until the top is golden brown and puffy. Slide on to a heated serving platter, and cut in half with a fork to serve. Serves 2.

Prawn omelette

This is really a cross between an omelette and a pancake, as it contains a little flour, and is served cut in strips.

6 eggs
3 tablespoons milk
1 tablespoon self raising flour
1 teaspoon salt
Dash cayenne pepper
¼ teaspoon freshly grated nutmeg
1 cup chopped, cooked prawns (or you may use flaked crab)
30 g (1 oz) butter
1 tablespoon oil
Shredded lettuce and soy sauce to serve

Beat the eggs with the flour and milk until well combined. Stir in the salt, pepper, nutmeg and prawns.

Heat the butter and oil in a large frying pan. Pour in the batter and cook over moderate heat until edges set. Pull edges towards middle, tilt the pan, and allow uncooked batter to run underneath. Repeat until omelette is set underneath and golden brown. Cut the omelette in half with the edge of an egg slice and turn each half over to brown the other side.

Turn omelette out of the pan and cut into 1 cm (½ in) strips. Arrange on a bed of shredded lettuce and sprinkle with a little soy sauce. Serves 2-3.

Feta sausage flan

(photograph page 178)

Use your favourite salami or other continental sausage in this flan, with its interesting combination of flavours.

60 g (2 oz) butter, melted
8 sheets of filo pastry
3 eggs
½ cup milk
1 cup of cream
60 g (2 oz) salami, finely shredded
45 g (1½ oz) Feta cheese, crumbled
6 black olives, sliced
2 teaspoons chopped fresh oregano, or ½ teaspoon dried
Salt and freshly ground pepper

Grease a 23 cm (9 in) flan tin generously with butter and line with filo pastry. Butter the pastry, place another sheet on top, and continue until filo is used up. Fold in any overhanging edges, or trim with scissors.

Beat eggs, milk and cream together and stir in half the salami and the remaining ingredients. Pour into the flan tin. Bake on the bottom shelf of a pre-heated moderate oven (180°C/350°F) for 45 minutes or until pastry is crisp and golden and filling firm. Sprinkle rest of salami over the top and serve warm or cold. Serves 6.

Eggs with tomato and hot sausage

| 2 tablespoons olive oil |
| 1 medium onion, finely chopped |
| 1 small green pepper, finely chopped |
| 1 clove garlic, crushed |
| 2 medium-size ripe tomatoes, peeled and chopped |
| Salt and freshly ground pepper |
| Dash cayenne pepper |
| 1 chorizo or pepperoni sausage, sliced |
| ½ cup chicken stock |
| 6 eggs |

Heat the oil in a large, heavy frying pan and fry the onion, green pepper and garlic until soft, about 5 minutes. Add the tomatoes, seasonings, sausage and stock. Cover the pan and simmer for 5 minutes.

Carefully break the eggs over the top and cover the pan again. Poach for 6 minutes, or until eggs are set. Serves 3-6, depending on appetites.

Good health flan

(photograph page 178)

You'll enjoy the cheese and leek filling in its wholemeal crust.

For pastry:

| 1 cup wholemeal plain flour |
| ½ teaspoon salt |
| 1 cup wheatgerm |
| 2 tablespoons grated tasty cheese |
| Pinch cayenne pepper |
| 90 g (3 oz) butter or margarine, cut in small pieces |
| About ½ cup water |

For filling:

| 60 g (2 oz) butter |
| 1 leek, trimmed and thinly sliced |
| 2 eggs |
| ¾ cup light sour cream |
| ¾ cup milk |
| 1½ cups grated tasty cheese |
| 1 tablespoon finely chopped parsley |
| 1 tablespoon finely chopped fresh mixed herbs, or 1 teaspoon dried |
| Salt and freshly ground pepper |

Place flour, salt and wheatgerm in a bowl and stir to combine. Add cheese and cayenne. Rub in butter until mixture resembles coarse breadcrumbs, then stir in enough water to make a firm dough. Knead gently on a lightly floured surface, then roll out to line a 23 cm (9 in) greased flan tin.

Heat the butter in a small saucepan and gently fry the leek until soft but not brown, about 4 minutes. Put aside to cool. Beat the eggs, sour cream and milk together, then stir in cheese, herbs and seasoning. Spread the leek over the pastry crust, and gently pour in the cheese mixture. Place on the bottom shelf of a preheated moderate oven (180°C/350°F) and bake for 50 minutes, or until pastry is cooked and filling set. Serve warm or cold. Serves 6.

Pickled eggs

(photograph page 178)

| 12 hard boiled-eggs, shelled |
| Vinegar to cover |
| Sprigs of herbs, such as thyme, oregano, tarragon, rosemary |
| 12 peppercorns |

Arrange eggs in a large jar. Pour sufficient vinegar to cover the eggs into a large saucepan (not aluminium). Add herbs and peppercorns, bring to the boil, and simmer gently for 10 minutes. Cool, then pour over the eggs (including herbs and peppercorns). Cool and seal. Allow to stand for at least 24 hours before eating. Delicious for a picnic. Serves 6-12.

Simple boiled artichokes

The large, leafy artichokes are the ones we usually think of in Australia as artichokes. The little, knobbly brown tubers called Jerusalem artichokes are not as common (and in fact, are not related in any way to the large artichoke, so it's a mystery why they share the same name!)
There is not much to cooking an artichoke, but eating it may be a bit of a mystery — hence the rather detailed explanation.

| 4 globe artichokes |
| Salted water |
| Lemon juice |
| 2 tablespoons vinegar |
| Hot melted butter and lemon juice to serve |

Try to get tightly closed artichokes. If they aren't closed, soak them upside down in a large bowl of salted water to remove any earth that may have lodged in the leaves. Cut the stalks off close to the head and snip off the sharp points of the leaves with a pair of scissors. Rub the cut edges of leaves with lemon juice to prevent them turning dark.

Bring a large pot of salted water to the boil with the vinegar. Add the artichokes and cook for about 30 minutes uncovered, or until the soft little pad at the base of a leaf is tender to the bite.

Drain artichokes upside-down in a colander. Serve hot with melted butter and lemon juice, or cold with French dressing or mayonnaise. Serves 4.

To serve: Have a large bowl on the table for discarded leaves, a finger bowl at each place setting, and plenty of napkins. To eat an artichoke, pull away the leaves one by one, beginning at the bottom. Dip the soft base of each leaf in sauce, then chew it off the leaf, which is discarded.

When you have pulled away all the leaves, you will see a circle of greyish fibres in the centre, called the "choke". Remove with a small spoon, or slide it off with a knife and discard.

The artichoke bottom — the last part and the delicacy — is now revealed, and can be eaten with a knife and fork.

Pumpkin salad

(photograph right)

A golden salad with a delightful combination of textures.

| 1 kg (2 lb) pumpkin, peeled and cubed |
| ¾ cup walnut pieces |
| 6 shallots, chopped |
| ¼ cup finely chopped parsley |
| Salt and freshly ground pepper |
| About 1 cup mayonnaise, homemade or bought |

Cook pumpkin in boiling, salted water until just tender. Drain in a colander, then run cold water through. Drain on paper towels, cover and chill.

When ready to serve, toss pumpkin with walnuts, shallots, parsley and salt and pepper to taste. Add enough mayonnaise to moisten, and fold through lightly. Serve with grills, or hot or cold roast meats. Serves 6.

Note: You can vary the salad by adding finely sliced celery, extra herbs, or using a mixture of pumpkin and potato.

Cauliflower cheese

For many of us, cauliflower just isn't cauliflower if it's served without white sauce and cheese.

| 1 small, firm whole cauliflower |
| 1 cup lightly salted water |
| ½ cup milk |
| ½ teaspoon salt |
| 45 g (1½ oz) butter |
| 2 tablespoons plain flour |
| Extra milk |
| Salt and freshly ground pepper |
| 1 cup grated tasty cheese |
| 1 cup sieved, fresh breadcrumbs |
| An extra knob of butter |

Separate cauliflower into floret clusters, wash and drain. Heat water, milk and salt to boiling, add cauliflower and cook partially covered for 4-5 minutes, or until just tender. Drain, reserving liquid, and place in a greased casserole dish.

Melt the 45 g of butter in a clean saucepan, stir in the flour and cook for 1 minute. Make up the cooking liquid to 1½ cups with extra milk, and gradually stir into the flour. Continue stirring over medium heat until smooth and thickened. Season with salt and pepper and stir in half the grated cheese. Spoon over cauliflower.

Mix remaining cheese with breadcrumbs and sprinkle over the top. Dot with little pieces of butter and bake in a preheated hot oven (200°C/400°F) for 10 minutes or until sauce is bubbly and topping golden. Serves 4-6.

Glazed parsnips

| 500 g (1 lb) young parsnips |
| 60 g (2 oz) butter |
| 1 tablespoon brown sugar |
| Salt and freshly ground pepper |
| Chopped parsley to garnish |

Wash parsnips (no need to peel young ones) and cut into 1 cm (½ in) slices. Cook in boiling salted water until just tender, about 6 minutes. Drain, and dry on paper towels.

Heat the butter in a heavy frying pan and stir in sugar until sugar melts. Add parsnips and gently toss over high heat until nicely glazed. Season with salt and pepper and serve sprinkled with parsley. Serves 4.

Carrot-cheese salad

Very healthy — and a lovely sandwich filling, as well as a salad.

| 1 small carton cottage cheese |
| 1 clove garlic, crushed |
| 1 tablespoon finely chopped chives or shallots |
| 1 tablespoon lemon juice |
| 2 tablespoons walnut or olive oil |
| Salt and freshly ground pepper |
| 2 medium carrots, grated |
| 2 tablespoons chopped walnuts (optional) |
| Lettuce leaves to serve |

Combine all ingredients and serve in lettuce leaves. Serves 4.

Spinach with cream and cheese

We like to cook the white stalks of spinach as well as the green leaves.

| One large bunch spinach weighing about 1 kg (2 lb) |
| 1 tablespoon olive oil |
| 1 fat clove garlic, crushed |
| ½ cup cream |
| Dash freshly grated nutmeg |
| Salt and freshly ground pepper |
| 2 tablespoons freshly grated Parmesan cheese |

Remove any discoloured or stringy stalks from the spinach. Remove the leaves from the tender stalks and ribs remaining. Slice the stalks and ribs finely and wash. Wash the leaves and slice thinly.

Place leaves and stalks in a heavy saucepan with a little salt (don't add water) and cook, covered, for 5 minutes or until tender. Shake the pan during this time to prevent sticking.

Drain spinach well, pressing down to extract as much liquid as possible.

Heat the oil in a heavy frying pan and fry garlic for a minute. Add spinach and toss, then stir in cream, nutmeg and pepper and salt. Heat through, but do not boil. Serve in a heated serving bowl, sprinkled with cheese. Serves 6.

Note: In some states of Australia, silver beet is called spinach. This has coarse white stalks. English spinach has softer, more delicate leaves and green stalks which do not need trimming or slicing.

Broad beans and onions

Fresh broad beans are in our shops now for a brief season. Serve this buttery, spicy mixture over rice, and you have a complete main course.

| 60 g (2 oz) butter |
| 2 large onions, thinly sliced |
| 1 clove garlic, crushed |
| 750 g (1½ lb) broad beans, shelled |
| Salt and freshly ground pepper |
| Dash freshly grated nutmeg |
| 1 teaspoon paprika |
| 1½ cups hot chicken stock |
| Finely chopped parsley |

Heat the butter in a heavy saucepan and fry the onions and garlic until softened, about 4 minutes. Add the broad beans and seasonings, and stir for another minute. Add the stock, bring to the boil, then simmer covered for 20 minutes, stirring now and again. Taste for seasoning and serve piping hot, sprinkled with parsley. Serves 4.

Note: If there is too much liquid in the pot after beans are cooked, reduce by rapid boiling.

Quick broccoli and ham casserole

| 500 g (1 lb) firm, bright green broccoli |
| 6 slices cooked ham |
| 1 medium-size can cream of mushroom soup |
| 1 tablespoon dry sherry |
| ½ cup thickened cream |
| Salt and freshly ground pepper |
| 1 cup breadcrumbs |
| 45 g (1½ oz) butter, melted |

Cut tough ends from broccoli, but leave tender stems on. Split broccoli into 6 pieces and cook in boiling, salted water until barely tender, about 5 minutes. Drain well.

Wrap a slice of ham around each piece of broccoli, and arrange side by side in a buttered shallow casserole dish.

Mix together undiluted soup, sherry, cream and salt and pepper to taste. Spoon over broccoli and sprinkle with breadcrumbs and melted butter. Bake in a preheated hot oven (200°C/400°F) until sauce is bubbly and crumbs golden. Serves 3-4.

Cheese and mushroom ring

A savoury custard is baked in a ring tin, then turned out and filled with creamy mushrooms. It's not difficult, but it certainly looks impressive.

| 4 eggs, separated |
| ¾ cup cream or evaporated milk |
| 45 g (1½ oz) butter, melted |
| 125 g (4 oz) grated tasty cheese |
| Salt and freshly ground pepper |
| Pinch cayenne pepper |

| **For filling:** |
| 60 g (2 oz) butter |
| 250 g (8 oz) small mushrooms, sliced |
| 2 teaspoons lemon juice |
| Salt and freshly ground pepper |
| ⅓ cup cream |
| Paprika to garnish |

Beat egg yolks and cream together, then stir in melted butter, cheese and seasonings. Beat egg whites until stiff peaks form and fold into the yolk mixture with a large metal spoon. Pour into a 4-cup, greased ring mould and set the mould in a baking dish with enough warm water to come half-way up the sides.

Bake in a preheated moderate oven (180°C/350°F) for 30 minutes, or until a knife inserted in the custard comes out clean.

Leave in the mould for a couple of minutes, then run a knife around the outer and inner edges to loosen them, and carefully invert the custard on to a serving plate. Fill the centre with mushroom mixture, sprinkle with paprika, and serve at once. Serves 4-5.

For filling: Heat the butter and toss mushrooms over high heat for a few minutes. Add lemon juice and salt and pepper and toss for another minute to evaporate some of the liquid. Stir in cream and heat just to boiling.

Cheese and onion castles

Serve as a snack, or instead of bread with grills and pasta dishes.

| 1 loaf unsliced white sandwich bread |
| 90 g (3 oz) butter, melted |
| 1 large onion, finely chopped |
| 1½ cups grated tasty cheese |
| Freshly ground black pepper |

Cut the crust from the top of the loaf and also the crusty ends (leaving just the bottom crust). Slice the bread lengthwise through the middle, almost to the bottom crust. Make crosswise slices at 2.5 cm (1 in) intervals, almost to the bottom crust. Brush all over with melted butter, and sprinkle grated onion and cheese between the slices. Grind black pepper over and place on a greased baking tray.

Bake in a preheated moderate oven (180°C/350°F) for 20 minutes, or until bread is crisp and brown and cheese melted. Serves 6.

Cucumbers with garlic and parsley

Try cucumbers this way, as an interesting hot vegetable.

| 2 medium-size cucumbers |
| 60 g (2 oz) butter |
| Salt and freshly ground pepper |
| 2 cloves garlic, crushed |
| 2 tablespoons finely chopped parsley |

Peel cucumbers, cut in half lengthwise, and scrape out the seeds with a teaspoon. Cut into 1 cm (½ in) pieces and boil in lightly salted water for 5 minutes. Drain well, and dry on paper towels.

Heat the butter in a heavy frying pan and add the cucumbers and garlic. Season with salt and pepper and stir over moderately high heat for 4-5 minutes, or until golden. Sprinkle parsley over and stir through. Serve at once. Serves 4.

Coconut vegetable curry

Coconut milk gives this curry rich flavour. As a main course, serve it with boiled rice and poppadums. As an accompaniment, it's excellent with kebabs, meat balls or grilled sausages.

| 45 g (1½ oz) butter |
| 1 teaspoon tumeric |
| ½ teaspoon grated fresh ginger |
| 1 teaspoon ground cumin |
| 1 teaspoon curry powder |
| 1 teaspoon brown sugar |
| 1 medium carrot, thinly sliced |
| 2 medium potatoes, cut in cubes |
| 250 g (8 oz) young green beans, topped and tailed |
| 2 cups coarsely chopped cabbage |
| 1 small eggplant, peeled and cut into cubes |
| 2 cups canned coconut milk |
| Salt to taste |

Heat the butter in a large saucepan and gently fry the tumeric, ginger, cumin, curry powder and sugar for a minute or two. Add prepared vegetables and toss to coat with spices. Add coconut milk and salt to taste and bring to the boil. Cover and simmer for 20 minutes, or until vegetables are tender. Taste for seasoning and serve in a heated bowl. Serves 4.

Macaroni with vegetables

It's much more flavoursome and colourful than it sounds.

| 250g (8oz) macaroni (any shape) |
| 2 tablespoons olive oil |
| 1 large onion, finely chopped |
| 2 medium carrots, cut into matchsticks (julienne) |
| 2 cloves garlic, crushed |
| 250g (8oz) mushrooms, sliced |
| 2 large ripe tomatoes, peeled and chopped |
| ½ cup chopped black olives |
| ½ cup dry white wine |
| 1 tablespoon chopped fresh oregano, or 1 teaspoon dried |
| Salt and freshly ground pepper |
| Pinch sugar |
| 2 tablespoons finely chopped parsley |
| ½ cup freshly grated Parmesan or Pecorino cheese |

Cook the macaroni according to packet directions, and drain. Meanwhile, heat the oil in a large pan and toss the onion, carrots and garlic over medium heat for 3-4 minutes. Add remaining ingredients except parsley and cheese and bring to the boil. Cover and simmer for 5 minutes. Taste for seasoning.

Spoon the freshly cooked macaroni into a large, heated bowl. Pour the sauce over and toss together. Sprinkle with parsley and cheese and serve at once. Serves 4.

Cucumber and yoghurt salad

An excellent salad to serve with fish.

| 1 large cucumber |
| 2 teaspoons salt |
| 2 tender sticks celery, chopped |
| 1 small carton natural yoghurt |
| 2 tablespoons finely chopped mint |
| Freshly ground pepper |

Peel the cucumber and cut into very thin slices. Place in a colander, sprinkle with salt and leave for 30 minutes. Drain well, pushing down on cucumber slices to extract as much moisture as possible.

Dry cucumber on paper towels, then mix with remaining ingredients. Chill before serving. Serves 4.

Leeks with Ricotta herb sauce

(photograph below)

This pretty green and white dish can be served hot or cold, as a first course, vegetable accompaniment or salad.

| 6 leeks, trimmed and washed |
| 1½ cups chicken stock |
| 125g (4oz) Ricotta cheese |
| ¼ cup finely chopped mixed fresh herbs (parsley, chives, oregano, thyme, marjoram etc.) |
| Salt and freshly ground pepper |

Poach the leeks in the chicken stock until tender but still firm, about 20 minutes. Drain and arrange in a serving dish.

Beat the Ricotta and herbs together with just enough of the cooking liquid to give a creamy consistency. Season with salt and pepper and spoon over the leeks. Serves 6.

Braised witloof with cheese

Witloof is delicious raw in salads, or cooked. It is really a member of the chicory family, but is sometimes called "Belgian Endive". By any name, look for white heads without brown or withered leaves.

| 6 medium-size witloof |
| 1 teaspoon sugar |
| 2 tablespoons lemon juice |
| 1½ cups hot chicken stock |
| 6 slices Swiss cheese |

Trim root ends and remove any discoloured leaves. Place in boiling, salted water, with sugar and lemon juice added, and cook for 10 minutes. Drain. Arrange side by side in a greased, shallow casserole dish, and pour hot stock over. Cover with aluminium foil and bake in a preheated moderate oven (180°C/350°F) for 15 minutes. Arrange cheese slices over the top and bake for another 5 minutes, or until cheese is melted and liquid in the casserole reduced. Serves 4-6.

Stuffed peppers

Here's an excellent way of using up leftover roast lamb or beef.

3 large green or red peppers
1½ cups finely chopped or minced cooked meat
1 small onion, grated
1 clove garlic, crushed
125 g (4 oz) mushrooms, finely chopped
1 large ripe tomato, peeled and chopped
Salt and freshly ground pepper
1 teaspoon dried basil
1 tablespoon finely chopped fresh mint
1 teaspoon sugar
¾ cup tomato juice or beef stock

Cut peppers in half from top to bottom and remove ribs and seeds. Cover with boiling water, leave for 10 seconds, then drain and rinse in cold water. Arrange side by side in a greased baking dish. Combine remaining ingredients, except tomato juice, and stuff peppers. Pour juice over and around peppers, and bake in a preheated moderate oven (180°C/350°F) for 30 minutes. (Add a little extra juice or water to the pan if necessary to prevent drying out). Serves 3-6.

Ginger butternuts

Choose butternuts that are fairly small, so each diner receives half as a serving.

2 small butternut pumpkins
90 g (3 oz) butter, melted
Salt and freshly ground pepper
2 tablespoons brown sugar mixed with ½ teaspoon ground ginger

Cut butternuts in half and scoop out seeds. (Do not peel). Brush all over with melted butter, and pour leftover butter into the hollows. Sprinkle with salt and pepper and place 2 teaspoons of sugar mixture in each hollow.

Place in a baking dish, and add 2.5 cm (1 in) of water to the dish. Bake in a preheated moderate oven (180°C/350°F) for 45 minutes, or until tender when pierced with a fork. Baste tops two or three times with butter — sugar mixture during baking. Serves 4.

Potato pancakes

Enjoy them for breakfast, with grilled bacon or tomatoes — or serve with meat as an interesting changes from mashed potatoes.

500 g (1 lb) old potatoes
2 eggs, beaten
2 tablespoons self raising flour
2 tablespoons chopped chives or shallots
1 tablespoon finely chopped parsley
Salt and freshly ground pepper
Oil for frying

Peel and grate the potatoes. Squeeze tightly in a tea towel to extract as much moisture as possible, then mix with eggs, flour, chives, parsley and salt and pepper to taste. Heat enough oil in a frying pan to give a depth of about 5 mm (¼ in) and drop in large spoonfulls of the mixture.

Cook over medium heat until brown and crisp on the bottom, then turn and cook the other side — about 8 minutes altogether. Drain on paper towels, and serve at once. Serves 4.

Broccoli cheese custard

This is like a quiche, but without the pastry. It's substantial enough to serve for lunch or a light dinner, or would make a lovely first course before chicken or fish.

750 g (1½ lb) firm, bright green broccoli
4 eggs
1 teaspoon salt
Pinch cayenne pepper
¾ cup milk
¾ cup evaporated milk or cream
4 shallots, finely chopped
1 cup grated tasty cheese

Cut off the hard ends from broccoli stems. Slice the tender stems thinly and separate the heads into florets. Cook stems and florets in boiling salted water until just tender, about 4 minutes. Drain and arrange in a greased casserole dish.

Beat eggs with salt, cayenne, milk and evaporated milk. Stir in shallots and cheese and pour over broccoli. Bake in a preheated moderate oven (180°C/350°F) for 45 minutes, or until custard is set. Serve warm. Serves 4-6.

Eggplant and tomato pie

2 medium eggplant
Plain flour
About ½ cup olive oil
Salt and freshly ground pepper
2 large, ripe tomatoes, peeled and cut in thick slices
1 tablespoon chopped fresh basil or 1½ teaspoons dried
Sprinkle of sugar
8-10 thin slices Mozarella or Swiss cheese

Peel the eggplant and cut into slices about 1 cm (½ in) thick. Dip in flour and shake off excess. Heat ½ cup of oil in a heavy frying pan, and brown the slices on both sides, about 2 minutes each side. (Do this in batches to avoid crowding the pan, and add more oil as necessary).

Arrange half the eggplant slices in a shallow casserole dish and season with salt and pepper. Place tomato slices on top and add salt and pepper, basil and a sprinkle of sugar. Top with remaining eggplant slices and season them. Arrange cheese slices over all.

Place the casserole in a preheated moderate oven (180°C/350°F) and bake for 25 minutes, or until vegetables are tender and cheese melted and brown. Serves 4-6.

Cumquat rice
(photograph page 178)

If you have a little cumquat tree, use them in this interesting savoury rice to serve with spicy meat dishes or roasts.

60 g (2 oz) butter
4 cups cooked brown or white rice (1½ cups raw)
6 cumquats, cut in thin slices and seeds removed
3 tablespoons sultanas
1 tablespoon chopped fresh mixed herbs, or 1 teaspoon dried
Salt and freshly ground pepper

Melt the butter in a deep frying pan, add all other ingredients and stir gently until rice is heated through. Serves 4-6.

Note: If cumquats aren't available, use the flesh of half an orange and its finely shredded rind.

Pan-fried zucchini

This way of cooking zucchini makes them golden brown and crispy around the edges.

| 6 small, firm zucchini |
| 2 tablespoons olive oil |
| 30g (1oz) butter |
| 2 cloves garlic, crushed |
| Salt and freshly ground pepper |
| 2 tablespoons finely chopped parsley |

Wash the zucchini, trim ends and cut into thin slices. Heat the oil and butter to sizzling point in a heavy frying pan. Add garlic and zucchini slices and toss and turn with a spatula over high heat until zucchini is golden brown. (This will only take about 3 minutes). Season with salt and pepper and serve at once, sprinkled with parsley. Serves 2-3.

Hot shredded beetroot with orange

| 2 large raw beetroot |
| 45g (1½oz) butter |
| 1 tablespoon grated orange rind |
| 1 tablespoon sugar |
| Salt and freshly ground pepper |
| 1 tablespoon vinegar |
| Finely chopped parsley to garnish |

Peel beetroot, and grate on a coarse grater.

Heat the butter in a heavy frying pan and toss the beetroot over high heat for 2-3 minutes. Add remaining ingredients except parsley and toss for another 2 minutes. Serve in a heated bowl, sprinkled with parsley. Serves 3-4.

Beans billabong
(photograph above)

So easy, you can cook it when you're camping out — and absolutely delicious.

| 500g (1lb) young green beans |
| 4 rashers streaky bacon, rind removed |
| A little pepper |

Top and tail the beans, and string if necessary. Cook in a small amount of boiling, salted water until just tender, about 5 minutes, then drain.

Cut the bacon into pieces and fry until crisp. Add beans to the pan and toss until coated with bacon fat and heated through. Season with pepper and serve piping hot with grills or cold roast meats. Serves 3-4.

Spinach-mushroom-bacon salad

The intriguing thing about this salad is the hot bacon dressing. It must be served the moment it's made, so it's a good idea to toss it at the table.

| 10-12 small spinach leaves |
| 125g (4oz) button mushrooms, sliced |
| 1 small onion, thinly sliced |
| Salt and freshly ground pepper |
| 3 rashers streaky bacon, rind removed |
| 2 tablespoons oil |
| 1 clove garlic, crushed |
| 1 tablespoon wine vinegar |

Remove stalks from spinach. Wash leaves, pat dry, and tear into small pieces. Place in a bowl with onion and mushrooms and season with salt and pepper.

Heat the oil in a frying pan. Chop bacon into small pieces and add to pan with the garlic. Cook for a few minutes, stirring, until bacon is crisp. Add vinegar to the pan and bring to the boil. Pour the hot dressing over the salad, toss lightly and serve at once. Serves 3-4.

Green beans with ham and almonds

| 500g (1 lb) young green beans |
| 60g (2 oz) butter |
| 2 teaspoons chopped fresh oregano or ½ teaspoon dried |
| Salt and freshly ground pepper |
| Pinch sugar |
| 2 slices cooked ham, cut in strips |
| 2 tablespoons toasted, slivered almonds |

Top and tail beans, but leave whole. Cook uncovered in rapidly boiling, salted water until just tender, about 5 minutes. Drain. Heat the butter in a frying pan and add the beans, oregano, salt and pepper to taste, a pinch of sugar and the ham strips.

Toss just until heated through, about 2 minutes. Serve in a heated dish, sprinkled with almonds. Serves 3-4.

Note: Green peas are also delicious treated this way, but use chopped fresh mint instead of the oregano.

Cheese souffle
(photograph below)

| *Make it with your favourite tasty cheese for lunch, or as a first course for dinner.* |
| *Butter and dry breadcrumbs to prepare dish* |
| 60g (2 oz) butter |
| 2 tablespoons plain flour |
| Salt and freshly ground pepper |
| Pinch each of cayenne pepper and nutmeg |
| 1 cup milk |
| 3 eggs, separated |
| 1½ cups grated Cheddar cheese |

Grease a 4-cup souffle dish or straight-sided dish with butter and sprinkle with breadcrumbs. Tie a collar of doubled, greased greaseproof paper around the outside of the dish to extend about 5 cm (2 in) above the rim.

Melt the butter over medium heat, stir in the flour, salt and pepper, cayenne and nutmeg, and cook for a minute. Gradually stir in the milk and continue stirring until mixture is smooth and thickened. Remove from heat and cool a little. Beat egg yolks and add little by little, then stir in the cheese.

Whisk egg whites until stiff peaks form and fold a couple of spoonfulls through the cheese mixture, then fold in the rest. Pour into the prepared dish and place dish on a metal tray that has been heated in a moderately hot oven (190°C/375°F).

Bake for 35 minutes, or until souffle is puffed and golden and feels firm to the touch. Serves 4.

Lemon-buttered Brussel sprouts

| *Try to get tiny sprouts. They should be bright green, with tightly closed leaves.* |
| 500g (1 lb) Brussel sprouts |
| 60g (2 oz) butter |
| 1 tablespoon lemon juice |
| Salt and freshly ground pepper |

Trim base of sprouts even with heads, and cut a slit in the bottom with a sharp knife. Place in a pan of boiling, salted water, using just enough water to cover the sprouts. Boil rapidly, uncovered, until just tender — about 5 minutes for small sprouts. Drain well. Heat the butter in a frying pan until it sizzles, and add the sprouts. Sprinkle with lemon juice and season with salt and pepper. Toss for a minute over high heat to coat with the butter, then serve at once. Serves 4.

Sweet potato puff

| *A hint of orange makes the delicious difference!* |
| 500g (1 lb) sweet potatoes |
| 30g (1 oz) butter |
| 2 eggs |
| 1 cup milk |
| Salt and freshly ground pepper |
| 1 tablespoon grated orange rind |
| 2 teaspoons sugar |

Scrub potatoes, cut in thick slices and boil in lightly salted water until tender, about 20 minutes. Drain thoroughly and mash with butter.

Beat eggs with remaining ingredients, then combine thoroughly with potatoes. Spoon into a buttered casserole dish and bake in a preheated moderate oven (180°C/350°F) for 45 minutes, or until puffed and golden brown. Serves 4.

Stuffed pork surprise

(photograph below)

4 pork fillets of equal length
1 cup soft breadcrumbs
30 g (1 oz) butter, melted
1 clove garlic, crushed
½ teaspoon dried sage
½ teaspoon dried rosemary
2 shallots, finely chopped
Salt and freshly ground pepper
1 cup plain flour
An extra 45 g (1½ oz) butter
125 g (4 oz) mushrooms, chopped
1 cup chicken stock
½ cup thickened cream

Trim the pork fillets and flatten out a little with a rolling pin. Mix together breadcrumbs, melted butter, garlic, herbs, shallots and salt and pepper to taste and spread over two of the fillets. Top with remaining fillets and press together. Cut into serving pieces and secure with tooth picks. Roll in flour and shake off excess.

Melt the 45 g of butter in a heavy frying pan and fry the fillets until golden brown on both sides. Add the mushrooms and stock and stir to get up the brown bits from the bottom. Cover the pan tightly and simmer until pork is tender, about 45 minutes.

Remove pork to a heated serving platter. Season sauce in pan with salt and pepper, stir in cream and heat gently. Spoon around pork and serve with buttered spinach and boiled potatoes.

Triple decker pork

(photograph right)

Use thin slices cut from the leg for this party main course, and ask your butcher to hammer them out very thinly, as for schnitzel.

6 thin slices pork
3 teaspoons Dijon mustard
3 thick slices ham
6-8 slices Mozarella cheese
6 fresh sage leaves or 1 teaspoon dried sage
Salt and freshly ground pepper
2 eggs, beaten
About 1 cup fine breadcrumbs
60 g (2 oz) butter
3 tablespoons oil

Spread 3 of the pork slices with mustard. Top with slices of ham, cut to fit, and then cheese. Place a couple of sage leaves on top or sprinkle with dried sage. Press remaining slices into place to make 3 "sandwiches". Season both sides with salt and pepper. Dip in beaten eggs, then in breadcrumbs, and chill for 20 minutes.

Heat the butter and oil in a large frying pan and fry the pork on both sides until golden brown and tender, about 4 minutes each side. Cut in thick slices to serve. Serves 6.

Note: This recipe is also excellent using thin slices of veal instead of pork. To accompany it, we like buttered noodles tossed with poppy or sesame seeds and a salad of mixed greens.

Farmer's pork platter

This is a lovely old-fashioned dish, uncomplicated but full of flavour. If you wish, you can use thin pork chops instead of the more expensive fillet.

60 g (2 oz) butter
3 large old potatoes, peeled and sliced
2 large onions, sliced
Salt and freshly ground pepper
2 tablespoons oil
750 g (1½ lb) pork fillet, cut into 1 cm (½ in) slices
½ cup white wine or water
125 g (4 oz) mushrooms, finely chopped
1 clove garlic, crushed
½ cup finely chopped parsley
30 g (1 oz) butter, softened
Extra chopped parsley

Grease a square or oblong shallow casserole, and add potatoes and onions in layers. Season each layer with salt and pepper and dot with butter. Cover with aluminium foil and place in a preheated hot oven (200°C/400°F) for 30 minutes, or until vegetables are tender.

Meanwhile, heat oil in a large frying pan and fry pork slices on both sides until golden brown and cooked through, about 10 minutes altogether. Season with salt and pepper and arrange over potatoes and onions.

Add wine or water to the frying pan, and stir over medium heat until it boils. Pour over pork and vegetables.

Mix together mushrooms, garlic, parsley and softened butter and sprinkle over the top. Return to the hot oven and bake for 10 minutes longer. Serve from the casserole, sprinkled with chopped parsley. Serves 6.

Chicken in caper sauce

(photograph right)

2 chickens weighing about 1.5 kg (3 lb)
2 cups water
1 bay leaf and a few sprigs of thyme and parsley tied together
1 small onion, stuck with 4 cloves
1 small carrot, chopped
Salt and freshly ground pepper

For sauce:

45 g (1½ oz) butter
2½ tablespoons plain flour
1¾ cups stock (from cooking chicken)
2 tablespoons finely chopped parsley
1 tablespoon chopped capers
¼ cup cream

Place chicken in a pan with water, herbs, onion, carrot and salt and pepper to taste. Bring to the boil, then cover the pan and simmer chicken for 40 minutes or until tender, turning once or twice.

Remove chicken and strain stock. Skin chicken, cut into joints, and place on a serving dish in a very slow oven to keep warm until ready to serve.

Melt the butter in a small saucepan, stir in the flour, and cook for 1 minute. Remove from heat, and stir in warm stock.

Return to heat and stir until smooth and thickened. Add parsley, capers and cream, taste for seasoning and spoon sauce over chicken. Serves 4.

Chicken pasties

You can make these fairly large for lunch and dinner, or small to serve as cocktail snacks.

2 sheets ready-rolled puff pastry
4 rashers streaky bacon, rind removed
2 cups finely chopped cooked chicken
2 tablespoons mayonnaise
4 shallots, finely chopped
1 tablespoon finely chopped parsley
1 tablespoon finely chopped gherkins
Olives
Squeeze of lemon juice
Salt and freshly ground pepper
Beaten egg to glaze

Cut pastry into squares about 10 cm (4 in). Grill bacon until crisp, and crumble into small pieces. Combine with remaining ingredients except egg (be sparing with the salt, as bacon is salty).

Place about a tablespoon of filling on each pastry square. Moisten the edges, press firmly together, and crimp with the tines of a fork. Make a slit in top of each pastry for steam to escape and glaze with beaten egg.

Bake in a preheated hot oven (200°C/400°F) for 15 minutes, or until crisp and golden brown. Makes about 8 luncheon-size pasties.

Chickens in a basket of cress

(photograph page 178)

An easy but spectacular chicken dish, marvellous for a picnic or casual outdoor meal.

6 spatchcocks (small chickens weighing about 500 g (1 lb) each)
3 lemons, halved
375 g (12 oz) butter
Freshly ground black pepper
3 bunches of watercress

Trim any fat from inside cavity of the chickens and wipe inside with damp kitchen paper. Rub a cut lemon half over the skin of each chicken, then place the lemon in the cavity. Melt butter and brush very generously over each bird, retaining any butter which isn't used.

Arrange chickens in two baking tins and roast in a preheated moderate oven (180°C/350°F) for about 1 hour. (Time will depend on size of birds). From time to time, brush more butter on to the chickens, and baste with juices in the baking dish.

Remove chickens when cooked, sprinkle with freshly ground pepper and allow to cool. Line a basket with watercress and arrange the whole or halved cold chickens among the cress. Serves 12.

Onion salad

A delightfully simple salad that goes with anything . . . at its best with the purple Spanish onions, but ordinary onions will do.

2 large onions (Spanish if possible)
Salted water to cover
1 tablespoon vinegar
1 tablespoon lemon juice
3 tablespoons olive or walnut oil
Salt and freshly ground black pepper
3 tablespoons finely chopped parsley

Peel the onions, slice as thinly as possible and separate into rings. Cover with lightly salted water with vinegar added. Leave for 15 minutes, drain, and dry on paper towels. Mix lemon juice with oil, a dash of salt, and plenty of pepper. Pour over the onions and toss to combine. Sprinkle with parsley to serve. Serves 3-4.

Note; Thin slices of orange may be added to the salad, and a garnish of black olives.

On these pages we show beautiful Australian butter and cheeses — just naturally part of our cuisine.

Fresh asparagus with walnuts and parmesan

500 g (1 lb) fresh asparagus
Salt and freshly ground pepper
90 g (3 oz) butter, melted
½ cup coarsely chopped walnuts
½ cup freshly grated Parmesan cheese

After snapping off the woody ends, peel stalks thinly with a vegetable peeler if necessary. Young asparagus shouldn't need peeling. Soak for a minute in cold water and drain.

Tie the asparagus in bundles of 6, and place in a deep saucepan of boiling salted water that covers only the stems. Leave the tips out of the water. Cover the saucepan with a lid, or a "tent" of aluminium foil, and cook for 15-20 minutes, or until stems are tender. Drain, untie strings, and arrange in one layer in a flameproof serving dish.

Sprinkle with salt and pepper and then drizzle melted butter over. Sprinkle with walnuts and cheese.

Place under a preheated griller for 2 minutes, or just until cheese begins to brown. Serve at once. Serves 4.

Super carrot cake

Our grandmothers would have been surprised at the thought of putting vegetables in cakes — now they're popular everywhere. This one has fruit as well!

2 eggs
¾ cup brown sugar
Grated rind 1 medium-size lemon
¾ cup oil
1½ cups self raising flour
¼ teaspoon salt
1 large ripe banana, mashed
1 cup grated carrot
¾ cup canned crushed pineapple, drained
½ cup chopped walnuts
Sifted icing sugar to decorate

Beat eggs, sugar and lemon rind together until thick. Gradually beat in the oil. Sift flour and salt together and beat in. Stir in banana, carrot, pineapple and walnuts.

Spoon into a greased 20 cm (8 in) square cake tin or a ring tin. Bake in a preheated moderate oven (180°C/350°F) for 1 hour, or until cooked when tested with a fine skewer. Leave in the tin for 5 minutes, then carefully turn out on to a wire rack. Sprinkle with sifted icing sugar when cold.

Pumpkin scones

Overseas visitors are always intrigued by this Australian specialty. Our favourite version has the added touch of sultanas.

45 g (1½ oz) butter
2 tablespoons brown sugar
½ cup mashed, cooked pumpkin
1 egg, beaten
½ cup milk
2½ cups self raising flour
Pinch salt
½ cup sultanas
Melted butter to glaze

Cream butter and sugar, then mix in the pumpkin. Stir in egg and milk.

Sift the flour and salt and add to creamed mixture with the sultanas. Knead a few times on a lightly floured surface, then pat out to a rectangle about 2 cm (¾ in) thick.

Cut into rounds with a floured scone cutter, or into squares with a sharp knife. Brush tops with melted butter.

Bake in a preheated hot oven (200°C/ 400°F) for 15 minutes, until well risen, golden brown on top and cooked through. Serve hot, split and buttered — with honey also, if you wish.

Australian MATURED CHEDDAR
Australian SWISS
Australian GOUDA
Australian EDAM
Australian CAMEMBERT
RIESLING
RIESLING
RIESLING

AUSTRALIA ENTERTAINS

Australians love to entertain and at the ring of a telephone will turn on a barbecue, throw a pool party, organise a picnic lunch, ask neighbours over for a drink, or bring friends home to dinner.

Our kind climate and our country's abundance of beautiful food makes it easy for us to be spontaneous. Visitors from abroad often comment that we also seem to have an inherently happy and unfussy approach to entertaining. Meticulous attention to every tiny detail of food, flowers, table setting and seating arrangements may not always be our most important priority, but perhaps we enjoy ourselves all the more for having a casual approach!

In this chapter, we have tried to give you a selection of party dishes that are already popular in Australian homes. They range from a "big occasion" masterpiece such as a whole glazed ham, to easy casseroles which will carry well when you're asked to "bring a dish".

Here's to the pleasure of getting together with family and friends!

Captions to preceding 6 pages.

Page 202/203 Terrace house party, Eastern Suburbs, Sydney. (photography: Colin Beard)

Page 204/205 Entertaining in Australia can mean anything from a backyard barbecue to a bountiful buffet, with an endless variety of savoury and sweet dishes. (photography: Andrew Elton)

Page 206/207 Sydney's waterfront restaurant, Pier One, with Sydney Harbour bridge in the background. (photography: Colin Beard)

Facing Page: Sydney Skyline. (photography: Colin Beard)

Chestnut soup

Now that fresh chestnuts are available in Australia, you can serve this wonderful soup for a special dinner party.

500 g (1 lb) chestnuts
1 tablespoon olive oil
2 medium carrots, coarsely chopped
2 leeks, cleaned and chopped
2 sticks celery, chopped
1 large onion, chopped
6 cups chicken stock
8 sprigs parsley
3 whole cloves
½ teaspoon salt
½ cup light cream
2 tablespoons brandy
Salt and freshly ground pepper
Finely chopped parsley to garnish

Make a small slit in the bottom of each chestnut with a sharp knife. Cover the chestnuts with boiling water, and simmer for 30-40 minutes, until soft. Drain, and peel off the skins when cool enough to handle. Heat the oil in a heavy saucepan and brown the carrots, leeks, celery and onion for 5 minutes. Add the chestnuts, chicken stock, parsley, cloves and salt and simmer until vegetables are very soft. Remove the cloves. Rub the soup through a fine sieve, or puree in a blender, and return to the pan. Add the cream and brandy. Adjust the seasoning, and heat just to boiling point. Serve in warmed soup bowls and garnish with chopped parsley. Serves 6.

Pumpkin soup

A creamy, golden soup that's become a favourite all around the country.

60 g (2 oz) butter
1 small onion, sliced
4 shallots, chopped
750 g (1½ lb) pumpkin, peeled and diced
4 cups chicken stock
¼ teaspoon freshly grated nutmeg
2 tablespoons plain flour
An extra 30 g (1 oz) butter
¾ cup cream
Salt and white pepper
Whipped cream
Tiny croutons (see note)

Melt the 60 g of butter in a large saucepan and add the onion and shallots. Cook gently until they are soft but not brown. Add the pumpkin, chicken stock and nutmeg. Simmer, covered, until pumpkin is very soft. Knead together the flour and 30 g of butter and stir into soup until blended. Stir until soup thickens, then rub through a sieve or puree in a blender. Add cream and bring to boiling point, but do not boil. Season with salt and pepper to taste. Serve in warmed soup bowls and garnish with dollops of whipped cream and croutons. Serves 4-6.

Note: To make croutons, cut slices of stale white bread into small squares, or using a cutter, into rounds, ovals or other desired shapes. Dry them on a tray in a slow oven (150°C/300°F) or cook on both sides in a frying pan in melted butter until golden. Drain on absorbent paper.

Fireside chicken soup

(photograph right)

500 g (1 lb) chicken soup pieces
8 cups water
Salt and freshly ground pepper
1 parsnip, sliced
1 stick celery, sliced
2 carrots, sliced
1 turnip, sliced
2 tablespoons chopped parsley
½ teaspoon dried thyme
1 teaspoon grated lemon rind
1 clove garlic, crushed
An extra tablespoon chopped parsley

Place chicken pieces, water and salt and pepper in a large saucepan. Cover and simmer for 1 hour. Add vegetables and thyme and simmer a further 25 minutes. Remove chicken from soup and pick meat from bones. Return to the pan and taste soup for seasoning. Mix together lemon rind, garlic and parsley. Ladle soup into heated bowls and sprinkle with the parsley mixture. Serves 6.

Vichyssoise

(Leek and potato soup)
(photograph page 204)

This classic soup made its way to Australia from France, where it began as a satisfying hot potage among the country folk. Served chilled, it makes a first course for a dinner party. Served hot with crusty bread and a tossed salad, it's a satisfying luncheon or supper dish.

60 g (2 oz) butter
2 leeks, washed and trimmed and sliced into rings
1 medium onion, peeled and chopped
4 cups chicken stock
1 large potato, peeled and sliced
1 tablespoon chopped parsley
Salt and white pepper
1 cup cream
Finely chopped chives to garnish

Melt butter in a heavy saucepan. Add leeks and onion and fry very gently with the lid on for 10 minutes. Do not brown. Add chicken stock, potato and parsley, bring to the boil, and simmer covered for 30 minutes. Remove from heat and cool. Puree the mixture in a blender or push through a sieve. Reheat and adjust seasoning with salt and pepper. Cool, then chill thoroughly. Just before serving, stir in the cream. Serve chilled, in individual soup bowls, sprinkled with finely chopped chives, mint, parsley or mixed herbs. Serves 4-6.

Note: Vichyssoise can be served hot or cold depending upon the season. Make it the day before for chilling in the refrigerator.

Fireside chicken soup is easily made from simple, economical ingredients; with thick slices of crusty bread, it's a warming meal in itself.

Tomato-garlic prawns

(photograph right)

60g (2 oz) butter
1 large onion, finely chopped
2 large ripe tomatoes, peeled and chopped
¼ cup dry white wine
1 teaspoon sugar
Salt and freshly ground pepper
750g (1½ lb) cooked prawns, peeled
An extra 60g (2 oz) butter, melted
2 fat cloves garlic, crushed
½ cup finely chopped parsley
1 cup breadcrumbs

Heat the butter and fry the onion until it starts to soften. Add tomatoes and fry another minute or two, then add wine, sugar and salt and pepper to taste. Simmer with the lid on for 5 minutes, then spoon the mixture into a shallow, greased ovenproof dish. Chop prawns into pieces if very large, and arrange over the tomatoes. Mix melted butter with garlic, parsley, breadcrumbs and salt and pepper to taste and sprinkle over prawns.

Bake in a preheated hot oven (200°C/400°F) for 8-10 minutes, or until topping is crisp and golden. Serve with boiled rice and a salad. Serves 4.

Prawn risi bisi

(photograph right)

One of the easiest prawn dishes to assemble — and very pretty on a buffet table.

60g (2 oz) butter
1 clove garlic, crushed
3 cups boiled rice (1 cup raw)
500g (1 lb) cooked green peas
500g (1 lb) small cooked prawns, peeled
Salt and freshly ground pepper
Dill sprigs and Parmesan cheese (optional)

Heat the butter in a large, heavy frying pan and fry the garlic for a minute or two. Add rice, peas and prawns, and season to taste with salt and pepper. Toss gently over low heat until heated through.

Spoon into a heated serving bowl and garnish with dill if desired. Parmesan cheese may also be sprinkled over the top. Serves 4-6.

Dipping sauces for prawns

Arrange these interesting sauces on a big platter with peeled prawns, crusty bread and butter and wedges of lemon. Add glasses of foaming beer, and you've got a feast!

Creamy olive sauce

⅓ cup sour cream
⅓ cup mayonnaise
1 hard-boiled egg, finely chopped
¼ cup chopped, stuffed olives
1 tablespoon chopped chives
½ teaspoon paprika
Salt and freshly ground pepper

Mix all together and use as a dip for prawns, crisp vegetable sticks, potato chips or corn chips.

Herb sauce

(photograph right)

⅓ cup French dressing
⅓ cup mayonnaise
1 teaspoon dried tarragon
2 tablespoons finely chopped parsley
1 tablespoon chopped fresh dill, or 1 teaspoon dried
1 tablespoon chopped chives
Salt and freshly ground pepper

Mix all together until well combined.

Pink cocktail sauce

2 tablespoons tomato sauce
½ cup thickened cream
1 teaspoon prepared horseradish
1 teaspoon sugar
2 teaspoons lemon juice
1 tablespoon finely chopped red pepper or canned pimento
Salt and freshly ground pepper

Mix all together until well combined.

Australians love prawns and here are some interesting ways to serve them: Tomato-garlic prawns are at the left, Prawn risi bisi at the back, a lovely herb sauce for dipping on the right, and eggs with chutney prawns in the foreground.

Garnished smoked salmon

(photograph page 204)

A side of smoked salmon adds
excitement to any buffet table.
It isn't outrageously expensive,
and goes a long way.

1 side smoked salmon
2 large onions, thinly sliced
½ cup malt vinegar
1 tablespoon sugar
1 small jar capers, drained
Fresh dill to garnish
Sliced French bread and rye bread and butter to serve

Serve the salmon cold, but not chilled.
Arrange on a wooden board or serving
platter, and slice about half into thin
slices. (The rest can be sliced as required).

About ½ an hour before serving time,
marinate onion slices in vinegar and sugar,
then drain and arrange around salmon.
Garnish with capers and dill, and serve
with bread and butter. Serves 30.

Salmon roll

(photograph page 204)

An Australian version of the
traditional Russian dish, Coulibiac,
but without the original's complicated
and elaborate preparation.
This pie makes an ideal buffet choice
and would be perfect for picnics.

For pastry:
4 cups plain flour
1 teaspoon salt
375 g (12 oz) butter
8 tablespoons chilled water

For filling:
250 g (8 oz) mushrooms, sliced
60 g (2 oz) butter
2 medium onions, chopped
1½ cups boiled rice (½ cup raw)
2 × 440 g cans red salmon
Juice 1 lemon
1 tablespoon chopped fresh dill, or 1 teaspoon dried
4 hard-boiled eggs
Salt and freshly ground black pepper

To glaze:

1 egg beaten with 2 tablespoons sour cream

Sift flour and salt into a bowl. Cut butter
in small pieces and rub into flour until
mixture resembles coarse breadcrumbs.
Work in chilled water, knead to form a
firm dough and cut into two portions.
Cover and refrigerate for an hour.

To make filling, fry the mushrooms in
butter for 5 minutes. Add onions and rice
and stir over moderate heat for a further 3
minutes. Add liquid from canned salmon
and simmer, covered, until all liquid has
been absorbed. Allow mixture to cool,
then fold in salmon and lemon juice, dill
and hard-boiled eggs.

Roll pastry out into two oblong shapes,
approximately 17 × 40 cm (7 × 16 in).
Place one in the centre of a large, flat
baking tray and pile prepared filling down
the centre. Brush the edges of pastry with
glaze. Place second pastry sheet on top,
pinch edges together and cut a hole in
the top for steam to escape. Brush with
glaze and bake in a preheated hot oven
(200°C/400°F) for 20 minutes. Reduce
heat to moderate (180°C/350°F) and
bake a further 20 minutes, or until pastry
is cooked through. Serve hot or cold, cut
in slices, with a bowl of sour cream mixed
with chopped fresh dill. Serves 8-10.

Saladia

(photograph right)

Potato and egg salad is moulded into
shape, than coated with
mayonnaise . . . a novel touch
for a party.

4 large old potatoes, boiled and skinned
2 tablespoons chopped chives
2 tablespoons chopped parsley
2 tablespoons finely chopped gherkin
½ cup finely chopped celery or green pepper
½ cup French dressing
Salt and freshly ground pepper
About 1½ cups mayonnaise
Tomato slices to garnish

Mash the freshly cooked potatoes, and
mix in chives, parsley, gherkin, celery,
French dressing and salt and pepper to
taste. Mould into a half-melon shape,
and chill. At serving time, cover the
salad completely with mayonnaise, and
garnish with tomato slices. Serves 6-8.

Kedgeree

This old-fashioned English dish
was originally adapted from the
Indian "Kitchre", a mixture of rice,
lentils and spices. It makes an ideal
party brunch or supper dish, served
with chutney and toast fingers.

250 g (8 oz) cooked smoked fish
125 g (4 oz) butter
4 cups freshly cooked rice (1½ cups raw)
1 teaspoon curry powder
Salt and freshly ground black pepper
3 tablespoons cream
2 hard-boiled eggs, chopped
2 hard-boiled eggs, sliced
Chopped parsley to garnish

Remove any skin and bones from the
fish, and separate flesh into large flakes.

Melt the butter, add the fish and heat
through. Stir in the rice with a fork
Season with curry powder, salt and pepper. Blend cream through mixture, stir in
the chopped eggs and cook gently for a
minute. Turn into a hot dish, garnish
with sliced eggs, and sprinkle with parsley. Mixture must be creamy, so add
extra cream or butter if rice seems dry.
Serves 6-8.

*Note: If you wish, add 1 small onion
sliced and fried until golden in butter, and
1 tablespoon sultanas which have been
"plumped" in hot water.*

Easy cheesies

250 g (8 oz) extra tasty cheese, grated
250 g (8 oz) butter
2 cups self raising flour
½ teaspoon cayenne pepper

Cream butter and cheese together, add
flour and cayenne and form into small
balls, approximately 2.5 cm (1 in) round.
Arrange on a greased baking tray and
bake in a preheated moderate oven
(180°C/350°F) for 25 minutes or until
crisp and golden. Makes approximately
48 cheesies to serve with drinks.

*Note: The dough can be rolled out and
cut into fingers, brushed with a little milk
and sprinkled with sesame seeds. Cook at
the same temperature but for only 15
minutes. Makes about 60 fingers.*

Saladia looks exotic, but is easy to make.

Paradise salad
(photograph page 204)

This is a version of an exotic dish we discovered in New York. It makes an exciting and substantial main course for a party and looks superb. The duck can be served in pieces garnished with the other ingredients, but the salad is perhaps even more flavoursome and eye-catching if they are all tossed together in a large bowl.

2-2.5 kg (4-5 lb) duck, roasted (see below)
500 g (1 lb) green beans, trimmed and cut into 5 cm (2 in) lengths
1 mango, peeled and cut into small pieces
2 red peppers, cut into narrow strips
½ cup macadamia or cashew nuts
14 canned lychees, cut in half
3 tablespoons lemon juice
½ - ¾ cup walnut or olive oil (or a mixture)
Salt and freshly ground pepper
2 tablespoons chopped parsley

To roast duck: Wipe the duck with a damp cloth and sprinkle inside and out with salt and pepper. Prick the skin on the thighs and breast with a skewer to allow fat to drain during cooking. Truss the bird, place on a rack in a roasting pan and roast for 2 hours or until tender in a preheated moderate oven (180°C/350°F). Remove fat from the pan as it accumulates. Take duck from the oven and discard trussing strings. Return to oven for 10 minutes. Take out and allow to cool.

The Salad: Remove the meat from the duck, discarding skin, fat and bones, and cut into bite-size pieces — about 2 cups. Set aside. Drop the beans into boiling water and simmer uncovered for 4 minutes after they return to the boil. Drain, and run quickly under cold water. Set aside to cool and drain thoroughly. Drop red pepper strips into boiling water and when the water returns to boil, drain and run under cold water. Set aside to cool and drain thoroughly. Combine the duck meat, beans, peppers, mango, nuts and other ingredients in a bowl and toss and blend well. Serves 8-10.

Note: This salad is best prepared as soon as possible before serving, and should be eaten at room temperature, not chilled.

Almond potatoes
(photograph below)

These tempting smooth and crunchy potato balls give an elegant touch to dinner party menus, accompanying fish, meat and poultry. We encountered them first in the Hotel de Paris dining room in Monte Carlo, at an international press party to launch a famous perfume.

750 g (1 ½ lb) potatoes, peeled
2 egg yolks, beaten
30 g (1 oz) butter
Salt and white pepper
Oil for frying
1 large egg, beaten
1 cup chopped or crushed almonds

Cook the potatoes in salted water until tender. Drain and shake over low heat to dry thoroughly. Mash until very smooth with the 2 egg yolks, butter, pepper and salt. (You can add extra flavour with chopped parsley, grated Parmesan or chives if you wish). Allow to cool, then form into balls with floured hands — approximately 8-16, depending on required size. Dip them in beaten egg and roll firmly in crushed almonds. Heat enough oil in a heavy frying pan to give a depth of about 2.5 cm (1 in). Fry balls, turning constantly with 2 spoons, until crisp and golden brown all over. Drain on paper towels and keep hot in a slow oven until ready to serve. Serves 8-10.

Almond potatoes. You can use the same recipe with mashed pumpkin, turnip or parsnips. A mixture of pumpkin and potato is especially delicious. Make sure vegetables are thoroughly drained and dried before mashing, or mixture will be too moist.

Curry puffs

These little appetisers are traditionally eaten in the fingers. They are a popular snack among Europeans in Malaysia, where we first tasted them at a "Club" party on an Australian tin mine compound.

2 tablespoons oil
2 cloves garlic, crushed
3 teaspoons curry powder
2 medium onions, chopped
500g (1 lb) minced beef, chicken or pork
1 large potato, grated
1 cup beef or chicken stock made from cubes, or 1 cup canned coconut milk
Salt
1 × 375g packet puff pastry
1 egg, beaten

Heat the oil in a heavy pan. Add the garlic and curry powder and blend. Add the onions and minced meat, and stir over moderate heat until meat changes colour, about 5 minutes. Add the potato and mix together, then stir in stock and salt to taste. Cover, reduce heat, and simmer for 10-15 minutes or until mixture thickens, but is still moist. Set aside and allow to cool. Roll out the pastry thinly on a floured surface and cut into 8 cm (3 in) squares. Place a portion of curried meat in the centre of each square of pastry, and fold over corner to corner to form triangles, sealing the edges with beaten egg. Brush tops of triangles with beaten egg and bake in a moderately hot oven (190°C/375°F) for 15-20 minutes, or until pastry has puffed and browned. Makes 20-30 puffs.

Note: Sultanas can be sprinkled into the curried meat mixture to give a sweeter flavour if desired.

Zucchini special

This is a particularly delicious way to prepare zucchini. Serve it hot as a vegetable with meat, poultry or fish, or cold as a salad, alone or in company with others on a buffet.

1 kg (2 lb) zucchini, coarsely grated on a hand grater or in a food processor
Salt
3 tablespoons oil
½ teaspoon sugar
1 tablespoon lemon juice
1 tablespoon each chopped fresh parsley and basil, marjoram or thyme
Freshly ground black pepper
Extra chopped parsley and herbs

Put grated zucchini in a strainer over a bowl and sprinkle with salt. Leave for 1 hour or longer to allow moisture to drain off. Squeeze excess moisture out before cooking and pat with paper towels, so that zucchini is as dry as possible.

Heat the oil in a heavy pan and cook zucchini with the sugar over moderate heat, stirring until tender, but not too soft. This will only take a minute or two. Add lemon juice and raise heat a little. Sprinkle with herbs and toss well. Spoon into a serving dish, grind black pepper over, and sprinkle with extra parsley and herbs. Serves 4-6.

Barbecued lamb kebabs

1 kg (2 lb) boneless lamb, cut from shoulder or leg
12 small onions
12 button mushrooms
1 green pepper
1 red pepper
Salt and freshly ground black pepper

Marinade:

2 tablespoons vinegar or lemon juice
2 tablespoons oil
1 tablespoon soy sauce
1 tablespoon chopped onion or shallots
1 clove garlic, chopped
2 bay leaves, crumbled
Freshly ground black pepper

Remove fat from lamb and cut meat into 5 cm (2 in) cubes. Mix marinade ingredients together in a bowl and add lamb. Marinate for at least 1 hour, turning now and then. Parboil the onions. Remove seeds and ribs from peppers and cut into 5 cm (2 in) squares. Wipe over mushrooms and trim stems. Season vegetables with salt and pepper.

Thread 4-6 skewers with ingredients, alternating meat, onions, peppers and mushrooms. Brush with marinade and barbecue over glowing coals for 5-6 minutes, turning and brushing with marinade during cooking. Serve with boiled rice, and tomatoes cooked on the grill. Serves 4-6.

Chicken salad Veronica

This an updated version of the old Waldorf salad, with chicken added. Best made when seedless grapes are in season, it's distinguished by delicious, curry flavoured mayonnaise.

4 whole chicken breasts or 8 half breasts
2 teaspoons curry powder
2 tablespoons chicken stock
1 egg yolk
2 teaspoons Dijon mustard
2 tablespoons lemon juice
Salt and freshly ground white pepper
1½ cups oil
Dash cayenne pepper and Worcestershire sauce
¾ cup chopped pecans, walnuts or blanched almonds
4 sticks tender celery, sliced
2 cups seedless white grapes, stems removed
2 tart apples, peeled and thinly sliced
Lettuce leaves to serve
Parsley sprigs or small bunches of grapes to garnish

Cover chicken breasts with lightly salted water, bring to the simmer, and poach for 8 minutes, or until cooked through. Cool in the stock, then remove skin and bones and cut flesh into neat, bite-size pieces. Reserve 2 tablespoons of the stock for this dish (the rest can be refrigerated for other uses).

Combine curry powder and the 2 tablespoons of stock in a small saucepan. Bring to the boil, stirring, then put aside to cool.

Place egg yolk in a bowl and beat in mustard, lemon juice and salt and pepper to taste. Gradually beat in the oil — drop by drop, using a wire whisk. When mixture begins to thicken, add oil in a thin, steady stream, and continue beating until mayonnaise is thick. Beat in the curry mixture, with cayenne and Worcestershire sauce to taste.

Place chicken pieces, nuts, celery, grapes and apples in a bowl and combine. Add curry mayonnaise and fold together. Arrange a bed of lettuce leaves on a pretty serving dish, spoon salad on top, and garnish with parsley sprigs or small bunches of grapes. Serves 8-10.

Eggs with chutney prawns
(photograph page 213)

Hard-boiled eggs are served with a spicy-sweet prawn sauce.

| 8 hard-boiled eggs, shelled |
| 60 g (2 oz) butter |
| 1 small onion, finely chopped |
| 1 large tart apple, peeled and finely chopped |
| 2 teaspoons curry powder |
| 2 tablespoons plain flour |
| 1½ cups chicken stock |
| 3 tablespoons chopped mango chutney |
| 1 tablespoon lemon juice |
| Salt and freshly ground pepper |
| 500 g (1 lb) prawns, peeled |

Cut eggs in half lengthwise and arrange cut-sides down on an ovenproof serving platter. Keep warm in a slow oven while preparing sauce. Heat the butter and fry the onion and apple until soft. Stir in the curry powder and cook for a minute, then sprinkle flour over and stir in. Gradually add the stock, stirring all the while. Bring to the boil and simmer for 2 minutes, then add chutney, lemon juice, salt and pepper to taste and prawns. Simmer until prawns are heated through, then spoon over eggs. Serves 6-8.

Rabbit and cheese pie

An unusual, delicious combination for an entree or luncheon dish, served with jacket or creamed potatoes, fresh green peas and redcurrant jelly. Mother's own recipe!

| 1 large rabbit, blanched and jointed |
| Plain flour seasoned with salt and pepper |
| 45 g (1½ oz) butter |
| 1 tablespoon oil |
| 2 large onions, thickly sliced |
| About 2 cups chicken stock |
| 1 tablespoon lemon juice |
| 1 teaspoon sugar |
| Salt and freshly ground pepper |
| 1½ cups grated, extra tasty Cheddar cheese |
| 2 cups fresh white breadcrumbs |
| Salt and freshly ground pepper |
| Extra butter |

Roll rabbit pieces in seasoned flour and fry in melted butter and oil over medium heat until browned all over, adding a little extra butter and oil if it is absorbed very quickly. Add onions and fry until golden. Drain rabbit pieces and onion and place in a casserole. Pour chicken stock into the frying pan and bring to the boil, stirring. Pour into casserole, adding enough to cover rabbit, and stirring gently to blend juices. Add lemon juice, sugar, salt and pepper. Cover and cook in a moderate oven (180°C/350°F) for 1 hour or until rabbit is tender. Allow to cool. Take rabbit meat from bones and cut into bite-sized pieces or slices. Strain gravy and reserve onions and gravy.

Sprinkle a well-buttered medium casserole on bottom and sides with breadcrumbs. Place a layer of rabbit in the bottom, then a layer of onion, a layer of cheese and a layer of breadcrumbs. Continue the layers until ingredients are used up, finishing with a layer of cheese and breadcrumbs.

Moisten layers with gravy as you go, making sure not to make mixture too moist. Dot surface with knobs of butter. Place in a preheated hot oven (200°C/400°F) and bake for 30 minutes or until heated through and crisp and golden on top. Heat any leftover gravy and serve separately in a gravy boat. Serves 6.

Steak alfresco

A hearty, unusual combination of steak and vegetables which makes an ideal one-dish meal on warm days.
It would travel well to a picnic, taking steak, vegetables and lettuce in separate containers, and assembling at the location.

| 1 kg (2 lb) rump steak, grilled or fried to medium-rare and allowed to cool |
| 500 g (1 lb) zucchini, trimmed and cut into 1 cm (½ in) "sticks" — about 4 cups altogether |
| 1 red pepper, cut into thin strips |
| 1 cup freshly cooked or canned whole kernel corn |
| 1 tablespoon Dijon mustard |
| 2 tablespoons red wine vinegar |
| 6 tablespoons oil |
| Salt and freshly ground pepper |
| 1 tablespoon chopped fresh tarragon, or 1 teaspoon dried |
| 1 large onion, thinly sliced |
| 1½ cups shredded lettuce |

Trim fat from steak and cut meat into very thin slices, reserving any juices. Drop zucchini and pepper into boiling water to cover. Drain quickly when water returns to boil, and run under cold water. Set aside to drain and chill. Put mustard in a bowl and add vinegar, stirring with a wire whisk or a fork. Gradually beat in the oil. Add salt, pepper and tarragon. Blend the mixture with the steak and steak juices, onion rings, corn, zucchini and red pepper and stir gently.

Spoon salad on to a serving dish and surround with shredded lettuce. Add a generous grinding of black pepper and serve at room temperature. Serves 6-8.

Smoked salmon pancakes
(photograph right)

| 1 cup plain flour |
| ¼ teaspoon salt |
| 1 egg, beaten |
| 1¼ cups milk |

For filling:

| 250 g (8 oz) cream cheese, softened |
| 2 tablespoons lemon juice |
| 2-3 tablespoons cream |
| 125 g (4 oz) smoked salmon, finely chopped |
| Dash white pepper |

Sift flour and salt. Beat egg and milk together, then gradually beat in flour. Cover and allow to stand for 30 minutes. Heat a greased frying pan and pour in about 2 tablespoons of the batter (easiest to do from a small jug). Cook over moderate heat until golden brown underneath and bubbly on top. Turn and cook the other side. There will be about 8 pancakes altogether.

To make the filling, beat cream cheese with lemon juice and enough cream to give an easy spreading consistency. Season with pepper, and fold in the chopped salmon. Divide the filling among the pancakes, roll them up, and arrange seam-side down in a shallow, greased baking dish. Place in a preheated hot oven (200°C/400°F) for 5 minutes, or until heated through. Serves 4-6.

Smoked salmon pancakes. This recipe makes a luxurious first course or luncheon dish, but if you wish to economise it's also delicious prepared with tuna, red salmon or chopped prawns instead of the smoked salmon.

Barbecued sausages with oysters

We believe this combination is an Australian original — a little brother to Carpetbag steak.

1 kg (2 lb) thick pork or beef sausages
2 dozen oysters
Barbecue sauce (recipe below)

Place sausages in a saucepan and cover with water. Bring slowly to the simmer, remove from heat, and leave in the water until cool. Separate sausages and store in a sealed container until ready to barbecue. Grill over glowing coals, basting with barbecue sauce and turning often. They should be ready in 6-8 minutes. Split each one down the centre lengthwise, and tuck 2-3 oysters in the middle. Serve with extra warm barbecue sauce in a side bowl. Serves 6-8.

Barbecue sauce

2 tablespoons brown sugar
1 teaspoon paprika
1 teaspoon salt
1/4 teaspoon cayenne pepper
1 teaspoon dry mustard
2 tablespoons Worcestershire sauce
1 cup tomato sauce
1/2 cup grated onion
2-3 tablespoons oil

Blend all ingredients together in a saucepan and bring to the boil. Simmer gently for 10 minutes, adjust seasoning, and leave to cool. This sauce will keep up to 2 weeks stored in a sealed container in the refrigerator.

Cold veal, ham and egg pie

For pastry:

2 1/2 cups plain flour
1 teaspoon salt
1 egg, separated
90 g (3 oz) butter
1/2 cup water

For filling:

500 g (1 lb) veal steak
750 g (1 1/2 lb) pork and veal mince
1 medium onion, finely chopped
1 clove garlic, crushed
Salt and freshly ground pepper
125 g (4 oz) ham, finely chopped
2 hard-boiled eggs, shelled and finely chopped
1/4 cup finely chopped parsley

For pastry: Sift flour and salt into a bowl, make a well in the middle and add egg yolk. Sprinkle some of the flour over yolk. Heat butter and water to boiling point. Pour around outside of flour, then quickly mix all together to make a firm dough. (Use a spoon first, then your hand). Knead dough until smooth, shape into a ball and set aside for 30 minutes.

Meanwhile, remove any fat and gristle from veal and chop meat into small pieces.

Place pork and veal mince, onion and garlic in a heavy frying pan and stir over medium heat until mince is brown and crumbly. Season with salt and pepper and put aside to cool.

Roll out two-thirds of the pastry to line the base and sides of a greased 20 cm (8 in) spring form tin. Roll out remainder to make a lid. Brush inside of pastry with lightly-beaten egg white, saving a little egg white to glaze top crust.

Place half the mince mixture in the pastry case, top with the chopped veal, then the ham and eggs. Season with salt and pepper and sprinkle with parsley. Add remaining mince, and press filling down lightly. Fit lid into place, press edges of dough together to seal, and cut away excess. Brush lid with egg white, and if desired decorate with leaves made from excess dough. Cut a few slits in top for steam to escape, and place in a preheated hot oven (200°C/400°F) for 20 minutes. Reduce heat to moderate (180°C/350°F) and bake for a further 1 hour. Remove from oven and leave in tin until cold. Serve cut in wedges. Serves 10.

Layered terrine

(photograph page 204)

This attractive terrine reveals its layers of meat dotted with juniper berries, white chicken breast and green spinach when sliced, and makes a superb first course for a special meal or a delicious main course with salads.

1.5 kg (3 lb) finely minced topside steak
1.5 kg (3 lb) finely minced pork and veal
2 teaspoons ground coriander
3 teaspoons ground allspice
3 teaspoons ground thyme
1 1/2 teaspoons salt
1 teaspoon pepper
1 tablespoon whole juniper berries
8 eggs
1 cup dry vermouth
1/2 cup brandy
2 bunches spinach — green leaves only — cooked and drained
4 cloves garlic, crushed
3 whole chicken breasts, deboned, skinned and flattened with a meat mallet
6 rashers bacon, rind removed
5 bay leaves

Combine minced meats with coriander, allspice, thyme, salt, pepper, juniper berries, 6 of the eggs, vermouth and brandy. Press half of the mixture into the base of a large, deep ovenproof casserole dish or crock. Chop the cooked and well-drained spinach, add crushed garlic and remaining two eggs and spread over minced meat layer. Arrange chicken breasts over spinach layer, then top with remaining layer of mince. Place bacon rashers over the top, then the bay leaves, and cover with a lid. Stand crock in a dish of cold water and bake in a preheated very slow oven (110°C/220°F) for 4 hours. Remove crock from dish of water, allow to cool, then refrigerate for at least 6 hours before serving. Serves 10-12.

Party Beef Curry is served with rice and traditional accompaniments. It's a popular dish all over Australia.

Party beef curry

(photograph page 221)

An easily-prepared curry that bakes in the oven, leaving you free to do other things.

750 g (1½ lb) round or topside steak
2 tablespoons ghee or oil
2 large onions, finely chopped
2 cloves, garlic, chopped
2 teaspoons finely chopped fresh ginger
1½ tablespoons curry powder
1 teaspoon salt
1 large tomato, peeled and chopped
1½ cups beef stock

Trim any fat from steak, and cut meat into 2.5 cm (1 in) cubes. Heat the oil, brown the meat on all sides over fairly high heat, then transfer to a casserole. Add onions, garlic and ginger to the same pan and cook for 2-3 minutes. Stir in curry powder and cook another minute or two. Add salt, chopped tomato and stock and bring to the boil, stirring. Taste for seasoning and pour over meat. Cover the casserole and bake in a preheated moderate oven (180°C/350°F) for 1½ hours, or until very tender. Serves 4-6.

Chicken livers Denholm

This simple, hot appetiser should be served in individual casseroles or ramekins. The flavour is unusual and rich, and the dish goes well before a light main course such as fish or cold meats.

Chicken livers (1-2 per person)
Butter
Spicy chutney
1 medium mushroom per person
Salt and freshly ground pepper
Thickened cream
Melba toast to serve

Remove any sinews or discoloured pieces from livers. Grease individual ovenproof dishes with butter and place 1-2 cleaned chicken livers in the bottom of each. Top with a teaspoon of spicy chutney, a single mushroom, pepper and salt and a dollop of thick cream.

Bake in a preheated hot oven (200°C/400°F) for 15 minutes. Serve with Melba toast or dry toast fingers.

Little chicken Wellingtons

(photograph above)

60 g (2 oz) butter
4 chicken fillets (skinless, boneless half-breasts)
Salt and freshly ground pepper
250 g (8 oz) mushrooms, finely chopped
1 tablespoon flour
3 tablespoons cream
Squeeze of lemon juice
2 sheets ready rolled puff pastry
1 egg, beaten

Heat the butter in a heavy frying pan and cook fillets over moderate heat for 3 minutes each side or until cooked through. Remove and season with salt and pepper. Add mushrooms to the pan, and stir until they are soft. Sprinkle flour over, and stir in. Add cream, lemon juice and salt and pepper to taste and continue stirring until mixture is smooth and thick. Allow to cool.

Cut each sheet of puff pastry into four. Chop the chicken into bite-size pieces.

Place a mound of chicken pieces on each square, and cover with mushroom mixture. Dampen edges of the pastry and roll neatly around filling, tucking in the ends. Place seam-side down on a baking tray and brush tops with beaten egg. Cut a small slit in the top for steam to escape and bake in a preheated hot oven (200°C/400°F) for 25 minutes, or until golden brown and crisp. Serves 4.

Chicken Mandalay

This delicate and subtly flavoured dish makes a satisfying buffet or luncheon party centre of attraction on a warm day. One of our favourites!

1.5-2 kg (3-4 lb) chicken
2½ cups water
2 strips lemon rind
1 onion, chopped
6 whole allspice
6 peppercorns
1 sprig thyme, 2 sprigs parsley, 1 bay leaf, tied together
1½ teaspoons salt

For sauce:

60g (2 oz) butter
2 tablespoons plain flour
1 tablespoon curry powder
2 cups chicken stock (from cooking chicken)
1 tablespoon lemon juice
2 tablespoons red currant jelly
½ cup cream
Salt and white pepper

Place chicken in a heavy saucepan with water, lemon rind, onion, allspice, peppercorns, bunch of herbs and salt. Bring to the boil and simmer, covered, for 45 minutes or until tender. When cool, remove chicken from stock and take meat from bones. Discard skin and cut flesh into thick slices. Reserve 2 cups of stock, and skim any fat from surface.

Sauce: Melt the butter, add the curry powder and flour and stir until smooth over low heat. Cook together for a few minutes. Slowly stir in the 2 cups of chicken stock and stir constantly over moderate heat until sauce thickens. Add the lemon juice and redcurrant jelly, beating into the sauce. Allow mixture to cool, whisking once or twice. Mix in the cream, then fold in the chicken pieces and adjust seasoning to taste. Serve cold. Serves 6.

Note: This is best made at least 6 hours before serving to allow the flavours to mature. Garnish with paprika, lettuce leaves and lemon slices and serve with Melba toast.

Finger chicken
(photograph right)

Nothing beats chicken pieces for informal entertaining — economical, so easy to cook, and perfect for eating in the hand.

60g (2 oz) butter
8-10 chicken pieces (thighs, drumsticks, etc.)
2 tablespoons finely chopped parsley
1 teaspoon salt
½ teaspoon each dried rosemary, thyme and oregano
1 teaspoon paprika
1 teaspoon crushed black peppercorns

Melt the butter in a baking dish, and roll chicken pieces in butter. Combine remaining ingredients and sprinkle over all sides of chicken. Bake in a preheated moderate oven (180°C/350°F) for 25 minutes. Turn pieces over and bake a further 25 minutes, or until crispy and golden brown. Serves 4-5.

Roast quail
(photograph page 204)

These delectable little game birds are now commercially produced in Australia. They can be served hot or cold.

6 quail
1 cup seeded muscatel grapes
2 sprigs fresh thyme, or pinch dried
1 cup red wine
¼ teaspoon salt
4 shallots, chopped
⅓ cup oil
6 streaky bacon rashers, cut in half
Hard-boiled quail eggs and watercress to garnish

Stuff the quail with the grapes. Bring the wine to the boil with the sprigs of thyme, then remove from heat. When cool, mix with salt, shallots and oil and pour over quail. Marinate, covered, for several hours or overnight. Drain quail, pat dry, and wrap each one in half a bacon rasher. Arrange in a greased baking dish and bake in a preheated moderate oven (180°C/350°F) for 15-20 minutes, until brown and tender. Serve at room temperature, garnished with quail eggs and watercress. Serves 6.

Honey glazed ham
(photograph page 204)

The traditional gesture to lavish entertaining, a ham, is expensive. But after its initial display and consumption for a special event, it can be used in various ways to supply after-the-party meals, ending its use with lovely pea soup made from the bone, so that not a scrap is wasted.

1 × 9kg (18lb) whole leg of ham
¼ cup whole cloves
½ cup honey
1 tablespoon Dijon mustard
2 tablespoon dry sherry
2 teaspoons soy sauce
¼ cup brown sugar

Carefully peel ham skin away from fat and pin back to form a scroll over the bone end. Cut the ham fat in a diamond pattern and insert a clove in the centre of each diamond. Combine the honey with remaining ingredients, brush over ham and place on a wire rack in a large baking dish. Bake in a preheated moderate oven (180°C/350°F) for 1 hour, basting occasionally with pan juices. Serve warm or cold. A whole ham of this size should serve 30-40 people with other dishes.

Note: Please see Cosmopolitan Cities chapter for Pea soup recipe using ham bone.

Kiwi fruit gateau
(photograph left)

1 cooked choux pastry ring (recipe below)
1 cup cold custard, homemade or bought
1½ cups cream, whipped with a little sugar and vanilla
4-5 ripe kiwi fruit, peeled and sliced

Choux pastry ring:

1 cup flour
1 cup water
125 g (4 oz) butter
3 eggs

To make ring: Sift flour. Put water and butter in a medium sized saucepan, stir until butter melts, then bring to the boil. Remove from heat immediately and add all the flour at once. Beat vigorously with a wooden spoon until mixture leaves the sides of the pan and forms a smooth ball. Cool a little, then add eggs one at a time, beating well after each. (Use an electric mixer for this if you have one). The mixture should look smooth and glossy when it has been sufficiently beaten.

Take about ⅔ of the pastry and shape into a circle 20 cm (8 in) in diameter on a baking tray which has been sprinkled with a little water. Use damp fingers to press the pastry into shape. Pipe the remaining pastry on the top edge of the circle (or shape the pastry into a long "sausage") to make the sides of the gateau.

Bake in a preheated hot oven (220°C/440°F) for 15 minutes, then reduce heat to moderate (180°C/350°F) and cook for a further 30-40 minutes. The pastry should be golden brown and have no beads of moisture visible. Cool on a wire rack.

Split the pastry shell through the centre and remove any soft mixture if necessary. Spread custard on the bottom of the pastry, then replace top. Spread prepared cream over the top of the pastry, then arrange slices of kiwi fruit over the cream. Refrigerate for an hour before serving. Serves 8.

Kiwi fruit gateau. Choux pastry is also used to make cream puffs and eclairs, and is excellent with savoury fillings as well as sweet. For a change with this gateau, you can use sliced strawberries, banana slices dipped in a little lemon juice, crushed pineapple, passionfruit, or a mixture of fruits.

Coffee liqueur cheesecake
(photograph page 205)

An absolutely superb cheesecake! Serve as a dinner party dessert, with other sweets on a buffet, or for special coffee mornings or suppers.

For pastry:

125 g (4 oz) butter
⅓ cup castor sugar
1 egg
1 egg yolk
1 cup plain flour
½ cup self raising flour
¼ cup cornflour
3 tablespoons finely chopped walnuts

For filling:

3 × 250 g packets cream cheese, softened
⅔ cup castor sugar
1 × 300 g carton sour cream
4 eggs
1 egg white
1 teaspoon vanilla
2 tablespoons cornflour
2 tablespoons coffee liqueur
1 tablespoon coffee essence

Whipped cream and marrons glace (sweetened chestnuts) for decoration

Beat butter and sugar together until light and creamy. Beat in whole egg and extra egg yolk, then work in sifted dry ingredients and walnuts. Wrap pastry in plastic film and chill for 30 minutes.

Grease a 23 cm (9 in) spring form cake tin and roll out pastry to line base and sides. Refrigerate while making the filling. Beat cream cheese and castor sugar together until smooth, then beat in sour cream, eggs, extra egg white, vanilla and cornflour. Pour half of the mixture into the prepared pastry case. Add coffee liqueur and essence to remaining mixture and spoon into pastry case.

Place cheesecake on a baking tray and bake in a preheated very hot oven (220°C/440°F) for 10 minutes. Reduce temperature to slow (150°C/300°F) and continue baking for a further 50 minutes. Turn heat off and allow cheesecake to cool in the oven with the door closed. Serve topped with whipped cream and chestnuts. Serves 10.

Note: Instead of chestnuts, you could decorate with candied coffee beans, strawberries or grated chocolate.

Superb pavlova
(photograph page 205)

Controversy continues to rage about the origin of this traditionally Australian sweet. The most popular and probably true version is that it was invented in Perth by an admiring chef when the great Russian dancer Pavlova was touring Western Australia at the beginning of the century. Although commercial pavlovas are available, there can be nothing more superb than the delicious rough-and-smooth of a home-made pavlova dressed with cream and fruit.

8 egg whites
Pinch salt
2 cups castor sugar
⅔ cups granulated sugar
3 tablespoons cornflour
3 teaspoons lemon juice
2½ cups cream, whipped
Pulp of 6-8 large passionfruit

Beat egg whites with salt until soft peaks form, then add castor sugar, 1 tablespoon at a time, and continue beating for 10 minutes. Combine granulated sugar with cornflour and fold into meringue mixture with lemon juice. Draw a 25 cm (10 in) circle on greased aluminium foil set on a baking tray. Pile meringue mixture inside the circle, and bake in a preheated very slow oven (110°C/220°F) for 2 hours. Turn heat off, and allow pavlova to cool in the oven without opening the door. Serve topped with whipped cream and passionfruit pulp. Serves 12.

Strawberry punch
(photograph page 205)

Perfect for special events such as weddings, christenings, anniversaries and important parties.

2 punnets strawberries, sliced
½ cup Grand Marnier liqueur
1 × 2 litre flagon rose wine, chilled
1 × 750 ml bottle champagne
Fresh borage flowers or orange and lemon slices to decorate

Combine strawberries and Grand Marnier and steep for 2-3 hours. Place in a punch bowl with chilled rose. Just before serving, add chilled champagne and float fresh borage flowers or orange and lemon slices on top. Serves 12.

Chocolate delights

Everyone loves chocolate, so here's a collection of special chocolate delights for entertaining.

Fudge squares
(photograph right)

| 125 g (4 oz) dark chocolate, chopped in small pieces |
| 185 g (6 oz) butter |
| 3 eggs |
| 1½ cups sugar |
| 1 teaspoon vanilla |
| 1½ cups plain flour |
| ¼ teaspoon salt |
| ½ cup chopped walnuts |
| Chocolate icing (see below) |

Melt chocolate pieces and butter over very gentle heat. Beat eggs and sugar until light and creamy. Stir in melted chocolate mixture and vanilla. Sift flour and salt together and stir into mixture with walnuts. Spread in a well greased 23 cm (9 in) square tin and bake in a preheated moderate oven (180°C/350°F) for 40 minutes. When cool, ice with chocolate icing. Cut into squares, and serve as a dessert or with coffee. Makes about 16.

Chocolate Icing: Stir together 1 cup sifted icing sugar, ¼ cup cocoa and 1 teaspoon cinnamon. Add hot water little by little to give a spreading consistency.

Banana chocolate treat
(photograph right)

| 4 scoops vanilla icecream |
| 2 medium bananas, sliced |
| Chocolate sauce (see below) |
| ½ cup whipped cream |
| Instant coffee or cocoa for dusting |

Place a scoop of icecream in each of 2 glasses. Add banana slices and chocolate sauce, then another scoop of icecream. Finally, top with cream and sprinkle with a little coffee or cocoa. Serve with long spoons. Serves 2.

Chocolate Sauce: Mix together in a small saucepan 1 tablespoon cocoa, 2 tablespoons sugar and ⅓ cup water. Bring to the boil, stirring, then simmer for 3 minutes. Cool before using.

Chocolate Delights include Fudge Squares, Rum Truffles, Banana Chocolate Treat, Devil's Mousse and Chocolate no-bake cake.

Devil's mousse

(photograph page 226)

One of the easiest recipes we know for chocolate mousse and quite delicious.

125g (4oz) dark chocolate
1 tablespoon sugar
1 teaspoon vanilla
3 eggs, separated
¾ cup cream, lightly whipped

Break chocolate into small pieces and place in the top of a double boiler or a small basin set over simmering water. Add sugar, vanilla and egg yolks to chocolate, then beat constantly until chocolate is melted and mixture thick. Leave to cool. Stir in cream, then fold in stiffly beaten egg whites. Spoon into mousse pots or pretty individual dishes and chill until set. Serves 5-6.

Note: The grated rind of an orange, or 2 teaspoons coffee essence makes a pleasant change if added to the chocolate with the sugar and egg yolks.

Rum truffles

(photograph page 226)

1 cup cake crumbs
90g (3oz) dark chocolate, melted
3 tablespoons sieved apricot jam
2 tablespoons rum
Chocolate sprinkles, desiccated coconut or crushed nuts

Mix all ingredients together thoroughly except chocolate sprinkles. Shape into small balls, then roll in sprinkles, coconut or crushed nuts. Chill until serving time and serve as a sweetmeat with coffee. Makes about 15 small balls.

Chocolate no-bake cake

(photograph page 226)

A wonderfully easy recipe for a continental-type cake to serve as a dessert, with coffee.

250g (8oz) sweet biscuits, crushed
½ cup chopped walnuts
125g (4oz) dried apricots, chopped
½ cup brown sugar
Juice and grated rind of one orange
1 tablespoon cocoa
125g (4oz) copha, melted
90g (3oz) dark chocolate, melted
Extra grated chocolate and walnut halves to decorate

Combine biscuits, walnuts, apricots, sugar, orange juice and rind and cocoa in a large bowl. Pour copha over and mix very thoroughly.

Grease a 20cm (8in) sponge tin, then line base with a circle of aluminium foil and grease again. Place biscuit mix in the tin, and press down firmly, using a flat-based glass. Chill for one hour.

Run a spatula around the edge of tin, then turn out on to a sheet of waxed paper.

Break chocolate into pieces and melt in a basin set over simmering water. Spread chocolate over top and sides of cake and decorate with extra chocolate or walnut halves. Cut in thin wedges, and serve with coffee. Makes 24 wedges.

Black Forest cherry cake

A luscious adaptation of the famous German gateau. Moist, dark and rich, it is a perfect companion to after-dinner coffee.

For cake:

6 eggs
½ teaspoon vanilla
1½ cups castor sugar
½ cup plain flour, sifted with ½ cup cocoa
150g (5oz) butter, melted and cooled

For syrup:

1 cup sugar
1 cup water
½ cup Kirsch

For filling and topping:

2 cups cream, whipped
⅓ cup sifted icing sugar
3 tablespoons Kirsch
1 can sour cherries, drained and stoned
Grated dark chocolate and Maraschino cherries to decorate

Beat the eggs and vanilla until light and creamy. Add the sugar 1 tablespoon at a time and beat for 5 minutes. Fold in sifted flour and cocoa, then add melted butter, one tablespoon at a time. Pour mixture into three round 20cm (8in) lined and greased cake tins. Bake in a preheated moderate oven (180°C/350°F) for 30 minutes. Remove from oven, then allow cakes to cool in tins for 5 minutes before turning out.

Make syrup by dissolving sugar in water over low heat. Bring to the boil, then reduce heat and allow to simmer for 5 minutes. Remove from heat, cool, then add Kirsch. Place cooled cakes on a shallow baking tray and pierce all over with a fine skewer. Pour over syrup, and allow to soak into cakes.

Combine whipped cream with icing sugar and Kirsch. Fold cherries through half of the whipped mixture and use to sandwich the three cakes together. Cover top and sides with the remaining cream, decorate with grated chocolate and Maraschino cherries, and refrigerate until ready to serve. Serves 8-10.

Brie surprise

(photograph right)

A perfect finish to a gala dinner party — a circle of creamy Brie cheese baked in a puff pastry crust.

10-12 celery leaves
1 sheet ready-rolled puff pastry
1 whole Brie or Camembert cheese
Beaten egg to glaze

Pour boiling water over celery leaves, leave for 2 minutes, then drain and pat dry. Roll the pastry out thinly to a circle big enough to wrap around cheese. Place half the leaves in the centre of the pastry. Put the cheese on top, then the rest of the leaves. Wrap the cheese completely in the pastry, sealing edges with beaten egg and trimming excess. Brush with beaten egg and place on a baking tray. Bake in a preheated hot oven (200°C/400°F) until pastry is puffed and golden, about 20 minutes. Serve cut in small wedges as a savoury after the dessert course. Serves 4-12, depending on size of cheese.

FROM THE VINE

Grape growing is a major industry in Australia, with vineyards occupying an impressive 30 per cent of our total crop area.

Latest figures show that 3 per cent of grapes are eaten as fresh fruit, 54 per cent are dried as sultanas, raisins and currants, and 43 per cent go into wines – of which the annual consumption in Australia is about 14 litres per head.

These percentages have changed vastly since the first half of the century, when the temperance lobby was powerful and wine was associated with sickly-sweet potions, seedy wine bars, and disreputable "winos".

The influence of migrants from Europe after World War II encouraged the production of dryer, lighter table wines and broadened existing attitudes. So much so that in the 1960's wine consumption had already increased fourfold!

Today we produce some of the world's best quality wines at the world's cheapest prices. We can afford to drink wine with our meals, offer it to friends, cook with it. Wine bars have become chic and wine appreciation courses are multiplying.

Here is a harvest of recipes to help you make the most of the fruits of the vine – whether they are fresh or dried, or come to your kitchen as wine or fortified wine to add special flavour to your cookery.

Captions to preceding 6 pages.

Page 230/231   Private vineyard near Seppeltsfield, Barossa Valley, South Australia. (photography: Colin Beard)

Page 232/233   Wine and fortified wines are produced in many areas of Australia and appear in such superb dishes as trifle and port wine jelly. (photography: Andrew Elton)

Page 234/235   Wine vats, Saltrams winery, near Angaston, South Australia. (photography: Colin Beard)

Facing Page: Barossa Valley, South Australia. View overlooking Bethany and Tanunda. (photography: Colin Beard)

Chicken-sherry soup

(photograph below)

A superb, delicate, creamy soup.

500g (1 lb) chicken soup pieces (necks, wings etc.)

5 cups water

1 small onion stuck with 2 cloves

6 peppercorns

Salt

½ cup cream

2 egg yolks, beaten

2 tablespoons medium sherry

Finely chopped parsley to garnish

Place chicken pieces, water, onion, peppercorns and salt to taste in a saucepan and bring to the boil. Cover and simmer for 45-60 minutes. Strain stock and reserve. Pick meat from chicken bones, and cut into small cubes.

Return stock to saucepan with chicken meat and bring to the boil. Whisk together cream, egg yolks and sherry. Remove saucepan from heat and whisk in cream mixture. Serve at once in heated bowls and sprinkle with chopped parsley. Serves 4-6.

Chicken livers with pasta

A wonderful party dish — and not too expensive!

2 tablespoons oil

2 medium onions, finely chopped

1 clove garlic, crushed

½ cup chopped lean bacon

500g (1 lb) chicken livers

2 tablespoons chopped parsley

1 medium-size green pepper, diced

750g (1½ lb) ripe tomatoes, peeled and chopped

½ cup red wine

2 teaspoons chopped fresh oregano or ½ teaspoon dried

Salt and freshly ground black pepper

500g (1 lb) small elbow macaroni

Extra chopped parsley to garnish

Heat the oil and gently fry onions until softened. Add the garlic and bacon pieces and continue cooking gently for a few minutes, stirring.

Meanwhile, remove any discoloured parts from chicken livers, and chop liver into small pieces. Add livers to pan and cook just until colour changes.

Pour excess oil from pan and add parsley, pepper, tomatoes, wine, oregano, and salt and pepper to taste. Simmer sauce for 15 minutes, stirring occasionally.

While sauce is simmering, cook pasta in plenty of boiling salted water until tender. Drain thoroughly and put into a warm serving bowl. Pour the chicken liver mixture over and toss lightly. Serve with crusty bread, a crisp salad, and a glass of red wine. Serves 6.

Stuffed chicken fillets in Marsala

This is a very special dish for a dinner party — a little bit fiddly to prepare, but that's no drawback to the cook who likes to serve something different.

8 chicken fillets (boneless half breasts of chicken)

Plain flour seasoned with salt and pepper

8 thin slices of ham

8 thin slices Swiss cheese

8 cooked asparagus spears

90g (3 oz) butter

½ cup Marsala wine

¼ cup chicken stock

Finely chopped shallots to garnish

Place fillets between sheets of plastic wrap and flatten out with a rolling pin. Dip in seasoned flour and shake off excess.

Place a slice of ham on each fillet, then a slice of cheese. Place an asparagus spear in the middle. Roll the fillets up neatly, tucking in the ends, and tie in place with string.

Heat butter in a large, heavy frying pan and slowly brown the chicken rolls on all sides. This will take 6-8 minutes altogether. Remove rolls and keep warm. Add Marsala and stock to the pan. Bring to the boil, stirring to get up the brown bits from the bottom, and simmer until reduced a little. Taste for seasoning.

Untie string from rolls, arrange on a heated platter, and spoon sauce over. Sprinkle with finely chopped shallots to serve. Serves 6-8.

Mussels in creamy wine sauce.

Almond sherry chicken

*A delicately flavoured dish, ideal
for a luncheon party.*

4 whole chicken breasts, boned

Plain flour seasoned with salt
and pepper

60 g (2 oz) butter

⅔ cup dry sherry

½ teaspoon dried tarragon

⅔ cup cream

2 tablespoons slivered toasted almonds

Lightly pound the chicken breasts with a mallet to flatten, coat with seasoned flour and shake off excess. Melt the butter, add chicken and cook over moderate heat for about 5 minutes each side, or until tender. Remove from pan and set aside.

Add sherry and tarragon to the pan and stir well to get up the brown bits from the bottom. When nearly boiling, stir in cream, replace chicken, and simmer until reheated. Taste for seasoning and add salt and pepper as required. Arrange on a heated serving platter and sprinkle with toasted almonds. Serves 4.

Wine-roasted duck

*Cooked this way, duck is tender
and beautifully glazed.*

1 large duck

Salt

Paprika

Ground ginger

1 small onion, grated

1 cup red wine

⅓ cup brown sugar

1 tablespoon cornflour

¼ teaspoon salt

2 teaspoons grated lemon rind

¼ cup toasted sesame seeds

Cut duck into quarters and remove any excess fat. Arrange duck pieces in a single layer in a baking dish and bake uncovered in a preheated hot oven (200°C/400°F) for 30 minutes.

Remove duck from oven and pour off fat that has accumulated in the dish. Season duck pieces generously with salt, paprika and ginger and return to the dish. Sprinkle with the onion, pour in half a cup of the wine, and cover dish with a lid or aluminium foil.

Continue cooking until duck is tender

(about 45 minutes) turning pieces now and then.

In a small saucepan, combine sugar, cornflour, salt, lemon rind, and remaining half cup of wine. Bring to the boil, stirring, and simmer until smooth and thickened. Spoon over duck and bake uncovered for another 10-15 minutes, basting often, until duck is glazed. Sprinkle with sesame seeds to serve. Serves 4.

Magic orange chicken

*The orange marmalade combines with
other flavourings to add a touch of
magic to an easy chicken dish.*

1 chicken weighing about 1.5 kg (3 lb)

Plain flour

60 g (2 oz) butter

1 tablespoon oil

1 cup orange juice

½ cup medium sherry

3 tablespoons orange marmalade

1 small onion, finely chopped

1 tablespoon light soy sauce

Salt and freshly ground pepper

Cut chicken into serving pieces and pat dry with paper towels. Roll chicken in flour and shake off excess.

Heat butter and oil in a large, heavy frying pan and slowly brown chicken on all sides. Mix remaining ingredients together and pour over chicken. Cover and simmer for 35-40 minutes or until chicken is tender, turning pieces several times. If gravy seems to be thickening too much, thin with a little extra orange juice or water. Before serving, taste for seasoning and add more salt and pepper if necessary. Serve with boiled rice and a green vegetable. Serves 4.

Cinnamon chops with prunes

60 g (2 oz) butter

6 lamb leg chops

Salt and freshly ground pepper

2 medium onions, thinly sliced

¾ cup red wine

⅔ cup water

12 soft prunes, stoned

One cinnamon stick about
4 cm (1½ in) long

3 strips lemon rind

Heat the butter in a large frying pan and brown the chops on both sides. Remove chops from the pan, sprinkle with salt and pepper and set aside. Add onion slices to the pan and cook gently until softened. Replace the chops and add wine, water, prunes, cinnamon stick and lemon rind. Bring to the boil, then reduce heat and cover with a tight fitting lid. Simmer for 45 minutes, or until chops are tender. Remove cinnamon stick and serve with buttered rice tossed with a few toasted almond halves, and a green vegetable. Serves 6.

Stuffed pork Wellington
(photograph right)

It's equally nice hot or cold.

4 pork fillets of equal size, weighing
about 625 g (1¼ lb) altogether

Salt and freshly ground pepper

1 teaspoon dried rosemary

1 cup finely chopped parsley

45 g (1½ oz) butter, softened

2 tablespoons grated Parmesan cheese

An extra 45 g (1½ oz) butter

1 × 375 g pkt puff pastry

1 egg yolk, beaten

Flatten the pork fillets between two sheets of plastic film, and season with salt, pepper and rosemary.

Mix together parsley, 45 g of softened butter, Parmesan and salt and pepper to taste. Spread this mixture on two of the fillets, top with the other two fillets and press firmly together. Tie into place with white string.

Heat the other 45 g of butter in a frying pan, and brown the stuffed fillets well on both sides. Remove, allow to cool, and remove string.

Roll the puff pastry out into two rectangles big enough to wrap around the fillets. Place a fillet on each, moisten the edges of the pastry, and press firmly together to enclose fillets completely. If desired make decorations from surplus pastry, moisten, and press into place on top. Brush all over with beaten egg yolk.

Arrange on a baking tray and bake in a preheated very hot oven, (220°C/440°F) for 20 minutes. Reduce heat to hot, (200°C/400°F) and bake for a further 10 minutes. (If pastry is browning too much cover with foil). Serve hot or cold, cut in thick slices. Serves 6.

*Stuffed Pork Wellington is easy to make
with prepared puff pastry.*

Spicy pot-roasted beef

Here's a German-inspired way with beef, which makes an economical cut tender and full of flavour.

2 kg (4 lb) fresh silverside, bolar blade or topside in one piece
1 cup red wine
½ cup wine vinegar
½ cup water
2 medium onions, roughly chopped
2 bay leaves
12 peppercorns
10 cloves
2 tablespoons sugar
2 teaspoon dry mustard
½ teaspoons powdered ginger
1 teaspoon salt
3 tablespoons bacon drippings or oil

Trim excess fat from beef and place meat in a deep bowl. Combine remaining ingredients except bacon drippings and pour over meat. Cover, and refrigerate for 3-4 days, turning meat over several times. Remove meat from marinade and dry well with paper towels. Strain marinade. Heat bacon drippings in a large heavy saucepan or Dutch oven, and brown meat slowly on all sides. Pour marinade over, cover tightly, and simmer for 3 hours or until beef is very tender, turning beef occasionally.

Remove beef to a platter and keep warm. Blot fat from surface of liquid in pan and if necessary reduce by boiling to gravy consistency. Serve beef in fairly thick slices, with gravy. Serves 8.

Holiday spareribs

Just a few simple ingredients and you can plan on beautifully glazed, tender pork spareribs for dinner.

2 kg (4 lb) meaty pork spareribs, cut into serving pieces
½ cup medium sherry
3 tablespoons vinegar
2 tablespoons brown sugar
½ teaspoon ground ginger
4 tablespoons light soy sauce

Place spareribs in one layer in a shallow baking dish. Bake uncovered in a pre-heated moderate oven (180°C/350°F) for 1 hour, then pour off fat that has accumulated in the pan.

Combine remaining ingredients and spoon over spareribs. Continue baking for another hour, turning frequently and basting with sauce. Serve with potatoes baked in their jackets, grilled pineapple slices and a salad. Serves 4-6.

Barossa rabbit casserole

Bacon, wine, herbs and mushrooms transform rabbit into a special-occasion casserole.

1 rabbit, cut into serving pieces
2 teaspoons vinegar
Plain flour seasoned with salt and pepper
1 tablespoon oil
30 g (1 oz) butter
3 medium onions, coarsely chopped
3 rashers streaky bacon, diced
1 tablespoon plain flour
1 cup dry white wine
½ cup chicken stock
1 tablespoon tomato paste
2 sprigs parsley
1 sprig thyme
1 bay leaf
Salt and freshly ground pepper
125 g (4 oz) button mushrooms, halved or sliced
30 g (1 oz) extra butter
Chopped parsley to garnish

Soak rabbit for 6-8 hours in cold salted water with the vinegar added. Drain pieces and dry thoroughly, then coat with seasoned flour.

Heat together oil and butter, add the rabbit pieces and brown all over. Transfer rabbit to an ovenproof dish. Add onions and bacon to the pan and gently fry until onions have softened.

Add the flour, stir for a minute or two, then pour in the wine and chicken stock. Add the tomato paste and stir until boiling. Pour over rabbit in dish, add the parsley, thyme and bay leaf, tied together, with salt and pepper to taste.

Cover and cook in a moderately slow oven (170°C/325°F) for about 1½ hours, or until tender. Just before cooking time is finished, quickly fry the mushrooms in extra butter for a minute or two and mix into the casserole. Remove bundle of herbs and serve garnished with chopped parsley. Serves 4.

Venison pork casserole
(photograph right)

The combination of meats makes this casserole unusual and quite delicious.

500 g (1 lb) venison steak
500 g (1 lb) pork fillet
20 juniper berries
1½ cups dry white wine
¼ cup port wine
Salt and freshly ground pepper
25 soft prunes, stoned
250 g (8 oz) mushrooms, sliced
⅓ cup cream
45 g (1½ oz) butter

Trim meat and cut into 2.5 cm (1 in) cubes. Crush juniper berries and mix with wine and port.

Place meat in a shallow dish with prunes and season with salt and pepper. Pour wine mixture over, cover with plastic film and leave overnight.

Drain meat and prunes and dry on paper towels. Heat butter in a large, heavy frying pan and brown meat on all sides. Remove with a slotted spoon and place in a casserole.

Fry mushrooms lightly in pan juices and add to casserole. Strain marinade into a small saucepan and boil uncovered until reduced by half. Pour over meat and add cream and prunes. Cover and bake in a preheated moderate oven (180°C/350°F) for 45-60 minutes, or until meat is tender. Serve with creamy mashed potatoes. Serves 4-6.

Venison Pork Casserole is a wonderful conversation piece for a dinner party.

Mushroom-wine steak sauce

When you're in the mood for a thick piece of tender steak, do it justice with this superb sauce.

60 g (2 oz) butter
1 tablespoon oil
125 g (4 oz) mushrooms, finely chopped
1 clove garlic, crushed
1 small onion, finely chopped
2 tablespoons plain flour
Dash of cayenne pepper
1 cup beef stock
¾ cup red wine
Salt and freshly ground pepper

Heat the butter and oil and fry mushrooms, garlic and onion over moderate heat until softened. Sprinkle flour and cayenne over and stir until flour is brown, about 3 minutes. Slowly stir in stock and wine, and bring to the boil. Simmer very gently for 20 minutes, stirring often. Season with salt and pepper to taste and serve over freshly grilled or pan-fried thick pieces of rump, sirloin or fillet steak. Enough for 4 servings.

Veal patties in mushroom-brandy sauce
(photograph below)

750 g (1½ lb) minced veal
½ cup cream or evaporated milk
2 eggs
Salt and freshly ground pepper
60 g (2 oz) butter
For sauce:
45 g (1½ oz) butter
185 g (6 oz) button mushrooms, sliced
Salt and freshly ground white pepper
2 tablespoons brandy
¾ cup cream
Paprika to garnish

Mix veal with cream, eggs and salt and pepper to taste until it forms a compact mixture. Shape into six patties and chill for 30 minutes.

Heat the 60 g of butter in a heavy frying pan, and cook the patties on both sides over moderate heat until golden brown all over and cooked through, about 8 minutes.

Meanwhile, make the sauce: Heat the 45 g of butter in a separate frying pan and toss the mushrooms over moderately high heat until tender but still firm, about 3 minutes. Season with salt and pepper and stir in brandy and cream. Simmer until sauce is thickened, and taste for seasoning. Arrange patties on a heated platter, spoon sauce on to each, and sprinkle with a little paprika. Serve with tiny boiled potatoes and a green salad. Serves 6.

Lamb's fry in wine sauce

Lamb's fry becomes a dinner party dish when you add a herby, red-wine sauce.

1 lamb's fry
Milk to cover
Plain flour seasoned with salt and pepper
3 tablespoons oil
2 large onions, thinly sliced
⅔ cup red wine
2 teaspoons tomato paste
1 teaspoon chopped fresh thyme or ¼ teaspoon dried
Salt and freshly ground black pepper
Pinch sugar

Soak the lamb's fry in milk to cover for an hour or so. Dry thoroughly with paper towels, cut into very thin slices, and lightly coat with seasoned flour.

Heat the oil in a large frying pan, add onions and gently fry until soft and golden. Season with salt and pepper, remove with a slotted spoon and keep warm.

Raise heat to moderately hot, add liver slices, and cook for 2 minutes each side, or until browned. Remove and keep warm. Add wine, tomato paste and thyme to the pan and stir well to get up the brown crusty bits from the bottom. Season with salt and pepper and a pinch of sugar and bring to the boil.

Arrange liver on a heated platter, pour the sauce over and top with the onion slices. Serves 4.

Sherried veal casserole

This casserole can be made ahead and reheated when needed.

750 g (1½ lb) stewing veal
Plain flour seasoned with salt and pepper
1 tablespoon oil
2 medium onions, thinly sliced
2 sprigs parsley
1 sprig thyme
1 bay leaf
½ cup beef or chicken stock
¾ cup dry sherry
Salt and freshly ground pepper
2 medium tomatoes, peeled
250 g (8 oz) shelled green peas

Trim fat from veal and cut meat into large squares. Coat with seasoned flour and shake off excess. Heat the oil, add meat and brown all over, then transfer to a casserole dish.

Add onions to the pan and cook until starting to soften. Add the parsley, thyme and bay leaf (tied together) the stock and sherry and stir until boiling.

Add salt and pepper to taste, pour over veal, cover dish and cook in a moderate oven (180°C/350°F) for 1¼ hours. Cut tomatoes into wedges and lightly mix in, with the green peas. Continue cooking until veal is tender and vegetables are cooked, about another 10 minutes. Serves 4-5.

Venison walnut casserole

Farm-reared venison is now becoming available in Australia and is at its best in this aromatic casserole.

1 kg (2 lb) stewing venison (cut from shoulder)
2 tablespoons plain flour
1 teaspoon dried mixed herbs
2 medium onions, finely chopped
2 large tomatoes, peeled and chopped
Salt and freshly ground pepper
Small piece cinnamon stick
5 pickled walnuts, sliced
2 teaspoons Angostura bitters
¾ cup red wine
Extra walnut slices and chopped parsley to garnish

Remove any sinews from venison, cut meat into cubes and roll lightly in flour. Arrange the cubes in a greased ovenproof dish in layers, sprinkling each layer with herbs, onions and tomatoes and seasoning with salt and pepper as you go.

Add the cinnamon stick and pickled walnut slices. Combine bitters and red wine and pour into the dish. Cover tightly and cook in a moderate oven (180°C/350°F) for 1½ to 2 hours or until venison is fork tender. Serve topped with a few pickled walnut slices and chopped parsley. Serves 6-8.

Wine, cheese and ham puff

It puffs up like a souffle, but is extra-easy to make.

8 slices white sandwich bread
Butter for spreading
½ cup dry white wine
1 cup finely chopped ham
250 g (8 oz) mature cheddar cheese, grated
4 eggs
2 cups milk
1 teaspoon Worcestershire sauce
Salt and freshly ground pepper

Butter the bread generously, then cut into bite-size squares. Arrange half in the bottom of a greased casserole about 20 × 20 × 5 cm (8 × 8 × 2 in). Sprinkle half the wine over the bread, then half the ham and cheese. Repeat the layers with remaining bread, wine, ham and cheese. Beat eggs with milk, sauce and salt and pepper to taste, pour into dish, and allow to stand for 30 minutes. Bake in a preheated moderately slow oven (170°C/325°F) for 1 hour, or until puffy and golden on top. Serves 4-6.

Mussels in creamy wine sauce
(photograph page 239)

40 fresh mussels
Water to cover
60 g (2 oz) butter
2 tablespoons plain flour
1½ cup cooking liquid from mussels
1 clove garlic, crushed
⅓ cup dry white wine
2 egg yolks
2 tablespoons lemon juice
⅓ cup cream
Salt and freshly ground pepper
Finely chopped parsley to garnish

Wash mussels in cold, running water and scrub with a stiff brush until clean. Discard any that are not tightly closed. Place in a wide saucepan, cover with boiling water, and boil rapidly for 5 minutes, or until they open. Discard any that do not open.

Remove mussels from their shells, reserving the best shells for serving the mussels. Strain the cooking liquid and save 1½ cups.

Melt the butter, stir in flour over low heat, and cook for 1 minute. Remove from heat and stir in the warm cooking liquid and the garlic. Bring to the boil and simmer for 5 minutes.

Whisk wine, egg yolks, lemon juice and cream together and stir into the pan. Continue stirring until sauce thickens, and season to taste with salt and pepper. Return mussels to the pan and gently reheat. Spoon into shells and sprinkle with chopped parsley. Serve with crusty bread. Serves 4.

Hawkesbury oyster soup

1 dozen oysters on the half shell, or 1 bottle oysters
2½ cups milk
½ cup cream
1 onion slice
1 stick celery, sliced
1 bay leaf
2 strips lemon rind
30 g (1 oz) butter
1½ tablespoons flour
Freshly grated nutmeg
Salt and freshly ground white pepper
4 tablespoons dry sherry
Finely chopped parsley to garnish

Drain oyster liquor into a saucepan. Chop oysters into pieces, add to saucepan and bring to simmering point. Pour into a bowl and set aside. In same saucepan, scald milk and cream with onion, celery, bay leaf and lemon rind. Leave to infuse for 5-10 minutes, then strain.

Melt butter in a clean saucepan over low heat and stir in flour. Gradually stir in flavoured milk and continue stirring until mixture boils and thickens.

Season with a touch of nutmeg, salt and pepper. Add oysters and their liquid and sherry and heat through but do not boil. Taste for seasoning, and serve in heated bowls, sprinkled with a little parsley. Serves 4.

Vermouth prawns

An intriguing appetiser. Prawns are marinated in an aromatic sauce, and served in the same sauce.

750 g (1½ lb) small cooked prawns, peeled
1 small onion, thinly sliced
2 cloves garlic, chopped
3-4 parsley sprigs
½ cup olive oil
½ cup dry vermouth
2 tablespoons wine vinegar
½ teaspoon dried tarragon
1 teaspoon sugar
Dash cayenne pepper
1 teaspoon salt

Place prawns in a bowl. Combine remaining ingredients and pour over prawns. Cover and chill overnight, stirring now and again.

Spoon into a serving dish, and supply toothpicks for spearing the prawns. Buttered French bread is a nice accompaniment. Serves 10 as an appetiser.

Poached trout with green mayonnaise

A beautiful cold main course for a summer party.

4-5 whole, medium-size trout
Lemon juice
Salt and freshly ground pepper
1 teaspoon dried dill
1½ cups dry white wine
1½ cups chicken stock
4 shallots, finely chopped
Green mayonnaise (see below)

Remove heads from trout if desired and trim fins with kitchen scissors. Make two or three diagonal slashes on each side of fish, through the skin. Season inside and out with lemon juice, salt and pepper and dill and allow to stand for 10 minutes.

Place wine, stock and shallots in a shallow pan and bring to a gentle bubble. Add trout in a single layer and simmer just until flesh is tender and opaque, about 15 minutes.

Cool fish in the liquid, then carefully lift out and remove skin. Arrange on a platter and spoon a little green mayonnaise over. Serve remaining mayonnaise separately. Serves 4-5.

Green Mayonnaise: In a blender or food processor fitted with the steel blade, combine 1 cup mayonnaise with half a cup of watercress leaves, 1 tablespoon lemon juice and salt and pepper to taste. (If watercress isn't available, use equal parts of chopped parsley and chopped young spinach leaves instead).

Fish in creamy grape sauce

Any fine-textured white fish may be used for this superb dish.

6 large fish fillets
4 shallots, finely chopped (including some green tops)
Salt and freshly ground pepper
1 cup dry white wine
Water to cover

For sauce:

45 g (1½ oz) butter
3 tablespoons plain flour
1½ cups stock from fish
½ cup cream
2 teaspoons lemon juice
Salt and freshly ground white pepper
125 g (4 oz) sultana grapes, stems removed
15 g (½ oz) butter, softened

Skin the fish fillets, fold them into halves or thirds and arrange in a buttered ovenproof dish. Scatter the shallots over fish and sprinkle with salt and pepper. Pour the wine over and add just enough water to cover.

Cover with buttered greaseproof paper and cook in a moderate oven (180°C/ 350°F) for 10 minutes, or until fish flakes easily when tested with a fork.

Remove from oven, drain stock from the dish and keep the fish in a warm place. For the sauce, melt the butter in a saucepan, remove from heat and stir in the flour. Cook over gentle heat for a minute or two, stirring. Add the fish stock and stir until sauce boils, then simmer for 2 minutes.

Gradually stir in the cream, lemon juice and season with salt and pepper. Fold in the grapes, simmer another minute, and whisk in the softened butter. Arrange the fillets on a heated serving platter and spoon the sauce over. Serves 4-6.

Cheese and port spread

Delicious spread on thinly sliced rye bread, or as a stuffing for celery sticks.

250 g (8 oz) grated cheddar cheese
2 shallots, finely chopped
2 tablespoons cream
4 tablespoons port wine
Dash of cayenne pepper
½ teaspoon paprika
Salt to taste

Mix together cheese, shallots and cream. Add port and beat well. Season with cayenne, paprika and salt to taste. Cover, and leave at room temperature for an hour or so before serving. Serves 8-10 as an appetiser with drinks.

Sunday mushroom rolls

Sunday supper calls for something quick to make but savoury and interesting. Here's a delicious answer!

1½ cups condensed cream of mushroom soup
½ cup cream
2 tablespoons medium sherry
Salt and freshly ground pepper
60g (2 oz) butter
250g (8 oz) mushrooms, finely chopped
Dash Worcestershire sauce
6 long bread rolls
Butter for spreading

Place undiluted soup in a saucepan with cream, sherry and Worcestershire sauce. Stir until smooth and boiling and put aside. Heat the 60g of butter, add mushrooms and toss over medium heat until moisture evaporates. Stir into sauce and season to taste with salt and pepper.

Meanwhile, prepare bread rolls. Cut a thin lengthwise slice from the top of each and pull out most of the crumbs to make a hollow. Spread inside with butter, including inside of top slice.

Place on a tray in a preheated very hot oven (220°C/440°F) for just a few minutes or until rolls and top slices are golden brown.

To serve, place toasted rolls on individual plates. Divide filling evenly among them and press top slices into place. Serve at once. Serves 6.

Broccoli in garlic and wine

This way of cooking broccoli results in a rich, peppery sauce, lovely with veal dishes, meat loaf or grilled sausages.

1 kg (2 lb) bright green broccoli
⅓ cup olive oil
2 cloves garlic, crushed
1 small dried red chilli, seeded and finely chopped
1 cup dry white wine
Salt

Cut off tough bottom stalk ends from broccoli, then slice remaining stalks into thin pieces. Separate heads into flowerets. Heat oil in a heavy saucepan and fry garlic and chopped chilli for a minute or two, until softened. Add broccoli stalks and wine, season with salt, and cook for five minutes or until stalks are softened. Place broccoli flowerets on top and cook covered for 10 minutes, or until flowerets and stalks are tender. Turn once or twice during this time.

Remove lid, raise heat and reduce liquid to about half a cup. Taste for seasoning, and serve very hot. Serves 6-8.

Luxury liverwurst

It's easy to turn liverwurst from the delicatessen into a beautifully flavoured pate.

250g (8 oz) liverwurst (chicken, Latvian, calf liver, etc.)
90g (3 oz) cream cheese
30g (1 oz) butter, softened
4 tablespoons medium sherry
1 clove garlic, crushed
2 teaspoons lemon juice
Salt and freshly ground pepper
Paprika and finely chopped parsley to garnish

Have liverwurst and cream cheese at room temperature and mash together in a bowl. Beat in the softened butter, then sherry, garlic and lemon juice. Season generously with salt and pepper and spoon into a lightly oiled mould. Chill until serving time, then turn out and garnish with alternate stripes of chopped parsley and paprika. Serves 8-10.

Sunshine Coast salad

Here's a pretty moulded salad to serve with cold meats.

1 small can crushed pineapple
2 packets lemon jelly crystals
Dash salt
2 tablespoons sugar
2¼ cups dry white wine
¼ cup white vinegar
1 medium-size cucumber
2 shallots, finely chopped
Lettuce leaves and mayonnaise to serve

Drain pineapple and measure syrup. Make syrup up to 1 cup with water if necessary, place in a saucepan and bring to the boil. Add jelly crystals, sugar and salt and stir until jelly dissolves. Remove from heat, and stir in wine and vinegar. Allow to cool until starting to thicken.

Meanwhile, peel cucumber and grate flesh into a colander. Press down well with a spoon to extract juice, then add cucumber to jelly mixture with shallots and pineapple. Taste for seasoning and add extra salt if desired. Spoon into a mould that has been rinsed in cold water, and chill until firm. Unmould on to crisp lettuce leaves and serve with mayonnaise. Serves 6-8.

Note: For a party you can chill the salad in individual moulds — small tea cups, custard cups etc.

Red wine salad dressing

A simple green salad becomes a talking-point when you toss it with this spicy wine dressing.

½ cup olive oil
½ cup safflower or sunflower oil
2 tablespoons red wine vinegar
3 tablespoons red wine
1 teaspoon salt
½ teaspoon freshly ground pepper
¼ teaspoon each of paprika and dry mustard
1 clove garlic, crushed
2 teaspoons sugar

Place all ingredients in a screwtop jar and shake vigorously until well blended. Taste and adjust seasoning to suit your own preference. Store in the refrigerator and shake well before using. Will dress enough green salad for 6-8.

Festival potato salad

This is a very special potato salad — nice enough for a main course in summer, with crisp lettuce leaves and buttered rolls.

500 g (1 lb) freshly cooked, peeled potatoes
4 sticks celery, thinly sliced
1 medium-size green or red pepper, cut into small dice
1 small onion, finely chopped
2 tablespoons chopped parsley
1 cup dry white wine
4 hard-boiled eggs, coarsely chopped
1 teaspoon celery seed
1 tablespoon Dijon mustard
½ cup mayonnaise
Salt and freshly ground pepper

Cut the warm potatoes into bite-size chunks and place in a bowl with celery, peppers, onion and parsley. Pour the wine over, cover and chill for several hours, gently turning now and again. Drain well. Sprinkle eggs and celery seed over salad. Combine mustard and mayonnaise and gently fold through mixture with salt and pepper to taste. Serve on a bed of lettuce leaves. Serves 4-6.

Apricot liqueur cake
(photograph right)

A quick idea for a dinner party. You buy a sponge from the cake shop, dress it up with canned apricots and apricot brandy, and serve warm.

1 sponge cake layer
1 medium can apricot halves
2 tablespoons apricot jam
¼ cup apricot brandy

Place the cake on a baking tray. Drain the apricots, and reduce the syrup to half its volume by boiling rapidly in a small saucepan. Stir in the jam, then strain mixture into a bowl and stir in the apricot brandy.

Spoon half the syrup over the cake. Arrange apricot halves on top, rounded sides up. Spoon rest of syrup over apricots. Place in a preheated moderate oven (180°C/350°F) and bake for 5 minutes, or until cake is heated through. Serve with custard, whipped cream or ice-cream. Serves 6.

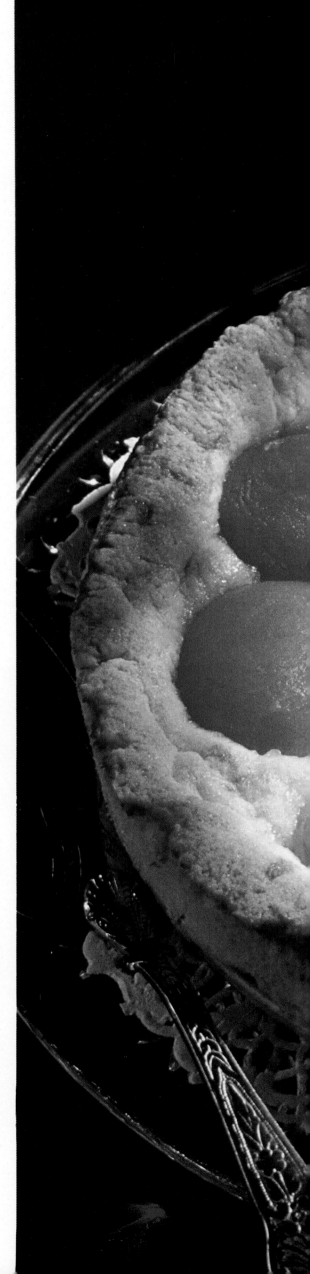

Ruby fruits

You can serve this pretty fruit cocktail as a first course or dessert. It's a great dish to remember when you have to entertain in a hurry.

¾ cup port wine

3 tablespoons red currant jam

1 tablespoon lemon juice

Pinch salt

1 can cherries, drained and pitted

1 can mandarin segments, drained

2 cups fresh or canned, drained pineapple pieces

Place wine and jam in a saucepan and stir over moderate heat until smooth. Remove from heat, add lemon juice and salt and allow to cool.

Place well drained fruits in a bowl, pour wine mixture over, cover and chill for several hours. Serves 6.

Port wine mousse

A subtle hint of orange blends beautifully with the flavour of port in this delicately-textured dessert.

½ cup water

¾ cup castor sugar

3 teaspoons gelatine

¼ cup hot water

3 eggs, separated

¼ cup port wine

2 teaspoons grated orange rind

1¼ cups cream

Extra whipped cream and walnut halves to decorate

Put water and sugar in a saucepan and bring to boiling point, stirring until sugar has dissolved. Sprinkle gelatine over the ¼ cup of hot water, stir until dissolved, then stir into the hot syrup.

Place egg yolks in a bowl set over simmering water and whisk until combined. Gradually add the syrup mixture, whisking constantly until slightly thickened.

Allow to cool, then stir in the port and grated orange rind and chill until mixture starts to thicken. Beat cream until soft peaks form and fold in. Beat egg whites until stiff and fold in.

Spoon into a serving bowl and chill until softly set. Serve topped with whipped cream and decorated with walnut halves. Serves 6.

Port wine jelly

(photographed page 232)

3 pkts port wine jelly crystals

3 cups boiling water

1 cup port wine

1 cup muscatel grapes, washed and stems removed

Whipped cream to serve

Dissolve jelly crystals in boiling water and allow to cool. Add port and grapes and pour into a chilled mould. Refrigerate until set.

Loosen jelly by standing mould in a container of hot water, then invert on to a serving platter. Serve in wedges, with whipped cream. Serves 6-8.

Chocolate souffle with foamy brandy sauce

(photograph right)

An unusual souffle, made with whipped cream.

125 g (4 oz) dark chocolate, chopped

1 cup cream, whipped with 3 tablespoon sugar

1 tablespoon brandy

3 egg yolks, beaten

4 egg whites

Icing sugar and grated chocolate to decorate

For sauce:

¼ cup sugar

Pinch salt

1 tablespoon cornflour

1 egg, beaten

3 tablespoons brandy

1 cup milk

1 cup cream, whipped

Make sauce first: Combine sugar, salt, cornflour, beaten egg and brandy in a bowl. Heat the milk to boiling point, and whisk into the cornflour mixture. Return to the saucepan and continue whisking over low heat until thickened. Cool, then chill. Just before serving, fold custard and whipped cream together.

To make souffle, place chopped chocolate, whipped cream and brandy in a basin set over simmering water. Stir until chocolate melts. Remove from heat and cool for 1 minute. Add beaten egg yolks a little at a time, beating well after each addition. Beat egg whites to a firm snow, and carefully fold in.

Butter 4 individual souffle dishes and sprinkle with sugar. Divide the souffle mixture among them, filling each dish about ⅔rd full. Place in a preheated moderately hot oven (190°C/375°F) and bake for 10 minutes or until well puffed and firm on top. Dredge with icing sugar and sprinkle with grated chocolate. Serve at once with chilled sauce. Serves 4.

Cherry brandy souffle

This is not a genuine souffle, but the flavour is marvellous — and even a beginner will find it foolproof.

4 eggs, separated

¼ cup castor sugar

2 tablespoons cocoa

1 cup cherry jam

½ cup cherry brandy

Icing sugar to decorate

Beat eggs yolks with sugar until thick and lemon coloured. Add cocoa and combine well. Beat egg whites until stiff and fold in.

Combine jam and liqueur, and spread in the bottom of a greased 4-cup souffle dish or straight-sided casserole.

Spoon egg mixture over, and bake in a preheated hot oven (200°/400°F) for 25 minutes, or until puffed and brown. Sprinkle with icing sugar and serve hot with whipped cream or icecream. Serves 6.

Strawberry wine trifle

(photographed page 232)

This is a very easy trifle to prepare, but looks and tastes spectacular.

1 Swiss roll filled with strawberry jam

½ cup Madeira wine

3 cups custard, home-made or bought

2 cups cream, whipped

1 punnet strawberries, hulled

Cut Swiss roll into 6-8 slices and arrange in a pretty glass bowl.

Sprinkle with ¼ cup of Madeira. Fold remaining ¼ cup of Madeira into cool custard, and pour over Swiss roll.

Chill well, then top with whipped cream and strawberries. Serves 8.

Chocolate Souffle is served hot from the oven with chilled brandy sauce.

Pineapple Marsala

(photograph left)

A most versatile recipe that can be served as a first course, a dessert, or as a luncheon salad with cold chicken or ham.

2 large, ripe pineapples
500 g (1 lb) black or green grapes, halved and pipped
2 large, ripe pears, peeled and cut into cubes
2 tablespoons lemon juice
2 tablespoons castor sugar
¼ cup Marsala wine
12-16 walnut halves

Cut pineapples in half lengthwise through green tops. Scoop out the flesh with a sharp knife, remove the core, and cut flesh in bite-size cubes. Toss with grapes, pears, lemon juice, sugar and Marsala. Cover and chill for 30 minutes. Fill back into pineapple shells and decorate with walnut halves. Serves 6-8.

Note: As a first course or salad serve with mayonnaise. As a dessert, serve with whipped cream or icecream and trickle a little extra Marsala over.

Grape surprise

A perfect dessert for the busy cook — just a few simple ingredients, a few minutes preparation, but it looks and tastes exotic.

750 g (1½ lb) sultana grapes
1 cup thick sour cream
3 tablespoons brandy
⅓ cup honey
3 teaspoons lemon juice

Wash the grapes, remove stems, drain well and chill. Combine the sour cream, brandy, honey and lemon juice and chill. Just before serving time, add grapes to the cream and toss lightly. Serves 6.

Pineapple with wine sauce

(photograph above)

6 eggs yolks
½ cup castor sugar
1½ cups dry white wine
1 tablespoon lemon juice
1 large ripe pineapple, peeled and sliced

Combine egg yolks, sugar, wine and lemon juice in a saucepan. Whisk constantly over gentle heat until sauce is thick and creamy. Do not let mixture boil.

Arrange slices of pineapple on a platter with the pineapple's leafy top in the centre. Serve sauce separately. Serves 6.

Brandy souffle

A fabulous dessert for a very special occasion.

2 tablespoons gelatine
½ cup cold water
5 eggs, separated
½ cup castor sugar
¾ cup brandy
⅓ cup medium sherry
2 tablespoons orange liqueur
½ cup almond macaroon crumbs
1¼ cups cream
Extra whipped cream and grated chocolate to decorate

Tie a double band of greaseproof paper around a 5-cup souffle dish or other straight sided dish, extending paper about 5 cm (2 in) above rim of dish. Lightly grease inside of paper above dish.

Sprinkle gelatine over the water, let soften, then dissolve in a bowl placed over hot water. Beat together over simmering water the egg yolks and sugar.

When very thick and creamy whisk in the brandy, sherry and liqueur and then stir in the dissolved gelatine.

Chill, stirring occasionally, until thickening, then fold in the macaroon crumbs. Whip cream lightly and fold in, then beat egg whites until stiff and fold in.

Spoon into the prepared dish and chill until firm. At serving time, carefully remove paper, easing it off with a spatula dipped in hot water. Decorate with extra whipped cream and grated chocolate. Serves 6-8.

Cherries in claret

This is a lovely way to enjoy fresh cherries during their brief season.

500 g (1 lb) cherries
1¼ cups claret
2 tablespoons sugar
Pinch cinnamon
2 tablespoons red currant jelly

Stone the cherries (use a cherry stoner or a new, clean hairpin). Put cherries in a saucepan with claret, sugar and cinnamon. Simmer until the cherries are soft, drain, and place in a serving bowl.

Simmer the juice until reduced by about a quarter, add the red currant jelly and stir until melted. Cook gently for another 3 minutes, cool a little, and pour over the cherries. Serve warm or chilled with cream or icecream and a crisp sweet biscuit. Serves 4.

Brandied dried fruits

*Top vanilla icecream with
this superbly-flavoured fruit medley.*

2½ cups water
1½ cups sugar
2 thin strips orange rind
2 thin strips lemon rind
One cinnamon stick about 5 cm (2 in) long
1 cup chopped dried apricots
¾ cup sultanas
¾ cup currants
⅔ cup coarsely chopped raisins
¾ cup brandy
2 tablespoons orange or cherry liqueur

Place water, sugar, orange and lemon rinds and the cinnamon stick in a saucepan. Slowly bring to the boil, stirring until sugar has dissolved. Boil for 2 minutes.

Add the dried apricots, reduce heat, and simmer for 5 minutes. Add rest of fruit and simmer for another 5 minutes. Remove from heat and cool.

Remove rinds and cinnamon stick and stir in the brandy and liqueur. Spoon into jars and seal tightly. Leave for 2 weeks in a cool place to mature before using. Serves 6-8 with icecream.

Rose punch

*A pink and beautiful party
punch flavoured with strawberries,
spice and peaches.*

½ cup rose wine
½ cup sugar
Pinch each nutmeg, cinnamon and ground cloves
½ cup fresh orange juice
1 punnet strawberries
2 fresh ripe peaches
2 bottles sparkling white wine, chilled

Put rose wine into a saucepan with the sugar and spices and gently heat, stirring until sugar has dissolved. Stir in the orange juice, and allow to cool.

Wash and hull the strawberries (halve them if large) and peel and dice the peaches. Add these to the rose mixture and chill thoroughly. To serve, pour over ice cubes in a punch bowl and add the sparkling wine. Makes about 15 punch-size servings.

Mulled wine

*A good hot drink for your
winter parties.*

½ cup sugar
1½ cups water
Grated rind ½ lemon
6 whole cloves
One cinnamon stick about 4 cm (1½ in)
1 bottle burgundy or claret
¾ cup brandy
Freshly grated nutmeg

Put sugar, water, lemon rind, cloves and cinnamon in a saucepan, bring to the boil, and stir until sugar has dissolved.

Reduce heat and simmer gently for 10 minutes, then strain. Stir in the wine and brandy and gently reheat, but do not boil. Pour into heated mugs and serve topped with a sprinkling of nutmeg. Serves 6.

Minted sherry cup

⅓ cup mint leaves, tightly packed
½ cup lemon juice
2 tablespoons sugar
⅓ cup sweet sherry
1 x 750 ml bottle lemonade, chilled
Lemon slices and small sprigs of mint to decorate

Put the mint leaves, lemon juice, sugar and sherry in a jug, stirring until sugar has dissolved. Chill for 2-3 hours. Just before serving, strain, and stir in the lemonade. Pour into 4 tall glasses and float a thin slice of lemon and a small sprig of mint on top of each. Serves 4.

Wine-tea punch

*Sauterne, tea and lemon juice
combine to make a perfect drink
for hot weather.*

5 cups boiling water
3 tablespoons tea leaves
½ cup lemon juice
4 cups sauterne
Lemon and orange slices to decorate

Pour the boiling water over the tea leaves, leave for 5 minutes, then strain into a bowl. Put aside until cold.

Chill the lemon juice and wine, add to the tea, pour over crushed ice in a jug or bowl. Float lemon and orange slices on top and serve at once. Serves 10.

OUR COSMOPOLITAN CITIES

Australia's capital cities are among the most cosmopolitan in the world. At last count, 36 major non-English languages are being spoken in our cities, plus 90 other languages or dialects.

First-generation Italians make up the largest group, followed by Greeks, Yugoslavs, Germans, people from Arabian countries, Chinese, Dutch, Maltese, Polish, Turkish, French, Hungarian, Russian and dozens more.

Naturally, this cosmopolitan make-up is repeated in the small cafes, take-away food bars, cafeterias, delicatessens, grocery shops, patisseries and restaurants which seem to jostle side by side in every second street and arcade.

Think of a food or ingredient and we can buy it here, from the most exotic Asian spices for spectacular treats, to crisp, buttery French croissants for breakfast. Eating out is just a matter of deciding what mood we're in and how much we can afford. Will it be classic French food or subtly-flavoured Thai dishes? Spicy Lebanese or sturdy Yugoslav? Will we make it a party and share a big table at the local Chinese restaurant, or go to a little Italian bistro for a candlelight dinner for two?

In Australian cities, the whole of the world's cuisine is literally within our reach, and home cooks, whether first or fourth generation Australians, are constantly experimenting and broadening their repertoire to include their neighbours' dishes and create what will eventually become a distinctive Australian culinary culture.

Here is a sample of our own favourite cosmopolitan dishes for you to try.

Captions to preceding 6 pages.

Page 256/257   Continental Delicatessen, Melbourne, Victoria. (photography: Colin Beard)

Page 258/259   Hahndorf Old Mill Restaurant, outside Adelaide, South Australia. (photography: Colin Beard)

Page 260/261   Dishes from all over the world are available in our cosmopolitan cities. This selection was arranged for photography in Mrs Sippy's stylish coffee shop in Sydney, New South Wales. (photography: Andrew Elton)

Facing Page: Lygon Street delicatessen, Carlton, Victoria. (photography: Colin Beard)

Minestrone

This hearty, national Italian soup makes a good first course for a winter meal or a satisfying meal-in-itself served with crusty bread and a crisp tossed salad.

2 tablespoons oil
125 g (4 oz) pickled pork, cut in small pieces
1 large onion, chopped
2 cloves garlic, crushed
8 cups beef stock
1 large carrot, diced
½ bunch celery, thinly sliced
½ small cabbage, shredded
2 large ripe tomatoes, peeled and chopped
1 cup sliced green beans
1 cup shelled green peas
250 g (8 oz) haricot beans, soaked overnight and cooked separately
1 teaspoon dried oregano or thyme
Salt and freshly ground pepper
1 teaspoon sugar
1 cup macaroni (tubes, shells, etc.)
½ cup finely chopped parsley
2 cups freshly grated Parmesan cheese

Heat the butter in a large saucepan and fry pork until golden brown. Stir in onion and garlic and cook for a few minutes. Add stock and bring to the boil, then add remaining vegetables and oregano and season to taste with salt, pepper and sugar.

Cover and cook gently for about 1½ hours, stirring now and then to help flavours blend. Half an hour before serving, add the macaroni and parsley. Adjust seasoning and serve in heated bowls, with grated Parmesan passed separately to sprinkle over the soup. Serves 8.

Dutch pea and ham soup

(photograph right)

To make a complete meal of this wonderful soup, heat continental frankfurts in it, and serve a frankfurt in each bowl.

500 g (1 lb) green or yellow split peas
1 ham bone or 500 g (1 lb) bacon bones
10 cups water
1 large onion, sliced
2 cloves garlic, crushed
1 large carrot, chopped
2 sticks celery, sliced
White pepper to taste

Wash peas and soak overnight in cold water. Next day, drain, and place in a large pan with ham bone, 10 cups water, and remaining ingredients. Bring to the boil, then cover and simmer for 3 hours, stirring occasionally to stop peas sticking to the bottom of the saucepan.

Remove bone from soup, take off the meat, and cut into small pieces. If you want a smooth texture, puree soup in a food processor or blender. If you like a coarse texture, leave it as it is. Return meat to the soup, reheat, and ladle into heated bowls. If desired, float a few croutons (small pieces of fried bread) in each bowl. Serves 8.

French onion soup

45 g (1½ oz) butter
2 large onions, sliced very thinly
4 cups beef stock
Salt and freshly ground black pepper
4 thick slices French bread, toasted
4 tablespoons freshly grated Gruyere cheese

Heat the butter in a heavy saucepan and fry the onions very gently until golden and very soft but not brown. Stir often as they cook, and don't try to hurry the process — it will take about 15 minutes. Add stock, cover the pan, and simmer for 15 minutes. Season with salt and pepper to taste.

Place a round of toast in each of 4 flameproof bowls, and sprinkle with cheese. Pour hot soup over. Place under a preheated hot grill until cheese is golden and bubbly. Serves 4.

Red cabbage salad

A central European dish that goes beautifully with cold roast pork, veal, corned beef or meat loaf.

1 small red cabbage, shredded
3 teaspoons salt
1 medium onion, finely chopped
1 crisp eating apple, peeled and thinly sliced
6 tablespoons oil
2 tablespoons wine vinegar
1 teaspoon sugar
Freshly ground black pepper
1 teaspoon caraway seeds (optional)

Place cabbage in a bowl and sprinkle with salt, cover and leave in a warm place for 1 hour. Put cabbage in a colander and press down well to remove as much moisture as possible. Place in a bowl with onion and apple. Mix oil, vinegar, sugar and black pepper together and toss with cabbage mixture. Add caraway seeds if desired and serve at room temperature or chilled. Serves 4-6.

French peas

1.5 kg (3 lb) young green peas
60 g (2 oz) butter
6 shallots
1 firm head of lettuce
1 bay leaf, 2 sprigs parsley, 1 sprig thyme, tied together
2 teaspoons sugar
Salt and freshly ground black pepper
2 tablespoons water

Shell the peas. Remove roots and green leaves from shallots, leaving white part whole. Wash and trim the lettuce, remove large outer leaves, and cut the heart into quarters. Butter a heavy saucepan, line with large lettuce leaves and add peas, shallots, salt and pepper. Bury the lettuce quarters in the peas and add a few dobs of butter. Cover tightly with foil or greaseproof paper and the lid. Place over low heat, and cook for 30 minutes without uncovering the pan, but tossing it occasionally to turn over the contents. Taste the peas, correct seasoning and add the remaining butter. Serves 6.

Dutch pea and ham soup makes a satisfying meal-in-itself. Crisply fried onion rings, croutons or frankfurts can be added for variety.

Salad nicoise
(photograph above)

There are several versions of this robust salad, but essential ingredients are potatoes, olives and anchovies, with a garlic-flavoured dressing.

1 lettuce (cos or mignonette if possible)
2 medium tomatoes, sliced
½ small green pepper, sliced
1 onion, sliced and separated into rings
8-10 black olives
1 small can anchovy fillets, drained
2 hard-boiled eggs, sliced
For dressing:
1 tablespoon wine vinegar
3 tablespoons olive oil
1 fat clove garlic, crushed
Salt and freshly ground pepper

Line a pretty salad bowl with lettuce leaves, and arrange salad ingredients over the top. Combine dressing ingredients by shaking in a screwtop jar, and spoon over salad when ready to serve. Serves 4.

Tabbouleh

This favourite Lebanese salad has become popular in Australia since its introduction in Lebanese restaurants, cafes and take-aways. Its preparation is highly individual, but the one essential ingredient is fine cracked wheat — burghul.

1½ cups burghul
3 tablespoons finely chopped shallots or 1 large onion, finely chopped — or both
2 cups finely chopped parsley
¾ cup olive oil
4 tablespoons lemon juice
Salt and freshly ground black pepper
½ cup finely chopped mint

Soak the burghul in plenty of cold water for about an hour to allow it to soften and expand. Drain, and squeeze out excess water with your hands. Spread the burghul on a clean tea towel or absorbent paper and dry off for 20 minutes.

Place burghul, onions, parsley and mint in a large bowl and mix well, squeezing with your hands so that the onion juice mixes with the burghul. Gradually add the oil, then the lemon juice and mix well. Season with salt and pepper and add additional lemon juice if necessary, as Tabbouleh should be quite tart. Serves 8.

Note: Tabbouleh is traditionally served on individual dishes, with vine leaves, lettuce or cabbage leaves on the side to be used as scoops. A little finely chopped cucumber and tomato (previously salted and drained of any excess juice) — may be added to the salad. If served in a large bowl, it can be decorated with black olives, tomato sections, slices of cucumber and sprigs of parsley.

Carrots Vichy

French style gives everyday carrots a gourmet touch.

6 medium carrots
125 g (4 oz) butter
1 tablespoon water
1 teaspoon sugar
½ teaspoon salt

Wash and scrape the carrots if necessary. Cut in long, very thin strips. Melt the butter in a heavy saucepan and add the carrots and water. Cover tightly with foil and saucepan lid and cook over slow heat for 1 hour, stirring gently now and then until water has evaporated and carrots are tender and glazed. Just before serving, sprinkle with sugar and salt. Serves 6-8.

Note: A little finely chopped mint may be added if desired.

Herring salad

Pickled and salt herrings are popular throughout Europe, and available in every second delicatessen in Australia. This recipe is one given us by an Austrian friend, but has its counterparts in Scandinavia, Germany and other countries.

3 pickled herrings
1 dill pickle, thinly sliced
2 gherkins, thinly sliced
2 crisp eating apples, peeled and chopped
1 medium-size beetroot, cooked and cut into small dice
500 g (1 lb) potatoes, peeled and cut into dice
½ cup olive oil
2 tablespoons vinegar
1 teaspoon dry mustard
2 tablespoons dry white wine
1 medium onion, finely chopped
1 teaspoon sugar
½ teaspoon salt
Good pinch white pepper
Lettuce leaves to serve

Chop herrings into 5 mm (¼ in) pieces. Place in a deep bowl and toss with dill pickle, gherkins, apples, beetroot and potatoes. Mix together oil, vinegar, mustard, wine, onion, sugar, salt and pepper. Pour over salad and toss together. Chill until ready to serve, then taste for seasoning and spoon into a pretty dish lined with lettuce leaves. Serves 6.

Potatoes Anna

A French way of turning sliced potatoes into a crisp, delicious potato cake.

1 kg (2 lb) medium-size new potatoes
180 g (6 oz) butter
Salt and freshly ground black pepper

Preheat the oven to moderately hot (190°C/375°F). Peel the potatoes and slice them as thinly as possible. Thickly butter a 23 cm (9 in) round sandwich tin and line the sides and bottom with potato slices placed close together and firmly attached to the butter. Sprinkle lightly with salt and pepper and dot with butter. Cover with another layer of potatoes, and salt, pepper and butter, and so on until potatoes are used up.

Cover with buttered paper and cook for 45 minutes or until tender when pierced with a sharply pointed knife. Run a knife around the potatoes and invert on to a heated plate. Let stand a few minutes to settle. The inside should be soft and the crust crisp and golden. Cut into wedges and serve with meat, fish or poultry. Serves 6.

Moussaka

A famous Greek dish which has become popular in Australia in many variations, for parties and family meals as well as on menus in restaurants, cafeterias and take-away cafes.

1 kg (2 lb) eggplant
Salt
Oil for frying
2 medium onions, thinly sliced
2 cloves, garlic, crushed
1 kg (2 lb) minced beef or lamb
1 large tomato, peeled and chopped
2 tablespoons tomato paste
2 tablespoons chopped parsley
Salt and freshly ground black pepper
1 teaspoon sugar
½ teaspoon ground allspice or cinnamon
½ cup water

For cream sauce:
45 g (1½ oz) butter
2 tablespoons flour
1 cup hot milk
Salt and white pepper
Pinch grated nutmeg
1 egg yolk

Slice unpeeled eggplant thinly. Sprinkle generously with salt and leave in a colander to drain for 1 hour. Squeeze out excess moisture, and dry with paper towels. Shallow fry in oil, until browned on both sides, turning once. Drain on towels and set aside.

Fry onion and garlic in 2 tablespoons oil, until pale golden. Add the minced meat and fry until well browned, stirring to break up any lumps. Add tomato paste, tomato and parsley and season with salt, pepper, sugar and allspice or cinnamon. Stir in water. Cover and simmer gently for 30 minutes, until meat is cooked and liquid has been absorbed.

To make cream sauce: Melt butter in a saucepan, stir in flour, and cook gently for a minute until smoothly blended. Add the hot milk gradually, stirring constantly until it boils, and taking care no lumps form. Season with salt, pepper and nutmeg. Simmer until sauce is smooth and thick. Beat egg yolk and stir in a little of the hot sauce, then return to pan and blend, stirring constantly. Do not boil again.

To assemble the Moussaka, place one third of the eggplant slices in a greased, square or oblong casserole dish. Spread half the meat sauce on eggplant slices. Add another layer of eggplant and mince and top with remaining eggplant. Spread cream sauce over and bake in a preheated moderate oven (180°C/350°F) for 45 minutes to 1 hour, or until top is crispy and brown. Stand for 10 minutes to settle, before serving in squares with a tossed salad. Serves 6-8.

Note: A richer Moussaka can be made by sprinkling 3 tablespoons of grated Kaphalotini or Parmesan cheese over cream sauce before baking.

Pesto Genovese

This famous Italian green sauce is eaten with pasta or gnocchi. It is a dish for the summer, when fresh basil is available, and it cannot be made with dried basil.

3 cloves garlic, chopped
1 cup firmly packed fresh basil leaves
2 tablespoons pine nuts
½ cup grated Parmesan cheese
1 cup (approximately) olive oil
Freshly ground black pepper

With a mortar and pestle or in a blender or food processor fitted with the steel blade, pound together garlic, basil, pine nuts and cheese. Transfer to a bowl and gradually add the oil, whisking well after each addition. Continue whisking in enough oil to make a smooth, thick sauce. Stir in freshly ground pepper.

Note: This amount of sauce makes enough for 500 g (1 lb) pasta.

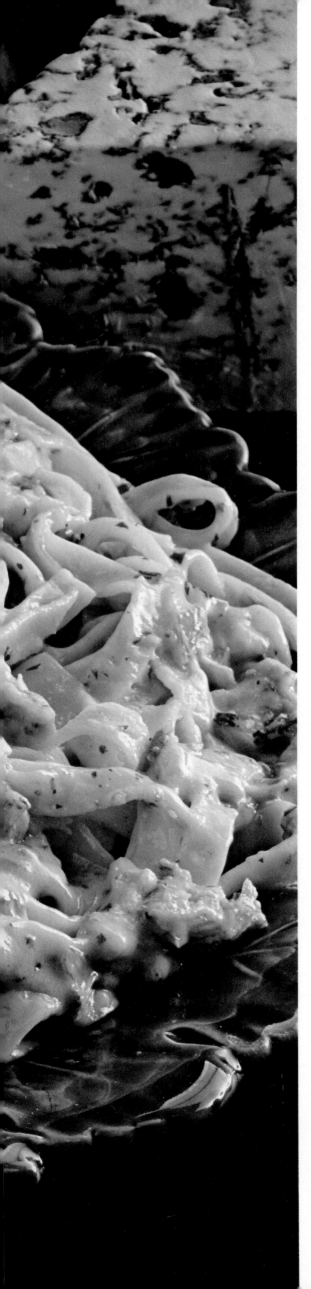

Vitello tonnato

This beautiful Italian cold dish features veal in a tuna sauce.

1 kg (2 lb) boned leg of veal
6 canned anchovy fillets
1 medium onion stuck with 2 cloves
1 bay leaf
1 stick celery with leaves, chopped
1 medium carrot, cut in quarters
Few sprigs parsley
Salt and freshly ground black pepper
1 cup tuna packed in oil
1 generous cup olive oil
Juice of 2 lemons
½ cup drained capers
Extra anchovies and capers to garnish

Remove the skin and fat from veal. Cut 2 of the anchovy fillets into small pieces, and insert into small slits in the meat. Roll up the meat and tie securely with white string. Put into a deep saucepan and cover with boiling water. Add the onion and cloves, bay leaf, celery, carrot, parsley and salt and pepper. Cover and simmer for 1½ hours or until tender. Cool the meat in the broth, then drain and pat dry. (You can use the broth in soup or another dish).

Pound the tuna and its oil with remaining anchovy fillets and gradually add the olive oil, working the oil into the tuna to make a creamy paste. Thin the sauce with the lemon juice and add the capers. The paste should be quite thick and very smooth. Taste, and if necessary season with salt and pepper.

Slice the veal thinly and arrange the slices neatly on a serving dish with shallow sides. Pour the sauce over and around the meat, cover with plastic film to stop sauce going brown, and chill overnight. Garnish with anchovies and capers. Serves 8-12.

Fettucine are the narrower, thicker ribbon noodles Romans love to eat with creamy sauces such as our blue vein cheese sauce. Green fettucine get their atttractive colour from spinach.

Fettucine with blue cheese sauce
(photograph left)

The simple sauce has a gourmet touch.

250 g (8 oz) green fettucine (ribbon noodles)
30 g (1 oz) butter
1 medium onion, thinly sliced
125 g (4 oz) blue vein cheese, diced
½ cup cream
2 tablespoons chopped walnuts
¼ cup dry white wine
2 egg yolks, lightly beaten
1 tablespoon finely chopped parsley

Cook fettucine in plenty of boiling salted water until tender. While pasta is cooking, prepare the sauce:

Melt butter in a saucepan and add onion and cheese, stirring until cheese melts. Gradually stir in cream, walnuts and wine. Bring to the boil, then whisk a little of the sauce into the egg yolks. Return this mixture to the saucepan and stir over gentle heat until thickened, but do not allow to boil. Stir parsley into sauce. Pour sauce over cooked fettucine and serve immediately. Serves 4.

Arni souvlakia

A traditional Greek dish of lamb kebabs flavoured with lemon and oregano and served with steamed rice and Greek salad.

1 shoulder of lamb, boned
Salt and freshly ground pepper
3 tablespoons olive oil
2 tablespoons lemon juice
1 tablespoon chopped fresh oregano or 2 teaspoons dried

Remove skin and excess fat from the lamb. Cut meat into 2.5 cm (1 in) cubes and put into a bowl. Sprinkle with salt and pepper, then add oil, lemon juice and oregano. Stir and set aside for 30 minutes or more.

Thread meat pieces on to skewers and grill until tender, brushing with the herb mixture during grilling. Serves 4-5.

Note: Greek salad is a mixture of tomato slices, onion rings, thick slices of cucumber, black olives and cubes of salty Feta cheese. It is tossed with a dressing of olive oil and lemon juice seasoned with salt and black pepper, and served by itself or on a bed of tender lettuce leaves.

Chicken Piraeus

(photograph right)

A lovely chicken dish from Greece, flavoured with cinnamon, wine and orange juice.

2 small chickens weighing about 750g (1½ lb) each

Salt and freshly ground pepper

2 teaspoons cinnamon

2 tablespoons lemon juice

3 tablespoons olive oil

¾ cup orange juice

¾ cup chicken stock

2 extra tablespoons oil

500g (1 lb) zucchini, unpeeled and cut into sticks

1 clove garlic, crushed

3 oranges, peeled and sliced

Split chickens in half lengthwise, and rub with salt, pepper, cinnamon and lemon juice. Cover and allow to stand for 30 minutes.

Heat the oil in a large, deep frying pan and brown the chickens on all sides. Add orange juice and stock to the pan, cover, and simmer until chicken is almost tender, about 25 minutes.

Meanwhile, fry zucchini quickly in extra oil until golden brown. Season with salt, pepper and garlic and add to chicken with orange slices. Simmer another 5 minutes, or until chicken is quite tender.

Remove chicken, zucchini and orange to a heated platter. Reduce liquid in pan to sauce consistency by rapid boiling. Taste for seasoning, spoon over chicken, and serve piping hot with boiled rice. Serves 4.

Dolmades

A dish found throughout the Middle East, especially in Greece.

1 × 250g pkt vine leaves in brine, rinsed in cold water and drained

500g (1 lb) minced lamb

1½ cups cooked rice (½ cup raw)

2 medium onions, finely chopped

¼ cup grated Parmesan cheese

1 tablespoon chopped mint

1 teaspoon salt

2 cups boiling chicken stock

Lime or lemon wedges to serve

Place a layer of vine leaves over the base of a large, greased, shallow casserole dish. Combine mince with onion, rice, cheese, mint and salt. Place a spoonful of mixture in the centre of 30 vine leaves, and roll them up to form neat packages. Arrange the prepared dolmades in a single layer in the dish, cover with another layer of vine leaves, and pour boiling stock over.

Cover, and bake in a preheated moderate oven (180°C/350°F) for 40 minutes, or until cooked through and tender. Remove rolls from dish to a heated serving platter, discarding vine leaves and liquid in pan. Serve garnished with wedges of lime or lemon. Serves 8 as an appetiser.

Note: Dolmades are also delicious cold, with a little oil and lemon juice poured over them.

Yugoslav lamb with rice

750g (1½ lb) boneless lamb, from leg or shoulder

1½ cups raw rice

250g (8 oz) mushrooms, sliced

1 large green pepper, sliced

Salt and freshly ground black pepper

60g (2 oz) butter, cut in pieces

1 fresh chilli, seeded and finely chopped

Water to cover

1½ cups freshly grated cheese

Remove fat from lamb and cut meat into 2.5 cm (1 in) cubes. Place in a deep saucepan and cover with the rice. Sprinkle mushrooms and pepper on top and season generously with salt and pepper. Dot with butter and chopped chilli.

Cover with enough water to come 4 cm (1½ in) above the level of rice, and bring gently to the boil. Simmer, covered, for about 40 minutes or until lamb is tender and rice cooked through. If mixture is still liquid, remove cover and cook until evaporated. Fluff up with a fork, spoon into a heated serving dish, and sprinkle with cheese. Serves 4.

Greek cookery is full of the sunny flavours of citrus fruits, spices and herbs. Chicken Piraeus is a typical dish, flavoured with lemons and garnished with oranges.

Paella

(photograph left)

The Spanish rice dish called Paella is justly famous around the world, and in many of our Spanish restaurants in Australia. We have simplified its preparation for the home cook — the rice and "toppings" are prepared separately, then baked together.

It is an absolutely splendid dish for a party, as the rice and topping can be cooked the day before and refrigerated, ready to bake.

For rice:

2 tablespoons olive oil
60 g (2 oz) butter
1 large onion, finely chopped
1 clove garlic, crushed
1 bay leaf
1 tablespoon chopped fresh thyme, or 1 teaspoon dried
Pinch dried rosemary
Salt and freshly ground pepper
Good pinch cayenne pepper
¼ cup raw long grain rice
½ teaspoon saffron threads soaked overnight in 1¼ cups chicken stock — or add 1 teaspoon turmeric to stock.

For topping:

2 cups diced, cooked lobster or peeled cooked prawns
250 g (8 oz) scallops, lightly cooked in a little butter
500 g (1 lb) boneless pork, cut into cubes and cooked in butter until brown and tender
1 cup cooked green peas
6 half-breasts of chicken, cooked in butter until brown and tender
2 small cans artichoke hearts, drained
12 black olives, stoned
1 small can pimento, drained and sliced
24 mussels, steamed until shells open (optional)

Paella lends itself to endless flavour variation. In the version pictured, chorizo or Spanish garlic sausage, tiny peeled tomatoes, green and red peppers and black and green olives have been included.

To prepare the rice, heat olive oil and butter in a large, heavy frying pan which has a tight-fitting lid. Add the onion, garlic, seasonings and rice, and stir over medium heat until rice is a light golden colour. Add the chicken stock and stir thoroughly. Cover tightly and simmer over low heat until liquid is absorbed and rice tender, about 25 minutes.

Spoon rice into a large, shallow oven-proof dish (the traditional paella pan is round, so use a round dish if you have it). Arrange meat, seafood and vegetables on top, and garnish with olives and strips of pimento. Cover with foil, and place in a preheated hot oven (200°C/400°F) for 10 minutes, or until heated through.

Take the dish to the table, so diners can see the splendid sight and help themselves. Serves 6.

Note: If ingredients have been refrigerated, you will need to reheat the paella in a moderately slow oven (170°C/325°F) for 20-25 minutes. Add a little extra chicken stock if rice seems dry.

Sausages in beer

Germany is a land of wonderful "wursts" or sausages, and sausage recipes, many of which have become Australian favourites. Here's a hearty combination of sausages and beer.

60 g (2 oz) butter
750 g (1½ lb) thick sausages, preferably pork
1 small onion, finely chopped
1 tablespoon plain flour
1 cup beer
Salt and freshly ground pepper
A little sugar and vinegar (optional)

Heat the butter in a large frying pan, and fry the sausages until brown all over and cooked through, about 8 minutes. Remove from pan, and pour off all but 1 tablespoon of fat. Add the onion to the pan and stir until soft, about 3 minutes. Sprinkle flour over and stir in, then slowly stir in the beer. Cook until smooth and thickened and season to taste with salt and pepper.

If you would like a sweet-sour flavour, add a couple of teaspoons each of sugar and vinegar. Return sausages to the pan, cover and simmer for 2-3 minutes until heated through. Serve with mashed potatoes and cabbage or sauerkraut. Serves 6.

Vienna schnitzel

This superb Austrian way with veal steak has become part of our national cuisine. To enjoy it at its best, ask your butcher to cut the veal from the leg or the boned loin. The slices should be beaten out between sheets of plastic film until they are almost wafer thin and the fibres broken.

4 slices veal, beaten out very thinly
Plain flour
2 egg yolks, beaten with 1 tablespoon water, ½ teaspoon salt and freshly ground pepper
1½ cups fresh white breadcrumbs, rubbed through a sieve
60 g (2 oz) butter
Slices of lemon to garnish (you may also like to add anchovy fillets and capers to the garnish)

Dip the slices of veal on both sides in flour, and shake off excess. Dip in beaten egg, and then in breadcrumbs, firming them on with a knife. Chill for 10 minutes until breadcrumbs set.

Heat the butter in a large, heavy frying pan until foamy. Cook each slice until golden brown on the bottom, then turn over and quickly cook the other side. It only takes a few minutes altogether. Garnish with lemon slices. Serves 4.

Note: For an Italian variation, place cooked schnitzels side by side in a shallow baking dish. Top with slices of cooked ham, then cheese. Place in a preheated very hot oven (220°C/440°F) for a minute, until cheese melts, and serve at once.

Chicken Marengo

This famous classic, said to be created for Napoleon during battle, is popular on the menus of French restaurants.

4 tablespoons olive oil

1 × 2 kg (4 lb) chicken, cut in pieces

Salt and freshly ground black pepper

1 bay leaf, 2 sprigs parsley,
1 sprig thyme tied together

1 clove garlic, finely chopped

2 tablespoons plain flour

¼ cup stock or water

½ cup dry white wine

1 tablespoon tomato paste

250 g (8 oz) mushrooms, cut in
thick slices

Chopped parsley to garnish

Heat the olive oil in a deep saucepan, and brown the chicken over medium heat, turning so all sides are brown and crisp. Remove from pan. Strain off any extra fat which may have accumulated, leaving about 3 tablespoons.

Stir in flour until well blended, then stir in stock and wine. When smooth add tomato paste, garlic, the bundle of herbs and mushrooms. Season with salt and pepper. Replace chicken and simmer, covered, for about 1 hour or until chicken is tender. Remove the herb bouquet and serve garnished with parsley. Serves 4-6.

Note: In France this dish is sometimes served with squares of oil-fried bread around it, and a fried egg per person.

Cassoulet

A superb ancient French peasant stew which provides a popular culinary exercise among Australian gastronomes who like to show off their cookery skills. Here is a simplified version of the original complicated recipe, in which goose fat or preserved goose was an essential ingredient.

500 g (1 lb) haricot beans

500 g (1 lb) pickled pork

5 cups beef stock

500 g (1 lb) boneless lamb

125 g (4 oz) lean bacon in the piece

30 g (1 oz) lard or butter

2 medium onions, coarsely chopped

2 cloves garlic, crushed

4 tablespoons tomato paste

1 bay leaf, 2 sprigs parsley,
1 sprig thyme, tied together

2 leeks, cleaned and sliced

2 large tomatoes, peeled and sliced

250 g (8 oz) garlic sausage, sliced

Salt and freshly ground black pepper

About 2 cups fresh white breadcrumbs

Extra butter

Soak the beans and pork overnight in cold water. Drain, and put pork aside. Place beans in a saucepan with the stock, cover and simmer for 1½ hours or until just tender. Cut the pork, lamb and bacon into 2.5 cm (1 in) cubes, discarding any skin and bone.

Heat the lard or butter in a large frying pan and brown the meats, onions and garlic. Transfer to an earthenware casserole and add the beans and stock, tomato paste, herbs, leeks, tomatoes and garlic sausage. Season with salt and pepper.

Cover and bake in a preheated moderately slow oven (170°C/325°F) for 3 hours. One hour before end of cooking time, sprinkle the breadcrumbs over the top of the cassoulet, to a depth of at least 2.5 cm (1 in). Dot with butter and bake uncovered for the remainder of cooking time, breaking the crust occasionally, and letting it reform until it is brown and crispy. Serve from the casserole. Serves 6.

Croque Monsieur

This simple sandwich-with-a-difference is a favourite lunch time snack in the brasseries of Paris.

2 slices white bread, crusts removed

Butter

1 slice leg ham

½ teaspoon French mustard

1 slice Gruyere cheese

Butter for frying

Butter one side of each bread slice. Place the slice of ham on the buttered side of one piece of bread and spread with mustard. Arrange the cheese on top. Place the second slice of bread, buttered side down, on top. Fry the sandwich in butter on both sides until cheese is melting and both sides of sandwich are brown, or grill on both sides and butter top when serving. Makes 1 sandwich.

Chicken liver pate

Of all the delicious pates and terrines that have come to us from France, this is possibly the Australian favourite.

125 g (4 oz) butter

2 rashers bacon, chopped

1 large onion, chopped

500 g (1 lb) sausage mince

500 g (1 lb) chicken livers, trimmed

2 cloves garlic, crushed

2 teaspoons chopped fresh basil, or
½ teaspoon dried

1 teaspoon Dijon mustard

1 teaspoon salt

½ teaspoon each ground mace
and cloves

1 cup dry white wine

½ cup cognac or brandy

½ cup sour cream

For aspic:

1 tablespoon gelatine

½ cup chicken stock

½ cup dry white wine

Sprigs of fresh thyme

Melt butter and lightly fry bacon, onion, sausage mince and chicken livers. Add garlic, basil, mustard, salt, mace, cloves and wine and simmer with the lid off for 20 minutes. Allow to cool. Put mixture in a blender, adding cognac and sour cream, and blend until smooth. Spoon into one large mould or 8 small moulds and refrigerate until firm.

Make the aspic by dissolving gelatine in chicken stock and wine and standing in a saucepan of simmering water until clear. Allow to cool. Place sprigs of thyme on top of pate, carefully spoon the aspic over, and refrigerate until set. Serve accompanied by crisp toast or crusty bread. Serves 8.

Russian meat pasties
(photograph right)

In this recipe, the pasties have a meat filling, but they can be made with fish, mushrooms or other vegetables. They can also be deep-fried instead of baked. Like Australia, Russia has many versions of the savoury pie.

1½ cups plain flour
Dash salt
90 g (3 oz) butter, cut in small pieces
2-3 tablespoons cream
Beaten egg to glaze

For filling:

60 g (2 oz) butter
250 g (8 oz) finely minced raw lamb or beef
1 small onion, finely chopped
2 tablespoons finely chopped parsley
1 cup boiled rice
Salt and freshly ground pepper

Sift flour and salt into a bowl, and rub in butter until mixture resembles fine breadcrumbs. Add cream, and mix with a knife to form a soft dough. Wrap in plastic film and chill for 30 minutes.

Roll pastry out thinly on a lightly floured surface and cut into circles about 10 cm (4 in) across. Divide the filling among the pastry circles, brush edges of pastry with water and press together in a half-moon shape. Cut a few slits on top for steam to escape and brush with egg.

Bake in a preheated hot oven (200°C/400°F) for 20 minutes, or until golden brown. Serves 4.

Filling: Heat butter and fry mince until brown, stirring to break up any lumps. Add onion and cook until onion is soft. Stir in remaining ingredients and allow to cool.

Chinese pancake rolls
(photograph page 276)

Light, tender pancakes wrapped around a spicy pork filling are just right for almost any occasion — a first course, a main course with rice and vegetables, a super luncheon snack.

2 eggs
¾ cup plain flour
1 cup milk
½ teaspoon salt
45 g (1½ oz) butter, melted

For filling:

250 g (8 oz) finely minced pork
2 tablespoons oil
1 tablespoon soy sauce
Salt and freshly ground pepper
1 teaspoon sugar
1 tablespoon dry sherry
Pinch Chinese 5 spice powder
3 cups finely shredded white cabbage
½ cup finely chopped shallots

To brush rolls:

1 tablespoon oil mixed with 2 teaspoons soy sauce

Beat eggs, then mix in flour, half a cup of the milk, and the salt. Beat for 2 minutes, stir in melted butter, then gradually beat in remaining milk.

Heat a greased crepe pan or small frying pan, and pour in enough batter to give a thin layer over the bottom of the pan — about 1½ tablespoons. Cook the pancakes on the underside only until golden. (The top should be set by this time, and not "runny").

Stack pancakes with sheets of plastic film or greaseproof paper between them. When all are cooked, place a heaped tablespoon of filling in the centre of each, tuck in the ends, and roll up.

Arrange the rolls in a greased baking dish and brush tops with oil-soy mixture. Bake in a preheated hot oven (200°C/400°F) for 6-8 minutes, or until piping hot. Serves 6.

Filling: Fry minced pork in hot oil until brown, stirring to get rid of any lumps. Add remaining ingredients and continue cooking until cabbage is tender but still firm. Allow to cool, and taste for seasoning before filling pancakes.

Chinese braised duck

1 duck about 2 kg (4 lb)
Neck and giblets from duck
2 tablespoons medium sherry
1 tablespoon soy sauce
1 teaspoon sugar
1 teaspoon salt
Sprinkling pepper
2 tablespoons oil
1 clove garlic, crushed
2 cups duck stock
¾ cup sliced celery
125 g (4 oz) mushrooms, cut in thick slices
6 shallots, cut into short sections, including green tops
2 tablespoons cornflour mixed to a paste with a little water
Extra shallots to garnish

Remove excess fat from the duck and wipe inside with a damp cloth. Make stock with giblets and neck simmered in 2 cups of water for 30 minutes. Combine sherry, soy sauce, sugar, salt and pepper.

Brown the duck all over in oil, in a large, deep pan. Pour oil from pan, add sherry mixture and garlic to the duck and cook for 2 minutes. Add stock, cover pan and cook gently for 1¼ hours. Add the celery, mushrooms and shallots. Replace lid and continue cooking gently for half an hour or until very tender.

Remove duck, cut into pieces, put on a serving platter and keep hot. Add cornflour mixture to liquid in pan. Stir until boiling, then simmer a minute or two and pour over duck. Garnish with extra shallots, shredded and scattered over duck. Serves 4.

In our recipe for Chinese pancake rolls on the previous page, we have made the filling with minced pork and sliced cabbage. For a variation, try chopped prawns or finely chopped ham instead of the pork — or a mixture of all three!

Honey prawns

Everybody seems to be ordering them in Chinese restaurants, and they're not difficult to prepare at home.

1 kg (2 lb) green prawns with the heads and shells removed but tails left on
½ cup cornflour
1 cup self raising flour
½ teaspoon salt
1 egg
1¼ cups water
Oil for frying
1 tablespoon extra oil
2 tablespoons honey
½ cup toasted sesame seeds
Shallots and fried prawn chips to garnish

De-vein prepared prawns and toss in cornflour. Sift flours and salt into a bowl, make a well in the centre, add egg and water and beat until smooth.

Heat enough oil in a wok or frying pan to give a depth of about 2 cm (¾ in). Dip prawns into the batter and quickly fry for approximately 1½ minutes, or until crisp and golden, then drain on kitchen paper.

Drain oil from wok, wipe clean, then add the extra oil, honey and sesame seeds. Heat, then add the cooked prawns and toss lightly to coat. Serve garnished with shallots and prawn chips, and accompanied by boiled rice and soy sauce. Serves 4.

Malaysian beef sates

125 g (4 oz) raw peanuts
1 tablespoon curry powder
1 teaspoon sugar
½ teaspoon salt
¼ cup light soy sauce
500 g (1 lb) round steak, cut in cubes
1 tablespoon oil
½ cup milk
⅓ cup tomato sauce
Cubes of fresh or canned pineapple, thin slices of cucumber and boiled rice to serve.

Toast peanuts in a dry frying pan, shaking pan frequently. Rub off the skins. When cool, put peanuts into a paper or plastic bag and crush with a rolling pin. (Or crush in a food processor fitted with the steel blade).

Mix half the curry powder with the sugar, salt and soy sauce. Add the cubed meat and marinate for 30 minutes.

To make the sauce for sates, mix remaining curry powder with the crushed peanuts and add enough of the milk to make a paste. Heat the oil in a small saucepan and fry the paste for 2 minutes, stirring constantly. Gradually stir in the rest of the milk and the tomato sauce. Cook gently, stirring until almost boiling, then simmer for 5 minutes.

Thread meat on to skewers and grill for about 7-10 minutes, basting frequently with the marinade, and turning skewers constantly.

Put skewers on a serving platter and garnish with pineapple cubes and cucumber slices. Gently reheat the sauce and serve separately, accompanied by a bowl of boiled rice. Serves 4.

Coconut beef with onions
(photograph page 279)

500 g (1 lb) round or topside steak
1 clove garlic, crushed
1 teaspoon tamarind or lemon juice
1 teaspoon ground coriander
1 teaspoon ground cumin
¼ teaspoon ground cloves
½ teaspoon cinnamon
½ teaspoon turmeric
½ teaspoon ground ginger
2 tablespoons oil
1 cup canned coconut milk
Salt to taste
2 tablespoons shredded or desiccated coconut
An extra 2 tablespoons oil
2 large onions, thinly sliced
Salt and freshly ground pepper

Remove any fat and gristle from steak and cut meat into finger lengths. Place in a bowl with garlic, tamarind juice and spices, and toss to coat thoroughly. Cover and leave for 30 minutes. Heat the oil in a heavy frying pan, add the meat, and brown quickly on all sides. Add the coconut milk and salt to taste. Bring to the boil, then cover and simmer for 1½ hours, or until meat is tender.

Stir in coconut, taste for seasoning, and top with fried onions. Serves 4.

Fried onions: Heat oil in a separate pan and fry onions slowly until soft and well browned. Season with salt and pepper.

Indonesian rice table
(photograph right)

In the old days, it is said as many as 100 side dishes would be served with rice for the traditional Rijstaffel in grand Indonesian restaurants and private homes. Today, a choice of three or four savoury dishes adds up to an interesting meal — good fun to prepare and eat.

Pork sates with peanut sauce
(photograph right)

500g (1lb) boneless lean pork
2 kemerie nuts or macadamia nuts, grated
1 teaspoon trassi (fish sauce)
2 tablespoons sweet soy sauce
2 tablespoons oil
1 clove garlic, crushed

Cut pork into 1 cm (½ in) cubes. Mix with remaining ingredients, cover, and marinate for 2 hours. Thread meat on to small bamboo skewers (soaked in water to prevent charring) and grill on both sides until brown and cooked through. Serve with Peanut sauce. Serves 4.

Note: Kemerie nuts, trassi and sweet soy sauce are all available at Asian food stores. If you can't get trassi locally, use 1 teaspoon anchovy paste instead. If you can't get sweet soy sauce, use ordinary soy and add 2 teaspoons sugar to the marinade.

Peanut sauce

¾ cup water
4 tablespoons peanut butter
1 clove garlic, crushed
¾ teaspoon salt
2 teaspoons brown sugar
1 tablespoon sweet soy sauce
1 tablespoon tamarind juice or lemon juice
½ teaspoon sambal ulek or dash chilli powder

Mix water and peanut butter in a small saucepan and bring to the boil. Remove from heat and stir in remaining ingredients. Taste, and add extra salt, sugar or lemon juice to suit your own preference. Serve warm, as a dip for sates, or over freshly cooked vegetables.

Prawn rolls
(photograph right)

3 eggs
½ teaspoon salt
½ cup plain flour
½ cup water
For filling:
250g (8oz) peeled, cooked prawns
60g (2oz) butter
4 shallots, finely chopped
3 sticks celery, finely chopped
1 teaspoon medium curry powder
Salt to taste
½ teaspoon grated lemon rind

Beat eggs, then whisk in salt, flour and water. Cover batter and allow to rest for 30 minutes. Heat a greased crepe pan or small frying pan and pour in enough batter (about 1½ tablespoons) to cover bottom of pan. Cook until golden underneath and small bubbles appear on top, then turn and cook other side.

Spread filling over crepes, and roll up or fold into an envelope shape. Arrange on a baking tray and place in a preheated moderate oven (180°C/350°F) for 5 minutes to reheat. Serve with a side dish of shredded fresh vegetables and light soy sauce or chilli sauce. Serves 4-6.

Filling: Chop prawns finely. Heat butter and fry shallots and celery until soft. Stir in the curry powder and cook for 1 minute. Remove from heat and add lemon rind, prawns and salt to taste.

Tandoori murg

Serve this Indian chicken on a bed of salad made up of sliced onion, tomato, cucumber and radish rings. Garnish chicken with fresh limes and coriander. Crisp fried poppadums and boiled rice are appropriate accompaniments.

2 × 1.5 kg (3lb) chickens, cut into serving pieces
1 teaspoon saffron threads or turmeric
½ teaspoon red food colouring
3 teaspoons salt
1½ teaspoons coriander seeds
1 teaspoon cumin seeds
2 teaspoons finely chopped fresh ginger

2 cloves garlic, crushed
¼ cup lemon juice
1 × 500g carton natural yoghurt

Place chicken pieces in a large bowl. Combine remaining ingredients and pour over chicken, turning pieces until well coated. Cover and refrigerate for at least 12 hours. Place chicken on a rack in a large baking dish, and spoon any remaining marinade over. Bake in a preheated moderate oven (180°C/350°F) for 40 minutes, basting often with juices that collect in pan. (If necessary add a little water to the pan to prevent scorching). Serves 8.

Yakitori

Chicken pieces and shallots are marinated, then grilled, in this classic Japanese dish. It is usually served as a first course or snack.

1 chicken, weighing about 1.25 kg (2½ lb)
10 large shallots
¾ cup light soy sauce
¼ cup sugar
⅓ cup dry sherry
Cayenne pepper

Disjoint chicken, remove flesh from bones and cut into 2.5 cm (1 in) pieces. Cut shallots into 2.5 cm (1 in) sections. Arrange pieces of chicken on skewers, with two or three pieces of shallot in between. Warm together soy sauce, sugar and sherry, pour over skewered chicken and shallots and leave for 10-15 minutes.

Grill slowly until tender, turning skewers and brushing frequently with the sauce. Serve sprinkled lightly with cayenne pepper. Serves 4.

In the Indonesian rice table pictured, from left to right: Pork Sates with peanut sauce, prawn rolls, and coconut beef with onions, accompanied by rice and shredded vegetables.

Beef teriyaki

Crisp vegetables, subtle flavourings and thin egg noodles combine with sliced beef in this Japanese favourite.

750g (1½lb) tender grilling steak
3 tablespoons oil
1 clove garlic, halved
1 large onion, sliced and separated into rings
1 large green pepper, halved and sliced
1 large red pepper, halved and sliced
4 small zucchini, sliced
2 medium-size carrots, cut into thin sticks
½ cup light soy sauce
1 tablespoon sugar
¼ cup Mirin or sweet sherry

250g (8oz) thin egg noodles
250g (8oz) small mushrooms, thinly sliced

Cut steak into paper-thin slices (if meat is placed in freezer until well chilled, slicing will be easier). Heat the oil with the garlic. Remove garlic, add meat a few pieces at a time, and quickly brown on both sides. Remove from pan. Add onion rings, fry for 2 minutes, then add peppers, zucchini and carrots. Cook for 2 minutes, stirring constantly. Add the soy sauce, sugar and Mirin or sherry. Stir for another minute, or until vegetables are just tender-crisp.

Meanwhile, drop noodles into boiling salted water, and when they begin to soften, separate with chopsticks, or a fork. Cook until just tender and drain thoroughly.

Return meat to the pan, lightly mix in the mushrooms and noodles, and cook for another 2-3 minutes. Serves 6.

Indonesian meatballs and rice
(photograph below)

These subtly-flavoured little meatballs are served with rice as a main course. As an appetiser, you can spear them on toothpicks and serve with mild chilly sauce for dipping.

60g (2oz) butter
1 small onion, finely chopped
1 teaspoon ground cumin
1 teaspoon ground coriander
½ teaspoon ground allspice
½ teaspoon ground ginger
2 teaspoons cornflour
1 egg, beaten
Salt and freshly ground pepper
500g (1lb) minced beef or pork

For rice:

60g (2 oz) butter
4 cups boiled rice (1½ cups raw)
3 small peppers (if possible, one green, one red, one yellow) cut into small cubes
1 can mandarin segments, drained
Salt and freshly ground pepper

Heat 30g of the butter in a frying pan and fry the onion until soft. Add the spices and cook for a minute, stirring. Allow to cool, then mix with cornflour, egg, salt and pepper and mince. Shape into walnut-sized balls, and fry in remaining 30g of butter until brown all over and cooked through, about six minutes. Serve in a ring of savoury rice. Serves 4.

Rice: Heat the 60g of butter, and toss the peppers over moderate heat until starting to soften. Add rice, and stir until piping hot. Fold in mandarins, and season with salt and pepper.

Vietnamese curry

In south Vietnam, where the Indian influence is greatest, this curry is often served with French bread — combining three cultures at the table.

In Australia small Vietnamese restaurants are introducing their delicious cuisine to a public eager to taste the flavour of other countries.

1 large chicken cut into 10 pieces, with breast cut into 4.
1 tablespoon dried lemon grass
3½ teaspoons curry powder
Sprinkle of freshly ground black pepper
1 teaspoon sugar
1 tablespoon salt
½ cup oil
3 small sweet potatoes or 3 potatoes peeled and cut into 5 cm (2 in) cubes
4 cloves garlic, chopped
1 large onion, cut in wedges and separated into "petals"
3 bay leaves
2 cups water
1 large carrot cut into 1 cm (½ in) slices
2 cups canned coconut milk
1 cup water

Soak lemon grass in water for 2 hours, drain, and chop finely. Combine curry powder, pepper, sugar and salt and rub into the chicken pieces. Leave to absorb flavours for 1 hour.

Heat the oil and fry the potatoes over high heat until well browned but not cooked, about 5 minutes. Set aside. Pour off most of the oil, leaving 2 tablespoons. Fry the garlic for a few seconds, then add onion, bay leaves and lemon grass, and toss for a minute.

Add chicken, stir-frying until meat is slightly seared. Add 2 cups water and carrot. Cover and bring to the boil, then turn down heat and simmer 5 minutes. Take off lid and stir, then cook covered another 10 minutes. Remove lid and add the browned potatoes, coconut milk and water. Simmer covered for another 15 minutes or until chicken and vegetables are tender. Serve with noodles or rice. Serves 8.

Chicken with mint

Serve this popular Vietnamese dish as an appetiser or entree.

2 chicken drumsticks and thighs, steamed until tender
1 small onion
White vinegar to cover
⅓ cup finely chopped mint leaves
¼ teaspoon salt
Freshly ground black pepper to taste

Remove chicken flesh from bones and discard bones. Slice flesh into shreds. Slice the onion into paper-thin rings, place in a bowl and cover with vinegar. Put aside for 10-15 minutes.

Place shredded chicken in a bowl and mix thoroughly with chopped mint, salt and pepper, stirring until salt has dissolved. Strain vinegar from onions and rinse onions quickly in cold water. Add to the chicken mixture, stir, and serve. Serves 4.

Creme caramel

A classic French dessert.
2 cups milk
½ cup raw sugar
1 teaspoon vanilla
4 eggs
3 tablespoons sugar
1 tablespoon water

Put the milk in a saucepan with the raw sugar, bring to the boil, then remove from heat and cool to lukewarm. Add vanilla. Beat the eggs in a bowl and gradually add the lukewarm milk.

Sprinkle the 3 tablespoons of sugar in a heatproof mould and place over a direct flame, heating until sugar turns dark golden brown. Be careful it does not overcook or burn (this can happen quickly if you're not alert!)

Add the water, and turn the mould in your hands until the liquid caramel has reached every part of the mould. Pour in the custard, and place the mould in a baking tin with enough cold water to come about 5 cm (2 in) up the sides of the mould. Bake in a preheated moderately slow oven (170°C/325°F) for 40-45 minutes, or until custard is set. Allow to cool, and then chill before unmoulding creme caramel on to a dessert platter. (When unmoulding, place the platter on top of the mould before turning it upside down). Serve with or without sponge fingers. Serves 4-6.

Kourabiethes

These Greek shortbreads should be placed in a sealed container and stored for 2 days before serving with coffee.

250g (8oz) unsalted butter, at room temperature
3 tablespoons icing sugar
1 egg yolk
1 tablespoon brandy
2½ cups plain flour
1 teaspoon baking powder
2 cups icing sugar

Put butter in a mixing bowl with the 3 tablespoons of icing sugar and beat until light and fluffy. Add egg yolk and brandy and beat well. Sift flour and baking powder twice, and lightly mix into butter mixture. Take walnut-sized pieces of the dough and shape into balls. Place on an ungreased baking tray and make 4 indentations by pinching twice on the tops, pressing down lightly to flatten the shortbreads slightly.

Bake in a preheated moderate oven (180°C/350°F) for 15-20 minutes or until pale gold. Leave to cool on the tray for a few minutes. Sift 1 cup of icing sugar on to a large piece of waxed paper, and place warm shortbreads on top. Sift more icing sugar over tops and sides, so shortbreads are sugared all over. When cool, put into a container and sift remaining sugar over the shortbreads. Seal and store for 2 days before using.

Coffee chiffon cake with mocha glaze

The United States has contributed many foods to our cuisine, from hamburgers, fried chicken and hot dogs to comparative newcomers like this beautifully-textured cake.

8 egg whites, at room temperature

½ teaspoon cream of tartar

1⅓ cups castor sugar

2⅓ cups plain flour

1 tablespoon baking powder

½ teaspoon salt

½ cup oil (safflower or sunflower)

5 egg yolks

¾ cup cold water

1 tablespoon instant coffee

For glaze:

45 g (1½ oz) butter

60 g (2 oz) dark chocolate, chopped

1 teaspoon instant coffee

¼ teaspoon cinnamon

1 cup sifted icing sugar

2 tablespoons hot water

Beat egg whites, half the sugar and cream of tartar in the large bowl of an electric mixer on high speed until soft peaks form. Sift flour, baking powder, salt and remaining sugar into a medium-size bowl. Make a well in the centre and add oil, egg yolks, water and instant coffee. Beat at medium speed for 2 minutes, or until smooth. Gradually pour this mixture over beaten whites, gently folding in until no streaks of white remain. Spoon into a deep ungreased tube pan or 25 cm (10 in) angel cake pan (available from some kitchen shops and gourmet cookware sections in department stores).

Bake in a preheated slow oven (160°C/320°F) for 1 hour and 10 minutes, or until top springs back when pressed. Suspend pan over a bottle or other container, so cake does not touch the bench. Allow to cool completely, then loosen around inside edges with a spatula and gently invert on to a serving dish held against the pan. Drizzle glaze over and allow to set.

To make glaze, melt butter and chocolate in a small, heavy saucepan over very low heat, stirring until blended. Remove from heat and stir in coffee and cinnamon. Add icing sugar alternately with hot water, beating until smooth.

Pineapple lychee ice

A Chinese dessert, very refreshing after any spicy meal.

¾ cup water

½ cup sugar

1 cup diced fresh or canned pineapple

1 medium can lychees

Juice of 1 lemon or lime

Ice cubes to serve

Boil water and sugar together, stirring until sugar has dissolved. Add pineapple cubes and simmer for 5 minutes. Let pineapple and syrup cool. Pour the lychees and their juice into a serving bowl. Mix in the pineapple and syrup and stir in the lime juice. Chill, and embed the bowl in a larger bowl of ice cubes to serve. Serves 3-4.

Crepes

Despite the awe in which Australian diners in local French restaurants have always held these delicious pancake morsels, they're really easy to make at home.

60 g (2 oz) butter

1 cup plain flour

¼ teaspoon salt

2 eggs

1 cup milk

Butter for frying

Melt the butter and cool. Sift the flour and salt into a bowl, add the eggs and gradually beat in the milk and butter to make a smooth batter. Let stand for 10 minutes.

Heat a knob of butter in a crepe pan or small frying pan until it sizzles. Add just enough batter to coat the bottom of the pan (about 1½ tablespoons), tilting the pan to distribute evenly. Cook until underside of the crepe is golden brown, then turn or toss and cook on the other side until golden. As each crepe is cooked, place it on a plate with greaseproof paper in between to prevent sticking. Makes 10-12 crepes.

Note: This mixture can be used for sweet or savoury crepes. If you wish to serve stuffed crepes, make all the crepes before filling.

For filling: Fill with your choice of sweet fillings for an elegant dessert. Our favourites include chopped hazelnuts with warmed apricot jam and a dash of brandy; strawberries and whipped cream with a little Kirsch; grated chocolate and raspberry jam; stewed apple and softened cream cheese; or that old Australian favourite, castor sugar and lemon juice. Delicious!

Baklava

This is one of the best known of Middle Eastern pastries, a great Greek favourite and available from Greek cake shops all over Australia.

500 g (1 lb) filo pastry, available frozen or fresh from delicatess and most supermarkets

250 g (8 oz) unsalted butter, melted

2 cups pistachio nuts or walnuts, coarsely chopped

1 cup almonds, coarsely chopped

2 tablespoons sugar

For syrup:

1 cup sugar

½ cup water

1 tablespoon lemon juice

2 tablespoons honey

5 cm (2 in) cinnamon stick

3 whole cloves

Thin strip lemon rind

Make the syrup first: Place all ingredients in a saucepan, and stir over medium heat until sugar dissolves. Simmer until thick enough to coat a spoon. Strain, cool, and chill for 30 minutes.

Take a deep square or oblong baking dish approximately 33 × 23 × 5 cm (13 × 9 × 2 in) and grease bottom and sides with a pastry brush dipped in melted butter. Fit half the pastry sheets one at a time in the dish, brushing each one with melted butter and overlapping or folding the sides to fit where needed. Mix the chopped nuts and sugar together and spread evenly over the pastry in the dish. Cover with the remaining sheets, brushing each sheet with butter and also the top layer.

With a sharp knife, cut through the top layers of filo diagonally, to make diamond shapes. Bake Baklava for 30 minutes in a preheated moderate oven (180°C/350°F) then raise heat to very hot (220°C/440°F) and bake another 15 minutes or until puffed and golden brown.

Remove from oven and spoon cold syrup over the hot pastry. Allow to cool. When cold and ready to serve, cut into diamond-shaped pieces, following the outlines on pastry.

Zabaglione

This delicious, light, fluffy concoction is one of the specialities of top Italian restaurants in Australian cities.

| 6 egg yolks, at room temperature |
| 6 tablespoons icing or castor sugar |
| Juice ½ medium-sized lemon |
| ¾ cup Marsala or sweet white wine |
| Coffee powder or crushed toasted nuts to decorate |

Put egg yolks into a mixing bowl with the sugar and beat until combined. Place bowl over a saucepan of simmering water, without letting the water touch the bowl, and beat until thick.

Gradually add the lemon juice, beating constantly, then beat in the wine. Continue beating until mixture is thick and creamy. Pour into individual glass or crystal sweet dishes, and sprinkle with a dusting of coffee powder, crushed toasted hazelnuts or almonds. Serve warm, with sponge fingers or macaroons. Serve 4-6.

Sponge fingers

In Italy, these delicate sponge fingers are known as Savoiardi. They are available in packets in Australia, and used as an ingredient in sweet dishes, as an accompaniment to custards and icecreams, or just to enjoy with coffee.

| ½ cup castor sugar |
| 2 large eggs |
| 1 cup plain flour |
| Extra castor sugar |

Put the sugar in a shallow pan and place in a moderate oven (180°C/350°F) for 3-5 minutes, until sugar is hot to the touch. Have eggs at room temperature and put into a bowl or small basin of electric mixer. Beat briskly with a hand beater or at high speed for 1 minute with electric mixer, then add hot sugar and continue beating for 10 minutes or until mixture is thick enough to hold a shape.

Transfer egg mixture to a larger bowl. Sift flour twice, then sift for the third time over egg mixture and lightly mix flour through. Put mixture into a large piping bag fitted with a plain 1 cm (½ in) tube. Cover 2 baking trays with aluminium foil.

Pipe mixture on to trays in 8 cm (3 in) lengths, spacing them about 4 cm (1½ in) apart. Spoon carefully into similar lengths if you have no piping bag. Sprinkle extra castor sugar evenly over fingers, and bake one tray at a time in a preheated moderately hot oven (190°C/375°F) for 4-5 minutes. Cool on trays. Store in an airtight container. Makes about 20 sponge fingers.

Pears with chocolate sauce

| A delectable French dessert. |
| 6 large, firm pears |
| ½ cup water |
| 60 g (2 oz) sugar |
| 1 vanilla pod |
| 125 g (4 oz) dark chocolate, chopped |
| 30 g (1 oz) butter |

Peel the pears, cut into quarters and remove cores. Place in a pan with water, sugar and vanilla pod. Cook gently for about 10 minutes or until just tender. Place the chocolate in a basin set over a pan of hot water, and stir until melted. Stir in the butter and 2 tablespoons of liquid from cooked pears. Drain the pears well, and arrange in an ovenproof dish. Pour the melted chocolate over them, cover, and bake in a preheated moderate oven (180°C/350°F) for 15 minutes. Serve with sponge fingers and whipped cream, or ice cream. Serves 4-6.

Gula Malacca

This is a traditional Asian dessert to be served after curry. It is on the tiffin table at Raffles Hotel in Singapore, and a favourite ending to Sunday curry tiffin in the bungalows of Europeans in Malaysia and Thailand, many of whom have brought the taste for it to Australia.

| 1 cup sago |
| 2 cups water |
| 2.5 cm (1 in) piece of cinnamon stick |
| 150 g (5 oz) palm sugar |
| Extra ½ cup water |
| 1 cup coconut milk, canned or home-made (recipe follows) |
| Pinch salt |
| Extra coconut milk and syrup made with palm sugar and water to serve |

Wash the sago and put into a saucepan with 2 cups water and the cinnamon stick. Simmer, stirring frequently, until thick and clear. Meanwhile, chop the palm sugar into small pieces, put into a pan with ½ cup water, and melt over very low heat.

Stir 1 cup of coconut milk and a pinch of salt into sago, then stir in the palm sugar syrup. Continue cooking, stirring constantly, until very thick. Pour into a mould rinsed with cold water and chill. Unmould and serve with coconut milk and extra palm sugar syrup. Serves 5-6.

Coconut Milk: Put 3 cups desiccated coconut into a bowl, add 3½ cups of hot water and cool to lukewarm. Knead firmly with the hand for a few minutes, then strain through a fine strainer or a piece of muslin, squeezing out as much as possible of the liquid from the coconut. This should give about 2¼ cups of coconut milk. Use 1 cup for the sago, and serve the rest from a jug for pouring with the finished dessert.

Note: Palm sugar is available in most shops specialising in Asian ingredients.

Apple flan with amber glaze

A chic French approach to apple pie.

| 185 g (6 oz) butter |
| ½ cup castor sugar |
| 3 egg yolks |
| Juice of 1 lemon |
| 3 cups plain flour |
| 2 teaspoons baking powder |
| Pinch salt |
| **For filling:** |
| 4 large Granny Smith apples, peeled, cored and sliced |
| 3 tablespoons sugar |
| 1 teaspoon cinnamon |
| 1 cup apple, grape or quince jelly, melted |
| Whipped cream to serve |

Make pastry by beating butter and sugar until light and creamy. Add egg yolks and beat well. Add lemon juice and work in sifted dry ingredients to form a firm dough. Roll pastry out between two sheets of plastic film to line the base and sides of a large flan tin. Place prepared apples over the flan base in a pinwheel pattern, dust with sugar and cinnamon mixed together and bake in a preheated moderate oven at (180°C/350°F) for 50 minutes. Remove from oven and brush with melted fruit jelly. Before serving, top with whipped cream. Serves 8-10.

The authors

JOY HAYES

Joy Hayes is a fourth generation Australian who began her career as a freelance artist specialising in fashion and interior decorating in Melbourne and Sydney before she became a fashion editor and writer.

She is married to a construction engineer with whom she travelled overseas for 10 years, having 14 homes in various countries including Malaysia, Thailand and England, where their daughter was born.

She worked as a journalist and artist on English newspapers, and as a fashion and food writer for advertising agencies and newspapers in Canada and Australia, before becoming editor of the Australian weekly magazine New Idea and editor-in-chief of the Australian monthly Family Circle.

Joy inherited her passionate interest in food and cookery from her Scottish maternal grandmother, who loved France and French food and adored entertaining her husband's circle of literary friends in Edinburgh. Joy's mother brought these family traditions with her when she came to Australia as a bride after World War I.

JULIE GORRICK

Julie Gorrick is a Sydney journalist, mother of 3 sons, and has a degree in English literature.

Like Joy, she is a 4th generation Australian with strong country links.

She was taught to love cooking by her own mother, a professional cook, and has concentrated on food and cookery in a writing career that has taken her to many parts of the world as well in Australia.

Julie has written about food products for advertising agencies in Australia, Canada, the Philipines and Japan, and has taken cooking lessons from local cooks in Britain, Morocco, France, Tahiti and other countries.

For 2 years she ran her own small restaurant in a Sydney harbourside suburb, and has worked with some of Australia's top home economists in developing recipes and writing food stories in keeping with our Australian way of life.

She has discussed food and prepared it for photography in a top travel magazine, and is now cookery editor for the Australian monthly magazine, Family Circle.

Acknowledgements

Sue Forster and Anne Creber, for preparing beautiful food and arranging settings for photography.

Jill Godfrey for double-checking recipes.

Brian Roberts for his help in direction of some food shots.

Pauline Holden for some delicious ideas with cheese.

Denise Shaw for typing the manuscript.

Index